ILLUSIONS OF PARADOX

Studies in Epistemology and Cognitive Theory
General Editor: *Paul K. Moser, Loyola University of Chicago*

ILLUSIONS OF PARADOX

A Feminist Epistemology Naturalized

Richmond Campbell

ROWMAN & LITTLEFIELD PUBLISHERS, INC.
Lanham • Boulder • New York • Oxford

ROWMAN & LITTLEFIELD PUBLISHERS, INC.

Published in the United States of America
by Rowman & Littlefield Publishers, Inc.
4720 Boston Way, Lanham, Maryland 20706

12 Hid's Copse Road
Cumnor Hill, Oxford OX2 9JJ, England

Copyright © 1998 by Rowman & Littlefield Publishers, Inc.

British Library Cataloguing in Publication Information Available

Library of Congress Cataloging-in-Publication Data

Campbell, Richmond.
    Illusions of paradox : a feminist epistemology naturalized /
Richmond Campbell.
        p.   cm.—(Studies in epistemology and cognitive theory)
    Includes bibliographical references and index.
    ISBN 0-8476-8918-2 (alk. paper).—ISBN 0-8476-8919-0 (pbk. :
alk. paper)
    1. Knowledge, Theory of.   2. Feminist theory.   3. Naturalism.
I. Title.   II. Series.
BD161.C32   1998
121'.082—dc21   97-52358
                                                               CIP

Printed in the United States of America

∞ ™ The paper used in this publication meets the minimum requirements of
American National Standard for Information Sciences—Permanence of Paper for
Printed Library Materials, ANSI Z39.48—1984.

For my father
Earnest Goodrich Campbell

In memory of my mother
Kathryn Mullowny Campbell

Contents

Acknowledgments

Preparation for this book began some ten years ago when I tried to develop a theory of feminist moral realism in response to Annette Baier's feminist but antirealist perspective on morals. Though drawn to her critique of rationalist and foundationist moral theory, I could not accept her Humean interpretation of the content of moral claims, yet my efforts to construct an alternative that is both feminist and realist appeared to lead me into contradictions. My book may be viewed in part as an attempt to come to terms with Baier's work.

During my 1988–89 sabbatical leave I was supported by Dalhousie University and a research stipend from the Social Sciences and Humanities Research Council of Canada. This period of relative freedom from distractions enabled me to read more extensively in the feminist philosophical literature and to begin to understand the tensions inherent in the conception of feminist naturalism that I wanted to defend. It was not, however, until I wrote "The Virtues of Feminist Empiricism" (*Hypatia* 9, no. 1 [Winter 1994]: 90–115) that I could see how these tensions might be successfully resolved. I am grateful for permission to reprint modified portions of this paper in chapters 2, 3, and 4.

Throughout the development of this project I have been stimulated and sustained by challenges, encouragement, and constructive criticisms from many persons. Among these, I am especially grateful to Susan Babbitt, David Braybrooke, Justin Campbell, Sue Campbell, David Copp, Ron Giere, Michael Hymers, Richard Keshen, Hilary Kornblith, Duncan MacIntosh, Bob Martin, Carolyn McLeod, Gordon McOuat, Lynn Hankinson Nelson, Phyllis Rooney, and Susan Sherwin. In particular, my colleague Sue Campbell forced me to clarify my conception of the project as a whole and expressed faith in the project in its late stages when my doubts were particularly severe. Hilary Kornblith reviewed the penultimate draft for Rowman & Littlefield. I admire his work greatly and am very glad to have his assessment. Lynn Nelson provided a powerful model for how to combine Quine's naturalism with feminist empiricism. She has also been an astute but sympathetic referee at various stages when I endeavored to formulate my own version of this combination. Her support has meant a lot.

Sue Sherwin, though she cannot be held responsible for the conclusions that I have drawn, has deeply influenced my work on this book. More than anyone else, she has helped me to see the radical import of feminist epistemology and also to appreciate the uncomfortable ambiguities inherent in male feminism. In this respect she has helped me to accept both the importance and the limitations of my project. Throughout the writing she has assisted me in countless points of philosophical detail, but what has meant the most to me is her own example of intellectual and moral integrity. She has taught me best that truth matters, and to her standards of honesty, justice, and intellectual care my ideas are continually playing catch-up.

I am grateful to Judith Fox and Jan Sutherland for their expert secretarial and technical assistance.

Finally, I express my thanks to colleagues and students at Dalhousie and the surrounding philosophical community who have listened to and tirelessly tried to make sense out of my ideas. Without their insights what follows would be much more imperfect than it is; without their generosity and faith I could not have completed this work.

Chapter 1

Introduction

Promise or Paradox?

This book joins two important concepts: feminist epistemology and natural-ized epistemology. Each has a well-developed literature, but the concepts are commonly thought to be incompatible. Though some philosophers have rec-ognized the benefits to be gained from combining them, the apparent para-doxes engendered by their union have not been squarely addressed, especially regarding the objectivity of value. This book aims to show that, despite ap-pearances, the concepts are genuinely complementary. More important, it aims to demonstrate that by joining them it is possible to provide a coherent and politically useful account of the objectivity of value.

Almost three decades ago, W. V. Quine introduced the concept of natural-ized epistemology by proposing that epistemologists should abandon their ef-forts to found the possibility of knowledge on first principles and should instead explain how knowledge is possible from within science.[1] Though other philosophers, such as Patricia Churchland and Hilary Kornblith, have followed Quine closely, still others, such as Alvin Goldman, Gilbert Harman, and Philip Kitcher, who also are drawn to mixing epistemology and science, have taken less radical approaches, seeing the theory of knowledge as incorporating scientific methods and results without being simply a part of science.[2] Either way, the prospect of combining epistemology and science has had widespread appeal.[3]

Feminist epistemology, on the other hand, such as found in the work of Linda Alcoff, Lorraine Code, and Alison Jaggar, incorporates into epistemol-ogy the theories and norms of feminism.[4] Like naturalized epistemology, this approach is sharply at odds with traditional methodology. For while tradition-alists have sought to explain the possibility of knowledge from a standpoint external to science, they have also sought to do so on the basis of principles that are politically neutral. Indeed, epistemology is still frequently viewed as being, by definition, a disinterested inquiry into the possibility of knowledge.[5]

1

Nevertheless, the prospect of explicitly feminist epistemologies has broad appeal among feminist theorists, and the literature on this subject, exemplified in recent anthologies, is rapidly expanding.[6]

It is striking that, although the two approaches individually enjoy wide appeal, not many theorists embrace both. The reasons are not hard to fathom. Feminist theorists tend to view science as androcentric in outlook and often sexist in methodology. Therefore, explaining knowledge on the basis of science is likely to be problematic from a standpoint committed to the elimination of androcentrism and sexism. On the other side, naturalized epistemologists have tended to take the traditional view that epistemology should be politically neutral and that the primary epistemic agent is the individual. This is surely Quine's perspective. Feminist theorists usually reject these assumptions. Since many of them see both assumptions and the fact-value dichotomy that is associated with them as integral to the project of naturalizing epistemology, they see the project as being suspect on this ground alone. In fact, a common criticism of naturalized epistemology is that its aim to reduce epistemology to science, and in Quine's case to psychology, robs epistemology of its essentially normative and social character and thus makes it into something that it is not.[7] The upshot is that the idea of a naturalized feminist epistemology is apt to be seen from the standpoint of both approaches as being deeply paradoxical in its premises.

In this work I attempt to dispel the illusions of paradox surrounding this idea by drawing on conceptual resources already present in the two approaches to construct a coherent epistemology that is feminist *and* naturalized. The conception will reinforce and extend the present feminist critiques of androcentric science and the fact-value dichotomy, but it promises to do so by contributing to a politically useful account of objectivity that is uncompromising in its realist implications. There is now a renewed interest in objectivity among feminist philosophers—for example, in the work of Susan Babbitt, Jean Hampton, Sandra Harding, Elizabeth Lloyd, Helen Longino, Susan Moller Okin, Kathleen Okruhlik, Elizabeth Potter, Naomi Scheman, Nancy Tuana, and Alison Wylie.[8] In fact, some theorists—notably Louise Antony, Jane Duran, and Lynn Hankinson Nelson—defend versions of feminist epistemology that are naturalized.[9] But they do not address directly the deepest puzzles that attend the prospect of treating values as existing independently of us as an objective part of nature. How, after all, can there be values that are socially constructed and yet also objective? We must understand the social construction *and* the objectivity of our judgment that women's subordination exists and is wrong. Is this really possible?

To address this question, I analyze what happens when feminist values enter into the process of testing hypotheses experimentally and argue that fairly orthodox views within naturalized epistemology about how testing works— views that are independently plausible—explain how the influence of feminist values can make the process of testing more likely to track the truth and hence more objective than it would otherwise be. This argument, developed over the next three chapters, has five noteworthy consequences. It undermines one of the main sources of resistance to feminist epistemology: the assumption that incorporating political values into epistemic methodology makes objective inquiry impossible. It also undercuts the objection to naturalized epistemology that once epistemology is included within science it would lose its normative dimension and answers the feminist worry that the methodology of naturalized epistemology is tied to the (twice) false idea that when done well science is centered in the individual and is value neutral. It reconciles realism—implying a world existing independently of how we think of it—with the plausible belief, held by many feminist philosophers, that there cannot be a unique all-encompassing true description of reality. Finally, it shows to be mistaken the common view that a realist conception of objective inquiry cannot take such inquiry to be inherently social and value laden. The argument will be that a realist conception of objectivity is more than compatible with feminist political goals—it requires them.

The second part of the book builds on these conclusions to formulate a general conception of naturalized epistemology and to show how its social and reflexive nature makes it conducive to feminist analysis. A serious objection that is commonly made to naturalized epistemology is that it cannot address the traditional problem of skepticism without begging the question. Though often ignored, a parallel objection arises for feminist epistemology in the case of skepticism about feminism. This part of the book aims to provide an answer to *both* objections based on the reflexive character of knowledge and the justifications that are implicit in it. In addition, this part will illustrate how, under feminist analysis, self-knowledge can exemplify the social and reflexive nature of justification that would be implied in a naturalized epistemology. The feminist theorists studied here are Annette Baier, Catharine MacKinnon, Robin Dillon, and Susan Sherwin in their investigations, respectively, of trust and distrust, sexual pleasure under patriarchy, basal self-respect, and relational autonomy.[10]

The third part of the book deals with meaning and value and attacks the fact-value dichotomy on two levels. First, even if it were true that a factual statement cannot express value, it would still be true that facts cannot be established without value commitments. This argument, which proceeds on the basis of a modest form of Quine's evidential holism, contradicts Quine's own fact-value dichotomy, which implies that facts can be ascertained independently of values. I argue further, based on an interpretation of Quine's reasons for rejecting the analytic-synthetic distinction, that there is a corresponding interdependence between facts and meanings. Putting the two interdependencies together yields the result that meaning and value cannot be ascertained independently of each other. The conclusion is significant, since it implies that metaethical inquiry cannot be expected to be politically neutral, contrary to what is assumed in the bulk of metaethical discussion. I call this conclusion *meaning-value holism*. It is used to argue that a factual statement *can* express value, contrary to even a minimal form of the fact-value dichotomy. This idea lays the groundwork to construct in the fourth part of the book a theory of *moral* knowledge that is both naturalized and feminist.

In this last part I propose and defend a feminist form of contractarianism, revising models developed by Jean Hampton, Susan Moller Okin, Thomas Scanlon, and Richard Miller.[11] New sources of paradox arise here. Would such a contractarianism, if naturalized, reduce moral facts to biological facts about evolution? I argue it would not. Then problems of circularity arise because the conditions of the contract appear to presuppose considerations of justice. The solution that I propose is the method of resolving problems of circularity that arose for nonmoral knowledge in the second part. Finally, there are the worries that feminists, among others, have raised about the individualism presupposed by contractarian theory and its failure to take the issue of real consent seriously enough, given the hypothetical nature of the contract. These objections are voiced, for instance, by Carol Gilligan, Annette Baier, Virginia Held, and Alison Jaggar.[12] They are met by appealing to the social and reflexive nature of knowledge, including moral knowledge, that is implied by naturalized epistemology.

The Paradoxes

This is the promise of a feminist epistemology naturalized. But is this kind of epistemology really possible? To explain how a feminist epistemology can be naturalized, it is necessary to resolve the apparent paradoxes or contradictions that stand in the way of this project. I locate seven sources of potential paradox. It will be helpful to state them at the outset.

The Problem of Normativity for Naturalized Epistemology

There is, first, the apparent contradiction to be found within naturalized epistemology itself. A naturalized epistemology attempts to explain the possibility of knowledge by appeal to facts revealed by scientific inquiry into the process of reasoning and coming to have beliefs. Such an explanation, however, appears to be at best purely descriptive rather than normative. It tells us at most how we *do* think (reason, come to have beliefs) rather than how we *ought* to think. This presents a problem. Epistemology is necessarily normative, if the term *epistemology* is used in anything like the sense that is usually intended. In attempting to explain the possibility of knowledge, epistemology must explain how we ought to think, what beliefs we ought to have, what inferences we ought to make. Therefore, naturalized epistemology either has changed the subject, with the term "epistemology" used perversely and misleadingly, or else it is a contradiction in terms. I will call this *the problem of normativity for naturalized epistemology*.

This problem is attenuated somewhat by the recognition that norms are operating in scientific inquiry that are reflected in the way that one theory comes to be accepted over another in the face of conflicting evidence. Thomas Kuhn made this clear in his study of the way scientific theorizing evolves, in a sometimes revolutionary manner.[13] Why can we not say, then, that science is both descriptive and normative? And, if so, would this not circumvent the problem? Not really. Though it is now generally conceded that science contains norms of inquiry—such as norms requiring scientists to heed relevant evidence and, other things being equal, to prefer theories with greater predictive power—and that some of these norms may even be constitutive of scientific inquiry, the presence of norms in science does not solve the original problem. The reason is that it is not the business of science to evaluate its own norms of inquiry. To engage in this kind of metanormative evaluation—to determine which norms of inquiry in general are worth heeding—is to pursue a distinctively epistemological activity. It is in this much deeper sense that epistemology is normative. It is normative with respect to seeking to define and defend the ultimate norms governing the justification of belief and the acquisition of knowledge. To overcome the problem of normativity and dispel the appearance of paradox, naturalized epistemology would have to be shown to be normative in this ultimate sense. But how can it, if by its own lights epistemology is to be contained within science?

Because this is a problem for naturalized epistemology, it is a fortiori a problem for any feminist naturalized epistemology, since the latter combines the methodology of naturalized epistemology with the pursuit of certain political goals. Adding such goals would appear to do nothing to make science or naturalized epistemology normative in the ultimate sense. At most it would raise the question of how anyone can know that certain political goals are worth pursuing. Arguably, this is a question to be answered by epistemology proper. Feminist naturalized epistemology, to the extent that it is genuinely a form of naturalized epistemology, thus inherits the problem of normativity without being able to offer anything by way of a solution. Or so it would seem.

The Problem of Normativity for Feminist Epistemology

A second problem about normativity arises within feminist epistemology more generally. How is it that feminist political norms can do anything but hinder serious inquiry about what is true, whether the inquiry is in science or everyday life? To conduct serious inquiry after truth is to pursue truth for its own sake or at least to be guided by norms that serve the goal of finding out what is true about the world, not by norms that serve to improve the world. Take the feminist goal of eliminating women's subordination to men. However laudable this norm might be from the standpoint of making the world a better place, it has no direct bearing on how to find out what the world is actually like. Consequently, when this feminist norm operates in conjunction with norms governing inquiry after truth, it can serve only to hinder or bias that inquiry. For example, it may help to combat the present gender hierarchy if women are not viewed as less intelligent on average than men. But if the question is whether women are or are not less intelligent, wanting one conclusion rather than another to be true will be the enemy of impartial inquiry and can only serve to make the inquirer less attentive to evidence that does not support the conclusion that he or she prefers. Since epistemology, when it is properly conceived, aims at discovering through impartial inquiry norms that best serve impartial inquiry after truth, feminist epistemology as such appears, by its very nature, to be a self-contradictory idea. I call this *the problem of normativity for feminist epistemology.*

This problem carries over directly to feminist naturalized epistemology, now from the other direction, because the naturalized element appears to do nothing to diminish the inherent tension between feminism, a political movement, and epistemology, an impartial inquiry after truth and after the conditions that make that inquiry possible. Some feminist philosophers may be inclined at this juncture to dismiss the problem by rejecting the possibility of truth or the possibility of impartial inquiry. This cannot be my way out, however, since the epistemology that I defend in the following pages incorporates both. To solve the problem, I need to face the paradox head-on.

The Problem of Circularity for Naturalized Epistemology

A third difficulty arises from the fact that naturalized epistemology appears to be constitutionally unable to address the traditional epistemological problem of skepticism. The skeptic challenges us to show how knowledge or even justified belief is possible. As long as we allow that epistemology is about how knowledge and the justification of belief are possible, it will be important to understand how naturalized epistemology can recognize the challenge of skepticism as a problem, whether or not it is able to solve it. The trouble is that naturalized epistemology begins from within science assuming that some knowledge is already at hand and moves on from there. For many philosophers, especially those who are schooled in traditional epistemology, whether they be foundationists or coherentists or some hybrid variety, building into the structure of one's epistemology the assumption that knowledge is possible makes it seem as if no skeptical challenge exists. For them this approach is at best uninteresting; at worse it is dishonest. Indeed, if one supposes, as I do, that an epistemology must explain, not merely assume, the possibility of knowledge, the complete inability to address the problem of skepticism would count as an incoherence within naturalized epistemology.

The difficulty is nicely illustrated by Hume's skeptical problem of induction. Hume asked how we can justify our natural confidence in the reliability of inductive reasoning. We cannot justify it by deduction alone, since inductive reasoning is such that the truth of its conclusions cannot be established independently of experience. On the other hand, we cannot justify our confidence by appeal to inductive reasoning, since we would then be reasoning in a circle. Given that no third possibility exists, Hume concluded that the reliability of induction cannot be established by reason. In his famous essay "Natural Kinds" Quine appeals to Darwin to solve Hume's problem.[14] If inductive reasoning were not reliable at least most of the time, Quine reasons, natural selection would have made sure that we are not here today to think about it. While Quine's response to Hume's problem may appear to concede its existence, further reflection reveals that, in assuming that we *know* the truth of Darwin's theory and hence the reliability of induction in this instance, Quine has simply begged the question against Hume's skeptic. He has assumed that the possibility of knowledge itself cannot be questioned. But this he must do, given what naturalized epistemology is. I will call the general problem, of which this is but one illustration, *the problem of circularity for naturalized epistemology*. A feminist naturalized epistemology would seem to fare no better, for how could adding political norms to the other norms of inquiry possibly serve to solve this problem?

The Problem of Circularity for Feminist Epistemology

A corresponding problem of circularity arises for feminist epistemology. Feminist epistemology begins with the assumption that feminist political goals are worth pursuing. This is a normative assumption. Are normative assumptions factual assumptions? That is, are they true or false? There are obviously two ways to go here. One position, known as cognitivism, is that evaluative statements have truth value: each is either true or false. The opposite position, noncognitivism, is that evaluative statements have no truth value. Either way a problem of circularity emerges for feminist epistemology. Consider cognitivism first. If the assumption that feminist political goals are worth pursuing has truth value, then it is appropriate to ask how this can be known, and an adequate epistemology should have an answer. The problem is that in order not to be quesion begging, an adequate answer must appeal to considerations that have merit independently of the knowledge that feminist goals are worth pursuing. But if so, feminist epistemology must rest on the merit of considerations that are independent of feminism. If that is so, however, why call this epistemology *feminist*? The problem is not that what feminists claim to be knowledge is not knowledge. The problem is that to avoid the charge of circularity, feminist epistemology must lose the justification for its label.

Consider next the noncognitivist view that the assumption in question has no truth value. It may appear that on this view there is no problem, since then it cannot be the job of a feminist epistemology to explain how this assumption can be known. Nevertheless, we can ask how this normative assumption is to be justified. Does an epistemology have to answer this question, if the assumption is without truth value? On the understanding of epistemology that I will develop in response to the problems of normativity, it does. This is because normative assumptions, whether or not they have truth value, play a central role in the acquisition of knowledge and need themselves to be justified if they are to play this role in the context of serious inquiry. But now the issue of circularity reemerges, for an adequate justification must appeal to considerations that are independent of feminism if it is not to beg the question at issue. It is, in sum, paradoxical that the normative elements of an epistemology that are supposed to make it distinctively feminist should rest ultimately on norms that have authority independent of feminism. The two versions of this problem form a dilemma that I will call *the problem of circularity for feminist epistemology*.

The Problem of Naturalizing Value

Perhaps the most difficult problem remains: that of accommodating values, such as the political values of feminism, within a naturalistic worldview. This I will call *the problem of naturalizing value*. This problem lies at the heart of any epistemology that aspires to be both naturalized and feminist. Though related to the earlier problems of normativity, it is distinct from them. Those problems are about how values, feminist values in particular, can be an integral part of scientific methodology, in the first instance, and epistemological inquiry, in the second. Whereas those problems are methodological, the present problem is ontological. It asks, What is value?

Classically, two answers are possible, if we assume a naturalisitic worldview. One is to argue that values are real and exist as part of nature; the other is to argue that values are unreal but projected onto nature as if they were real because of an instinctive response to our interests and desires.[15] What position will be taken here? Considerations of consistency and simplicity argue strongly in favor of realism regarding values.[16] Indeed, I will argue that this option gives the most straightforward interpretation of the commitment within feminism to eliminate the subordination of women. On a realist interpretation of this commitment, this subordination is morally wrong and wrong independently of what our moral beliefs and values happen to be. Many will regard this conclusion as paradoxical. Do any facts obtain apart from perspective?

How can moral wrongness in particular exist independently of perspective, and if it can, how can it be part of nature?

To suppose that wrongness can be part of nature, that there can be moral facts that are also natural facts, is to combine moral realism with moral naturalism. This century has seen an intense resistance to this combination, beginning with G. E. Moore's charge that ethics based on this combination commits the Naturalistic Fallacy.[17] According to Moore, to identify some natural property N with a moral property, like goodness, is to imply that it would not be an open question whether N is good. But, Moore contends, no matter what property N we might have in mind, the question "Is N good?" is always a legitimate, nontrivial question. This "open question" argument, however, whatever its merits might be in other respects, does not have much force against contemporary forms of naturalistic moral realism, since the latter claim the identity holds a posteriori on a par with identities in science. For example, it can be an open question whether the genetic material that is responsible for heredity is DNA even if that material is in fact identical to DNA. Still, other arguments have considerable force and apply against contemporary forms of naturalistic moral realism.

These arguments, while they do not question whether the facts that are revealed through scientific investigation might be given a realist interpretation, imply that a firm distinction exists between such facts and values. One such argument, from Hume but made famous in recent times by J. L. Mackie,[18] is that judgments about what has value, particularly moral judgments, carry with them some motivation to act accordingly, whereas mere judgments of fact have no such influence by themselves. Another, also endorsed by Mackie, is that the extent and depth of disagreement about matters of value, especially moral issues, are best explained by the assumption that these apparently unresolvable disagreements are not about matters of fact. A third argument, an appeal to Occam's Razor introduced into the current debate about moral naturalism by Gilbert Harman,[19] is that the postulation of moral properties is unnecessary to explain our natural responses (beliefs, judgments, feelings, etc.) to what we observe and think about and hence ought not to be included in our understanding of reality. These arguments, of which many variations are possible, have been prominent in the literature on moral naturalism over the past two decades and need to be answered by anyone who would defend a feminist moral realism within a naturalized epistemology.

It is noteworthy that by and large feminist philosophers have not engaged themselves in this debate. Why? The reason cannot be that most of them would reject the fact-value dichotomy, since this, although true, would explain only why they cannot endorse the arguments just cited, not why they reject the debate as such. A more plausible reason is that many feminists would object to realism of any form. Feminists who are postmodernists are of this mind.[20] They object to the fact-value dichotomy, but their reason is not that there are normative facts that obtain independently of what we might think about them. They hold instead that there are no facts at all in the sense of facts that obtain independently of perspective. This position, however, does nothing to alleviate the tension between the pull toward moral realism that is implicit in feminist moral claims and the reasons to resist it. To the extent that the latter have force, they serve only to deepen the apparent paradox.

The Bias Paradox

An important dimension of naturalized epistemology that has not been given attention in this catalog of paradoxes is its reflexive character. Naturalized epistemology treats the process of coming to know, and indeed the process of understanding that process, as a natural process that is itself open to empirical investigation. Reflections on the natural but also social process involved in gaining knowledge (even when these reflections are not made under the banner of naturalized epistemology) have led feminists to mistrust claims to impartiality on the part of would-be knowers. For reasons set out in detail in the next chapter, any empirical investigation is subject to the influence of contextual values—that is, values that operate in the social context of the inquiry. For example, the ability of a researcher to think of an alternative explanation of the evidence may turn on his or her values. In this case an effort to be impartial—and thus to ignore these values—may result in a failure to think of an alternative explanation with the consequence that the inquiry is less trustworthy than it would be if the researcher had been able to imagine the alternative and hence had less confidence in his or her present, narrow interpretation of the evidence. If the narrow interpretation implies that evidence suggests that women are inferior to men (e.g., in testing of spatial or mathematical ability), then impartiality appears to be sexist (favoring a stereotype of women as being inferior in the absence of compelling evidence). Many similar examples can be cited. Some feminist philosophers would go a step further to claim that treating impartiality as a value by its nature reflects a masculine and patriarchical point of view that is contrary to the aims of feminism.[21] Whether or not one goes this far, it seems evident that appealing to the ideal of impartiality can result in gender bias, whether or not that is the intention of the person making this appeal.

The difficulty is that rejecting this ideal gives rise to what Louise Antony calls *the bias paradox*.[22] If the problem with impartiality is just that it results in bias, then bias must itself be undesirable. But this means that it would be better to be impartial, so that impartiality both should be and should *not* be our aim. Another way to put the problem is that feminists think some biases are bad (those that are implicit in a gender-biased appeal to impartiality) but they also think that some are good (those needed in order to avoid the trap of impartiality). How is it, then, that good biases are to be distinguished from bad ones in a way that is not question begging? One might say, as Antony does, that what makes good biases good is that they facilitate the search for truth whereas bad biases impede it, but this does not tell how to recognize the truth independently of good biases. The worry is that there is no way to distinguish good biases from bad that is not arbitrary, but if there is not the critique of impartiality that is engendered by the reflexive character of naturalized epistemology results in the contradiction that it both accepts and rejects the same ideal.

The Paradox of Male Feminism

Consider finally *the paradox of male feminism*. This book purports to be feminist, but how is that possible? If its arguments come anywhere close to being convincing, one's chances of getting at the truth are directly affected by one's history, experiences, social position, race, motives, and sex, among many other things. These can affect one's prospects postively or negatively. In particular, being privileged is apt to blind one to the nature of oppression. But, if this is so, how can I, privileged with respect to gender as I am, have much insight at all about gender oppression? In fact, I am multiply privileged, being white, male, well educated, middle-class, heterosexual, and able-bodied. If this book succeeds in telling anything like the truth about how knowledge is possible and thus about how gender oppression can be known, then how could it not be a fraud? It might be suggested that we have not a paradox but a *reductio* of the hypothesis that the book is true and a genuine instance of feminism. (If it were such an instance, then we would get a contradiction; so it cannot be.) My hope, however, is that the book reveals itself to be feminist. Then there is more than a *reductio*. The book generates a paradox by its own argument. The paradox springs, moreover, from the naturalized and hence reflexive dimension of the theory that the book presents. The theory, applied to itself in the context of its own genesis, undermines itself.

Some men who write in support of feminism describe themselves as profeminist rather than simply as feminist. Their motive is understandable. Recognizing that they are not in a position to understand oppression of gender from the inside, they would rather not presume to speak from the inside. But refusing the label "feminist" has its own dangers. To identify oneself as feminist is to do more than recognize women's subordination and desire that it be eliminated. It is also to take responsibility for how one's own life contributes to that subordination and to assume some responsibility for eliminating it. Theoretically, one can do this without the label, but taking on the label helps, since it carries a force of its own. Presuming to call oneself a feminist makes it is much harder to escape confronting the contradictions between one's profeminist views and one's life. For privileged men like me the contradictions will tend to be more severe and the need to take responsibility more urgent.

In the present case, however, a prior problem exists: the book's argument would appear to undercut the viability of *any* feminist label, "profeminist" or otherwise, given the sex of its author.

Three Commitments

The perspective of this book combines three main theoretical and practical commitments: (1) that epistemology can and should be "naturalized," (2) that the subordination of women is unjust and should be eliminated, and (3) that the feminist commitment just expressed can form an integral part of epistemology. The combination of (1) and (2) is unremarkable, though few of those who espouse naturalized epistemology identify themselves in their epistemological writing as feminists. This combination, however, should not be confused with the commitment (3) to mix feminism with epistemology. Many philosophers who are naturalized epistemologists may also endorse the view expressed in (2). They can do this without believing that it is appropriate or even intelligible to integrate feminism with epistemology. On the other hand, there are certainly many who identify themselves as feminists and also believe that feminism can be integrated with epistemology. These philosophers who combine commitments (2) and (3) express their commitment to feminism as they practice their epistemology and are easy to locate in the literature. These philosophers, though, are hardly ever epistemologists who subscribe to naturalized epistemology. The combination (1) and (2) as well as (2) and (3) have their own paradoxes to contend with, due to the apparent contradictions and puzzles contained in the notions of naturalized epistemology and feminist epistemology. It is the union of all three commitments, however, that is the most puzzling, since it contains all the other apparent contradictions and more besides.

My contention is that the seeming contradictions are illusions and that there is no real paradox in the idea of a naturalized feminist epistemology. The book will address the appearance of paradox in four stages. In the first I will sketch a conception of empirical knowledge that explains how feminist norms can be integrated into the application of standards of good evidence in a way that makes clear the inherently social character of knowledge acquisition but does not undermine the possibility that knowledge can be fully objective. This stage entails solutions to the paradoxes of bias and male feminism. In the second stage I will interpret Quine's conception of naturalized epistemology in a way that makes clear its normative dimensions and allows again the integration of feminist norms. This part of the book will afford an opportunity to resolve the problems of normativity as well as the problems of circularity that surround the prospect of an epistemology that is both naturalized and feminist. In the third stage I will consider how feminist "end norms" might be naturalized and address the fact-value dichotomy that stands in the way of naturalizing value of any kind. This third part of the book will take up very general problems regarding the relation of fact to value in normative theories and indeed the relation of fact to meaning and argue that value and meaning are interdependent concepts in their applications. This conclusion will provide a basis for the possibility of a feminist normative realism in which moral facts are as fully "natural" as any facts that might be revealed by empirical inquiry. In the final and fourth stage, I will attempt to give substance to this theoretical possibility by outlining and defending a naturalized feminist contractarian theory of moral norms. Thus conceived, moral knowledge (when genuine) would be a part of empirical knowledge that is both social and objective.

Let us now begin at the beginning. We need to develop a concept of feminist empiricism. Can good sense be made of this notion? If so, we can take the first step toward the construction of a viable feminist epistemology that can be naturalized.

Notes

1. W. V. Quine, "Epistemology Naturalized," in *Ontological Relativity and Other Essays* (New York: Columbia University Press, 1969).

2. See, for example, Patricia S. Churchland, *Neurophilosophy: Toward a Unified Understanding of the Mind-Brain* (Cambridge, Mass.: MIT Press, 1986); Hilary Kornblith, *Inductive Inference and Its Natural Ground: An Essay in Naturalistic Epistemology* (Cambridge, Mass.: MIT Press, 1993); Alvin I. Goldman, *Liaisons: Philosophy Meets the Cognitive and Social Sciences* (Cambridge, Mass.: MIT Press, 1992); Gilbert Harman, *Change in View: Principles of Reasoning* (Cambridge, Mass.: MIT Press, 1986); Philip Kitcher, *The Advancement of Science* (Oxford: Oxford University Press, 1993).

3. A recent bibliography, prepared by Fredrick F. Schmitt and James Spellman, in *Naturalizing Epistemology*, Hilary Kornblith, ed. (Cambridge, Mass.: MIT Press, 1994), 427–73, lists 856 books and articles on the subject.

4. See, for example, Linda Martin Alcoff, *Real Knowing: New Versions of the Coherence Theory* (Ithaca, N.Y.: Cornell University Press, 1996); Lorraine Code, *What Can She Know? Feminist Theory and the Construction of Knowledge* (Ithaca, N.Y.: Cornell University Press, 1991); Alison Jaggar, *Feminist Politics and Human Nature* (Totowa, N.J.: Rowman and Allenheld, 1983); and Alison Jaggar, "Love and Knowledge: Emotion in Feminist Epistemology," in *Gender/Body/Knowledge*, Susan Bordo and Alison Jaggar, eds. (New Brunswick, N.J.: Rutgers University Press, 1989). Alcoff's book on coherence theory does not so much incorporate feminist norms within a coherentist theory of knowledge as explain how such norms can provide guidance in the process of coming to know, but inasmuch as success in this regard is for her an important desideratum for an adequate theory of knowledge, it would count as feminist epistemology in the sense that I am using this term.

5. Susan Haack, "Science as Social?—Yes and No," in *Feminism, Science, and*

the Philosophy of Science, Lynn Hankinson Nelson and Jack Nelson, eds. (Dordrecht: Kluwer, 1996), 79–93, and Ellen R. Klein, *Feminism under Fire* (Amherst, N.Y.: Prometheus, 1996), are recent illustrations of how to use the definition to argue that "feminist epistemology" is not proper epistemological inquiry.

6. See, for example: Lynn Hankinson Nelson, ed., *Feminism and Science, Synthese*, vol. 104 (Dordrecht: Kluwer, 1995); Louise M. Antony and Charlotte Witt, eds., *A Mind of One's Own: Feminist Essays on Reason and Objectivity* (Boulder, Colo.: Westview, 1993); Linda Alcoff and Elizabeth Potter, eds., *Feminist Epistemologies* (New York: Routledge, 1993); and Elizabeth D. Harvey and Kathleen Okruhlik, eds., *Women and Reason* (Ann Arbor: University of Michigan Press, 1992).

7. See Jaegwon Kim, "What Is 'Naturalized Epistemology'?" in *Philosophical Perspectives, 2, Epistemology*, James E. Tomberlin, ed. (Atascadero, Calif.: Ridgeview, 1988), reprint in Kornblith, *Naturalizing*, and the introduction by Kornblith to *Naturalizing* for the criticism that naturalized epistemology eschews normativity and Lorraine Code, "What Is Natural about Epistemology Naturalized?" *American Philosophical Quarterly* 33 (1996): 1–22, for the criticism that naturalized epistemology has tended thus far to be excessively individualistic.

8. For relevant works by these authors and others, see Antony and Witt, *A Mind of One's Own*; Alcoff and Potter, *Feminist Epistemologies*; Harvey and Okruhlik, *Women and Reason*; Susan Babbitt, *Impossible Dreams: Rationality, Integrity, and Moral Imagination* (Boulder, Colo.: Westview, 1996); Elizabeth A. Lloyd, "Science and Anti-Science: Objectivity and Its Real Enemies," in *Feminism*, Nelson and Nelson, eds.; Elizabeth Potter, "Underdetermination Undeterred" in *Feminism*, Nelson and Nelson, eds.; Naomi Scheman, "Feeling Our Way Toward Objectivity," in *Mind and Morals: Essays on Cognitive Science and Ethics*, Larry May, Marilyn Friedman, and Andy Clark, eds. (Cambridge, Mass.: MIT Press, 1996); Helen Longino, *Science as Social Knowledge* (Princeton, N.J.: Princeton University Press, 1990); Susan Moller Okin, *Justice, Gender, and the Family* (New York: Basic Books, 1989); Nancy Tuana, ed., *Feminism and Science* (Bloomington: Indiana University Press, 1989); and Nancy Tuana, "The Radical Future of Feminist Empiricism," *Hypatia* 7, no. 1 (1992): 100–13.

9. See, for example, Louise Antony, "Quine as Feminist: The Radical Import of Naturalized Epistemology," in *A Mind of One's Own*, Antony and Duran, eds.; Jane Duran, *Toward a Feminist Epistemology* (Savage, Md.: Rowman & Littlefield, 1991); Jane Duran, *Knowledge in Context: Naturalized Epistemology and Sociolinguistics* (Lanham, Md.: Rowman & Littlefield, 1994); Lynn Hankinson Nelson, *Who Knows: From Quine to Feminist Empiricism* (Philadelphia: Temple University Press, 1990); and Lynn Hankinson Nelson, "Empiricism without Dogmas" in *Feminism*, Nelson and Nelson, eds.

10. See Annette Baier, *Postures of the Mind: Essays on Mind and Morals* (Minneapolis: University of Minnesota Press, 1985); Annette Baier, "Trust and Anti-Trust," *Ethics* 96 (1986): 231–60; Catharine A. MacKinnon, *Feminism Unmodified: Discourses on Life and Law* (Cambridge, Mass.: Harvard University Press, 1987); Catharine A. MacKinnon, "Sexuality, Pornography, and Method: 'Pleasure under Patriarchy,' " *Ethics* 99 (1989): 314–46; Robin Dillon, ed., *Dignity, Character, and Self-Respect* (New York: Routledge, 1995); Robin Dillon, "Self-Respect: Moral, Emotional

and Political," *Ethics* 107 (1997): 226–49; Susan Sherwin, *No Longer Patient: Feminist Ethics and Health-Care* (Philadelphia: Temple University Press, 1992); and Susan Sherwin, "A Relational Approach to Autonomy in Health Care," in The Feminist Health Care Ethics Research Network, Susan Sherwin, Coordinator, *The Politics of Women's Health: Exploring Agency and Autonomy* (Philadelphia: Temple University Press, 1998).

11. Jean Hampton, "Feminist Contractarianism," in *A Mind of One's Own*, Antony and Witt, eds.; Okin, *Justice*; Thomas M. Scanlon, "Contractarianism and Utilitarianism," in *Utilitarianism and Beyond*, Amartya Sen and Bernard Williams, eds. (Cambridge: Cambridge University Press, 1982); Richard W. Miller, *Moral Differences: Truth, Justice, and Conscience in a World of Conflict* (Princeton, N.J.: Princeton University Press, 1992).

12. Carol Gilligan, *In a Different Voice* (Cambridge, Mass.: Harvard University Press, 1982); Annette Baier, "The Need for More Than Justice," in *Science, Morality, and Feminist Theory*, Marsha Hanen and Kai Nielson, eds. (Calgary: University of Calgary Press, 1987); Virginia Held, "Noncontractual Society: A Feminist View," in *Science*, Hanen and Nielson, eds.; Virginia Held, *Feminist Morality: Transforming Culture, Society, and Politics* (Chicago: University of Chicago Press, 1993); Alison Jaggar, "Taking Consent Seriously: Feminst Ethics and Actual Moral Dialogue," in *The Applied Ethics Reader*, Earl Winkler and Jerrold Coombs, eds. (Oxford: Blackwell, 1993).

13. Thomas Kuhn, *The Structure of Scientific Revolutions*, 2d ed. (Chicago: University of Chicago Press, 1970).

14. W. V. Quine, "Natural Kinds," in *Ontological Relativity and Other Essays* (New York: Columbia University Press, 1969).

15. The view that moral values are part of nature can be interpreted so that moral properties are natural properties but not necessarily identifiable with any properties that can be described by the vocabulary of the physical sciences—as in Nicholas L. Sturgeon, "Moral Explanations," in *Morality, Reason, and Truth*, David Copp and David Zimmerman, eds. (Totowa, N.J.: Rowman & Allanheld, 1985); Richard Boyd, "How to Be a Moral Realist," in *Essays on Moral Realism*, Geoffrey Sayre-McCord, ed. (Ithaca, N.Y.: Cornell University Press, 1988); and David O. Brink, *Moral Realism and the Foundations of Ethics* (Cambridge: Cambridge University Press, 1989); or the view can be interpreted reductively, so that this identification is assumed, as in Peter Railton, "Moral Realism," *Philosophical Review* 95 (1986): 163–207. The moral antirealist perspective is exemplified in Allan Gibbard, *Wise Choices, Apt Feelings* (Cambridge, Mass.: Harvard University Press, 1990). For a review of these views and their alternatives as they have developed in this century, see Stephen Darwall, Allan Gibbard, and Peter Railton, "Toward *Fin de siècle* Ethics," *Philosophical Review* 101 (1992): 115–89.

16. For a good summary of these considerations, see David Copp, *Morality, Normativity, and Society* (Oxford: Clarendon, 1995), chap. 1.

17. George Edward Moore, *Principia Ethica* (Cambridge: Cambridge University Press, 1903).

18. John L. Mackie, *Ethics: Inventing Right and Wrong* (New York: Penguin, 1977).

19. Gilbert Harman, *The Nature of Morality: An Introduction to Ethics* (New York: Oxford University Press, 1977).

20. See, for example, Elizabeth Fee, "Women's Nature and Scientific Objectivity," in *Woman's Nature: Rationalizations of Inequality*, M. Lowe and R. Hubbard, eds. (New York: Pergamon, 1981); and Jane Flax, "Postmodernism and Gender Relations in Feminist Theory," *Signs* 12 (1987): 621–43.

21. Evelyn Fox Keller, "Feminism and Science," in *Sex and Scientific Inquiry*, Sandra Harding and John O'Barr, eds. (Chicago: University of Chicago Press, 1987).

22. Antony, "Quine as Feminist," 188–91.

Part I

Feminism and Empirical Knowledge

Chapter 2

Understanding Feminist Empiricism

Internal Feminist Empiricism

Broadly speaking, feminist empiricism is any epistemology that combines empiricist methods with feminist political goals. What are empiricist methods and feminist political goals? The term *empiricist* is tricky. It can describe the theory of knowledge exemplified in the works of the classical empiricists, John Locke and David Hume, but it can also be used much more loosely. I will use it very generally to describe any methods of learning about the world by appeal to the evidence of our senses. These include methods used in orthodox science to test theories against the evidence of controlled experiments, where the outcome of the experiment is verified by observation. The expression *feminist political goals* needs qualification too, since feminists often disagree about political goals. Most would agree, however, that one fundamental feminist political goal is to remove from society the present subordination of women to men. In this book I will take it for granted that this is an important feminist political goal. Feminist empiricism, then, proposes to combine feminist opposition to the subordination of women with methods of learning about the world through sense experience, such as the methods used in experimental science.

It is a matter of controversy whether this combination is viable. Many feminists believe that empiricist methods are by their nature incompatible with the pursuit of feminist political goals. One of the most important critics of feminist empiricism is Sandra Harding. Sexism and androcentrism in science are two significant factors contributing to women's subordination. She argues that removing sexism and androcentrism from science is not best achieved by applying the existing empiricist norms of scientific inquiry. Though some progress can be made through the use of empiricist methods, much better strategies are available that are incompatible with these methods. For example, there is postmodernism, a philosophical movement that rejects what is arguably a central presupposition of modern science—that there is an underlying reality that can be revealed by empirical study. There is also feminist stand-point theory. This strategy, which Harding favors, implies that the experience of marginalized and oppressed groups has the potential to offer insights that are inaccessible through the application of empiricist methods.

Harding's argument is that empiricist methodology, because it is rooted in the philosophical assumptions of positivism, ignores the role of contextual values in science and lacks sufficient reflexivity to treat its own methods as being open to empirical investigation and criticism. In ignoring the impor-tance of contextual values and reflexivity, empiricist methodology has no hope of succeeding in countering the influence of sexism and androcentrism.

My aim in the present chapter is to show that the criticisms of Harding do not stand up to scrutiny and that, ironically, they presuppose the very positivist assumptions she means to correct. I will contend that feminist empiricism, when it is properly conceived, presents a conception of social knowledge that successfully combines the ideal of objectivity with the virtues of being politi-cally subversive and alive to the relevance of contextual values. In part, I will be defending feminist empiricism against certain important and influential objections. At the same time, however, I will be developing a new way of thinking about joining feminism with scientific methodology to build a posi-tive and useful conception of objective inquiry and knowledge.

Later, in chapters 3 and 4, I will move on to defend a realist interpretation of these results and argue that some of the central insights of feminist standpoint theory—commonly understood to be an alternative to feminist empiricism—are, in fact, grounded in feminist empiricism. In answer to Harding's point about reflexivity, my argument in chapter 4 will be that feminist empiricism is able to view its own methodology as the product of social construction and hence subject to empirical inquiry and revision. But we should move one step at a time. Consider first whether feminist empiricism can answer the charge that it incorporates the assumptions of positivism.

Empiricism in this century has been associated with logical positivism. But it is unfair to define feminist empiricism as logical positivism in the service of feminist political ideals. That would make it a nonstarter. At the core of logical positivism (or logical empiricism, as it is also called) is verification-ism, a deeply flawed conception of meaning and knowledge implying that nothing can be meant or known except that which can be verified as true or false by logic or the senses. This view of meaning and knowledge, as is now well known, cannot adequately explain what scientific practice is really like, let alone how it might change for the better.

Harding is careful not to define feminist empiricism this way. "*Feminist empiricism*," she says, "argues that sexism and androcentrism are social bi-ases correctable by stricter adherence to the existing methodological norms of scientific inquiry."[1] Still, Harding sees feminist empiricism as grounded in one of the fundamental assumptions of positivism—namely, that the norms of science should apply only to the context of justification, not that of discovery. She believes for this reason that such empiricism is incapable of correcting gender bias in science:

> [A] key origin of androcentric bias can be found in the selection of problems of inquiry, and in the definition of what is problematic about these phenomena. But empiricism insists that its methodological norms are meant to apply only to the "context of justification"—to the testing of hypotheses and interpretation of evidence—not to the "context of discovery" where problems are identified and defined.[2]

We might question, however, whether the artificial separation of contexts of justification from those of discovery has to be part of feminist empiricism. Must feminist empiricism incorporate this tenet of logical positivism?

It is not clear why it should. Let us agree that if feminist empiricism were to accept this tenet, it would be inadequate to correct androcentric bias. From this it does not follow that existing methodological norms of scientific inquiry are positivist or that feminist empiricism, as Harding describes it, is grounded in positivism.[3] One may, it seems, accept her definition of feminist empiricism and her reasons for believing positivist methodological principles are impotent to correct androcentrism but not accept her argument against feminist empiricism. For one may question the suppressed premise that the existing methodological norms of scientific inquiry incorporate the positivist norm separating justification from discovery.

The suggestion that the existing methodological norms of scientific inquiry are not positivist is worth exploring. An immediate difficulty is that in all probability there is no such thing as the existing norms of scientific inquiry if one means some set of norms of inquiry that all (or even most) scientists accept.[4] A further complication is that we need to distinguish the norms of inquiry that scientists may profess to accept from the norms that actually guide their inquiry.[5] These difficulties can be ameliorated to a great extent by focusing on a specific set of norms. Consider the following three empiricist[6] standards for a good test of a theoretical hypothesis.[7] Very briefly, they are that (1) one outcome of the test—call it *the predicted outcome*—must be predictable (or be within limits that are predictable) on the basis of the hypothesis being tested together with plausible auxiliary assumptions about the testing conditions and the theoretical background of the test, (2) whether this outcome obtains must be ascertainable through observation without assuming the hypothesis being tested, and (3) apart from the hypothesis in question, there must be no plausible alternative explanation of the predicted outcome, should it be observed. (Hereafter, I will call these, respectively, the norms of predictive success, observation independence, and explanatory power.[8]) It would be foolish to suppose that these are the only methodological norms operating in science or that they are always rigorously followed. Still, it is arguable that they play a central role in guiding the construction and evaluation of scientific tests.[9]

Consider, then, the view that sexism and androcentrism in science are correctable by stricter adherence to these particular norms of hypothesis testing.[10] Is it plausible? I do not think so, not because such empiricism is positivist (I will argue it is not) but because the feminist political goals of eliminating androcentrism and sexism are not internal to the methodology that is proposed. The view implies that these political goals can be accomplished as a by-product of strict adherence to norms with no feminist content. As many feminists, including Harding, have argued, that view is not credible. At this point it may appear that Harding is right after all. But there is an important distinction to observe. We can distinguish between forms of feminist empiricism where the feminist goals are internal to its methodology for testing hypotheses and forms where they are not. The view just described can be called *external feminist empiricism*, since the pursuit of feminist goals is not entailed in following the methodology specified for testing hypotheses.

Consider, however, the possibility of an internal feminist empiricism. Can it be effective in accomplishing feminist political goals? I believe it can. The internal feminist empiricism on which I will focus combines in its methodology the feminist norm of pursuing the elimination of social bias against women and the three empiricist norms just described.[11] Notice, though, that because feminist norms are not in any general way part of the existing methodological norms of scientific inquiry, this internal feminist empiricism does not count as feminist empiricism by Harding's lights. Nor does it count as feminist standpoint theory or feminist postmodernism—Harding's two alternatives to feminist empiricism. (Not feminist standpoint theory because by itself it does not accord epistemic privilege to women as a group or to some subgroup of women;[12] not feminist postmodernism because the latter implies the impossibility of objective knowledge.) Thus, it misses all three strategies that Harding identifies for dealing with the question of science in feminism. Why, we might ask, has this kind of feminist empiricism been excluded?

I suggest that it has been excluded for two reasons. First, one may argue that internal feminist empiricism is incoherent because of an irresolvable tension between feminism and empiricism. This objection is suggested by Harding's claims that the feminist component of feminist empiricism "deeply undercuts the assumptions of traditional empiricism" and creates "a tension between empiricist epistemology and its use by feminists."[13] A second basis for exclusion is the argument that internal feminist empiricism is not genuinely or purely empiricist, since its methodology includes a feminist and hence nonempiricist norm. This argument is implicit in Harding's claim that the recent feminist empiricisms that attempt to incorporate a political standpoint involve a revised conception of empiricism.[14] I will now try to answer these two objections.

Is This a Coherent Empiricism?

The issue of whether internal feminist empiricism is coherent is akin to the question of whether feminist science can exist. About the latter Harding has noted the following general epistemological problem:

> Feminism is a political movement for social change. Viewed from the perspective of the assumptions of science's self-understanding, "feminist knowledge," "feminist science," and "feminist philosophy of science" should be contradictions in terms. Scientific knowledge seeking is supposed to be value-neutral, objective, dispassionate, and disinterested. It is supposed to be protected from political interests by the norms of science.[15]

In other words, the problem is that science is supposed to be by nature apolitical. The problem for internal feminist empiricism would be parallel, since empiricism too is supposed to be apolitical. Harding does not believe, of course, that feminist empiricism is self-contradictory, but that is because she conceives of it in a way that makes feminism external to empiricist methodology for testing scientific hypotheses. She assumes that feminist empiricism is necessarily external. If feminism were internal to empiricism, then would it not contain the very contradiction that critics attribute to the concept of feminist science? For if empiricist norms by their nature demand that a researcher be apolitical in testing hypotheses, how can there be a methodology for constructing and evaluating scientific tests that is at once both empiricist and feminist?

But do empiricist norms demand that a researcher be apolitical in scientific testing? Do, for example, the empiricist norms of predictive success, observation independence, and explanatory power make this demand? To answer these questions, we need to reflect on what such norms imply regarding the familiar distinction between context of discovery and context of justification. Feminist epistemologists (among others, such as Thomas Kuhn) point out that the identification and definition of research problems, the invention of hypotheses worthy of testing, the availability of alternative explanations of the evidence, and the content of untested background assumptions—all matters belonging to the context of "discovery"—can be and usually are influenced by political, social, and religious factors. (This point is so common and well documented that I take it for granted in what follows.[16]) Such influence is inevitably reflected in what is justified by the evidence, since the context of discovery determines what gets put to empirical test in the first place. But from this premise one cannot conclude directly that empiricist norms of scientific testing are political, for such norms are intended here to apply to the process of justifying a theoretical hypothesis on the basis of test results. The norms are intended to apply, in other words, to the context of justification only, not that of discovery. One can, therefore, consistent with the admission that the context of discovery is subject to political influences, maintain that the process of justification of a given hypothesis on the basis of given evidence is apolitical and that it is the latter process to which the empiricist norms are supposed to apply. Thus, the problem of coherence appears to remain in full force, at least for internal feminist empiricism.

This problem of coherence is anchored in a particular understanding of how the two contexts of discovery and justification are related. First, the norms of empiricism (especially those that pertain specifically to the question of whether a given set of data supports a given hypothesis) are assumed to apply to the context of justification alone. They are about the "logic" of justification and thus have nothing to do with the origins of data and hypotheses. Second, these norms of logic are assumed to be inherently apolitical (much as norms for deductive logic are thought to be). These assumptions taken together have two important consequences. One is that internal feminist empiricism becomes a conceptual impossibility, for the feminism contained in it would have to be somehow internal to the logic of justification (to its empiricist methodology) which is impossible on the assumptions just given. This point would explain why Harding simply assumes that the feminism in feminist empiricism would have to be external to its empiricism and hence why she does not broach the question of an internalist alternative. The other consequence is that strict adherence to the norms of empiricism would be utterly incapable of correcting for the social biases that affect the context of discovery. The reason is simply that empiricism is assumed to pertain to the logic of justification alone—something inherently apolitical—and therefore to have no bearing on the factors that influence the context of discovery.

This understanding is evident in Lorraine Code's *What Can She Know?* in which she describes the radical potential of feminist empiricism. Echoing Harding, she writes:

> Feminist empiricism advocates a new empiricist project informed by the privileged vision of feminist consciousness and hence peculiarly equipped to eradicate sexism and androcentrism, represented as social biases. In its feminist dimension, it disrupts the smooth impartiality of the standard empiricist credo by introducing a specificity—a declaration of specific interests—to contest the very possibility of a disinterested epistemology. Hence it can claim subversive potential.[17]

Notice that in this passage the "feminist dimension" of feminist empiricism is conceived to be external to and in tension with its empiricist dimension.

This political dimension "disrupts the smooth impartiality" of its empiricist counterpart. The apolitical or "disinterested" character of the latter is, Code believes, likely to be subverted by aims of feminism. But notice that the effect of the subversion is not to make the empiricism political (which by nature it supposedly cannot be) but rather to demonstrate that its logic cannot possibly filter out the social biases that infect the context of discovery. Thus, Code adds, "In arguing that social biases permeate 'the context of discovery' in any inquiry so thoroughly that it would be naive to hope for their eradication in the 'context of justification', feminist empiricism demonstrates its radical potential."[18] The assumption again appears to be that the context of justification is inherently apolitical.

This understanding of how the context of discovery relates to that of justification is, I believe, profoundly mistaken. It is, ironically, part of the legacy of logical positivism. A positivist concedes that political concerns could influence the "discovery" of a certain hypothesis or certain data but insists that the question of whether this hypothesis h is supported by this evidence e is another matter. The positivist says that whether e confirms h, no matter where either came from, is a matter of logic, and this at least is beyond politics. Even granting this, Harding and Code are right that the norms that guide us in deciding whether e confirms h cannot begin to filter out the social biases that enter into the discovery of h and e. Consequently, what ends up being confirmed, if e confirms h, reflect these biases. And they are right that the positivists are oblivious to the significance of this point. Still, they concede too much—indeed, they buy into the positivism that they want to reject—if they imply that the confirmation relation taken just in itself is untouched by political concerns. I want to argue the contrary. The very logic of confirmation, according to the familiar empiricist norms cited earlier, depends on the context of discovery. That is, whether a given e confirms a given h cannot be determined independently of the context of discovery. If this is right, then the argument for the incoherence of internal feminist empiricism falls apart. For in this case there would be no apolitical core of empiricism to stand in conflict with the political nature of feminism.

Consider first the standard of predictive success. It is not credible to claim that an outcome of a test situation confirms a particular theoretical hypothesis if that outcome is not in principle[19] predictable on its basis (or is not within the bounds of statistical likelihood, in the case of a hypothesis applying a stochastic model). For, while predictive success is not a sufficient condition for empirical confirmation, it sets a minimum condition; unless it is met, the alleged evidence is not relevant to the truth[20] of the hypothesis. But it is a commonplace in the philosophy of science that any theoretical hypothesis predicts an outcome of a test only in the context of various auxiliary hypotheses about the test situation and other background assumptions. The role played by these additional hypotheses and theories becomes obvious when the predicted outcome is not observed. In this case the absence of a positive result counts as disconfirming evidence only when the connecting hypotheses and theories are themselves credible. (The original hypothesis can always be saved from refutation if one or more of the assumptions on which the prediction is based can be rejected instead.[21]) It only remains to be noted that these connecting links form part of the context of discovery. Given the premise (which, as indicated earlier, I am assuming throughout) that political factors can and often do play a part in forming the context of discovery, it follows that these factors can figure in determining whether the standard of predictive success is met. The context of discovery and the political forces that help create it form an intrinsic part of the context of justification.

The place of the context of discovery in applying the standard of observation independence is almost equally straightforward once it is understood that observation itself, at least in any interesting testing situation, also involves assumptions from the context of discovery. For observations relevant to testing theoretical hypotheses generally involve the use of instruments (e.g., microscopes, thermometers) whose reliability depends on theory (e.g., of optics, temperature); indeed, arguably all perception is mediated by theory. This does not mean that the observation of test results begs the question of whether the hypothesis being tested is true. As long as the assumptions underlying the observation do not include the hypothesis being tested, circularity is avoided.[22] What it does mean is that once again the context of discovery, together with whatever political influences that have shaped it, determines whether a given test meets the norms appropriate for the context of justification.

Most striking is the way matters of discovery help determine explanatory power. According to this norm, putative evidence for a hypothesis counts as confirming its truth only if no credible alternative hypothesis explains what is observed equally well. Put another way, what is observed confirms a hypothesis only if (on the assumption that the hypothesis is not true or close to the truth) what is observed is improbable, given what we now take to be believable (including any alternative hypotheses). The norm of explanatory power is important, since without it there is no straightforward way to discount cases of confirmation where agreement between observation and theory is created ad hoc or is coincidental and thus can be explained without assuming the truth of the hypothesis being tested. Yet the comparative nature of this norm is such that it cannot be applied without noting whether other relevant theories exist, and these are part of the context of discovery. The present putative evidence confirms only to the extent that the present hypothesis fares well in this comparison.

To conclude this section, I will note two consequences that follow from this analysis and support the coherence and viability of internal feminist empiricism. The first is that there is no sense to the idea of "pure" empiricism with respect to testing hypotheses against the evidence—that is, a methodology of testing that is completely apolitical in its application—if empiricism entails acceptance of anything like the empiricist norms just discussed. The reason is simply that these norms cannot be satisfied except by reference to a theoretical background subject to political influence. The idea of pure empiricism in this sense is incoherent. But then the objection raised earlier, that internal feminist empiricism is not a genuine empiricism because it is political in its methodology, is a nonstarter.

The second implication is that, while there is no such thing as apolitical empiricism, the norms of empiricism do not carry with them any one particular set of political aims. This point partly explains why empiricist norms appear to be such that their application has no political import. The political ramifications of their application depend on the nature of the theoretical context in which they are applied. If the assumptions in that context arise from androcentric or sexist thinking in the field of research, then what is confirmed or disconfirmed reflects that bias. For this reason I agree with Harding and Code that empiricist norms, taken just by themselves, have no real chance of ridding science of androcentrism or sexism. In my terms, external feminist empiricism cannot achieve the feminist goals that are set for it—from the outside, as it were.

The externalist approach takes the context of discovery as given and then hopes by the rigorous application of empiricist norms to achieve scientific results free of any kind of gender bias. This is a very philosophically naive empiricism. That any actual feminist scientist could practice it consistently is doubtful, for she would surely question the theoretical context in which the norms of empiricism are applied. Though she may, through a mistaken conception of what empiricism involves, characterize her approach in terms that fit the external view, in all likelihood her practice would be that of an internal feminist empiricist. There would be no way to separate the feminism from the empiricism, each having the potential to guide the other in testing any theoretical hypothesis.

Can It Be Objective?

But if there is no way to separate feminism from empiricism in this epistemology, can it possibly be objective? It may seem that it cannot be. If objectivity in science is identified with taking the standpoint of a neutral observer, then obviously a problem arises. One cannot be both neutral and politically committed. This fact, according to many feminists, is a reason for rejecting feminist empiricism.[23] Ironically, this response implies an acceptance of the positivist split between fact and value that most feminists want to avoid.

Two ways to deal with this objection are possible. One is to give up any commitment to objectivity; the other is to reject the notion of objectivity that identifies objectivity with neutrality. The course defended here is the second.[24] The way around the objection, however, demands that an alternative account of objectivity be developed and shown to cohere with empiricism. To keep the discussion within manageable bounds, I will confine my attention to objectivity in testing hypotheses in science. (In later chapters, the discussion of objectivity will be expanded to include that of scientific and moral norms.) As a first approximation: objectivity in testing consists simply of heeding the empiricist norms of testing already outlined. The reason why this is only a first approximation will become clear in the next chapter. Obviously, this notion of objectivity is fully consistent with empiricism as it has been understood here. It should also be clear that it does not stand in the way of feminist political commitment, given the argument of the last two sections.

Since the argument thus far has been relatively abstract, it may be helpful to illustrate with some examples.[25] I take the first from Anne Fausto-Sterling's study of biological theories about sex differences in her book *The Myths of Gender*.[26] A popular belief shared by many psychologists is that there are sex-related differences in visual-spatial ability (VSA). Various tests have been designed to test this hypothesis. One of the best known is the rod and frame test developed by psychologist H. A. Witkin. Fausto-Sterling describes the test as follows.

> In this test the subject sits in a totally dark room in a chair facing a large (forty inches on a side), vertically held, luminescent frame. Bisecting the frame is a lighted rod. In one version the experimenter tilts the frame in various ways and the subject adjusts the rod to the vertical of the room, ignoring the immediate context of the tilted frame. In a different version, the subject's chair is tilted, and again he or she must make the rod inside the frame perpendicular to the floor.[27]

One standard work on the psychology of sex differences cites twelve separate studies in which this test was run; in seven of these men scored better than women and in five there were no sex-related differences.[28] The question is, Does this observation of better performance by men confirm the hypothesis that men have on average superior VSA?

This hypothesis, together with the assumption that how one does on the test is a direct result of one's VSA, predicts that on average men will score better on the test. Moreover, the results of the test can be verified independently of the assumption that the hypothesis is true. The norms of predictive success and observation independence appear, therefore, to be satisfied. What about explanatory power? Is it true that if the hypothesis were false (if there were no sex-related differences in VSA), then it would be very improbable that men would do better in seven of the twelve tests and women would do better in none? Or is the test result what you might expect independent of the test hypothesis?

The answer depends on whether factors other than VSA may explain poor performance, as Fausto-Sterling argues:

> Picture the following: a pitch dark room, a male experimenter, a female subject. What female would not feel just a little vulnerable in that situation? Although one would expect experimenter-subject interactions to be different for males and females in such a set-up, the studies cited by Maccoby and Jacklin apparently don't take into account this possibility. In one version of the test, the subject must ask the experimenter to adjust the rod by small increments to the position he or she believes to be vertical. A less assertive person might hesitate to insist to the nth degree that the experimenter continue the adjustments. Close might seem good enough. If it is true that females are less assertive than males, then this behavioral difference, rather than differences in visual-spatial acuity, could account for their performances in the rod and frame test.[29]

In other words, the norm of explanatory power is violated, since a plausible alternative explanation of the data exists. For this reason we should conclude that the data do not confirm the original hypothesis.

Is there not some way to redesign the test so that it conforms better to the norms? Perhaps so. Fausto-Sterling reports that when, in a similar test, "the rod was replaced by a human figure and the task described as one of empathy, sex-related differences in performance disappeared."[30] But the point of drawing attention to this example is not to argue that the new test was better designed (though there is reason to think that it was). The point is rather to show how feminist motivation can have an effect on the application of empiricist norms without undermining objectivity in the sense defined. In this instance a researcher who is skeptical of studies appearing to support a gender stereotype is able to find an alternative explanation of the earlier results and to show how it is borne out in further tests. Her approach to the question of justification is obviously not disinterested (i.e., not objective in the sense often attributed to empiricism), yet it is fully consistent with the norms of testing cited. In fact, it is because of her political motivation that she is able to discover that the norm of explanatory power has been violated.

Consider next an example involving nonhuman subjects. In an article critical of the methodology of some sociobiologists, Stephen Jay Gould reports an experiment conducted by David Barash to test a certain model of aggressiveness in male mountain bluebirds toward males who might "cuckold" them.[31] In Barash's model such aggressiveness would be selected for, since if the males were cuckolded, then their nest mates would pass the genes of other males on to the next generation rather than their own. The experiment designed to test this model involved the observation of two nests at three times, ten days apart, first before the female in the nest had laid her eggs and then two times after she had laid them. On each occasion a stuffed male was put near the nest while its male resident was away foraging. The supposed similarity of the model to nature (together with Darwin's theory of natural selection and a number of other assumptions) predicts what was observed: the resident male was more aggressive toward the mock intruder (and toward his mate) before the eggs were laid than afterward. In fact, in the last trial little aggression was shown toward the intruder and none toward the female. (Degree of aggression was measured by counting the number of successive aggressive encounters with the stuffed bird and the female.)

In this example the norms of predictive success and observation independence appear to be met. Gould is, however, severely critical of the methodology, since mere consistency with Barash's model should not be enough to warrant concluding that the evidence confirms the reliability of his model. In addition, the test should be designed to rule out alternative models. Suppose, for example, that the aggressiveness diminished over the intervals because the resident male came to recognize, more quickly each time, that the apparent intruder was a fake. On this alternative model the timing of the intrusion relative to egg laying is irrelevant to triggering aggression. Since both models can be used to predict what was observed, it would be gratuitous to suppose, given the evidence, that one rather than the other fits more closely the aggression of male mountain bluebirds.

Gould suggests that it would be easy to test the relevance of the second model: expose a male to the mock intruder for the first time after the eggs are laid. Barash's model predicts that there will be little aggression shown toward the stuffed male; moreover, this outcome would seem improbable if his model does not fit reality. (The only other model available predicts that the level of aggression will not be much different from the first time in the first experiment—relatively high.) In our terms, we can interpret Gould's criticism as pointing out that the original test design did not meet the norm of explanatory power. To meet this norm, one would have to run (at minimum) the combination of experiments in testing the first model. In this case a set of positive outcomes would confirm the model if no credible third model were available that could explain these results.

It is presumptuous to suppose that we know just what Gould's motives are in this case. It is clear, however, that someone could be moved to raise the same challenge because she or he is opposed to the way a certain patriarchal view of male behavior is projected onto nature. The opposition in itself does not undermine the support for Barash's model, but coupled with an appeal to the norm of explanatory power it can. The examples show how values work in tandem with empirical norms to determine whether test results support a given hypothesis and how values can enhance objectivity in testing in the sense defined.

Does It Have Sufficient Scope?

A problem remains, however, about the scope of feminist empiricism. Recall Harding's objection that feminist empiricism confines itself to the context of justification and thus ignores issues concerning how research problems are identified and defined prior to the stage where the justification of specific hypotheses becomes the focus of interest. Her concern is that so confined, feminist empiricism cannot deal with the deep roots of sexism and androcentrism in science, since these roots feed off the context of discovery. Harding assumes, of course, that the context of discovery is not part of the context of justification, and we have now seen in detail why this view is mistaken and how it contributes to an untenable conception of objectivity. Still, a problem persists inasmuch as the foregoing argument brings in the context of discovery only to the extent that it is relevant to the question of justification for a specific hypothesis. Any sexism or androcentrism that arises independently will simply be ignored by feminist empiricism, it would seem, and Harding's complaint, though based on a false premise, would be essentially unanswered.

The difficulty may be illustrated by the fact that until very recently the main studies of coronary heart disease (CHD) have been done exclusively on men, even though CHD is known to be the single most frequent cause of death among women, just as it is among men. Recent studies show that important differences exist between the sexes in their manifestation of CHD.[32] The most common initial manifestation for men is myocardial infarction (MI), while for women it is uncomplicated angina pectoris, which may continue for years without MI (though some evidence suggests that an initial MI is more apt to be fatal in women). Another important difference is that coronary events like MI are rare in women under age sixty-five. Since the rates of CHD increase gradually in postmenopausal women until they experience MI at the same rate as men and since women comprise a much larger percentage of the population over age sixty-five, the number of cases of CHD are greater for women than for men in this age group.

Because most well-known studies of cardiovascular disease had not included any women participants, these and many other differences have been slow to come to light. A famous example is the Multiple Risk Factor Intervention Trial Research Group, which studied 12,866 high-risk men between the ages of thirty-five and fifty-seven but included no women.[33] Another is the Physician's Health Study, a controlled study of 22,071 male physicians to determine whether low-dose aspirin reduces the risk of MI and beta-carotene reduces the risk of cancer.[34] The problem is not that these studies were ill designed for the purpose of revealing relevant information about heart disease in men but that there was little interest in understanding how CHD might affect women differently from men. In this case androcentrism operates at the level of the context of discovery, where research problems are identified, and not at the stage of testing specific hypotheses. Still, because of this bias, the massive studies in question did not and could not yield definitive answers about the causes and prevention of heart disease in women. Critics have claimed, for example, that the exclusively male studies have no means of testing the effects of estrogen in women, which (some evidence suggests) may help to protect women from MI.[35] In sum, although there may be no gender bias operating in the testing of hypotheses as such, the research interests that give rise to those hypotheses can themselves reflect bias, if those interests ignore the needs of women. The implication is that apparently nothing in feminist empiricism, if it is tied solely to the context of justifying hypotheses, can dislodge this bias.

The problem is obviously very general. It can be formulated more exactly for the feminist empiricism defined earlier as follows. The empiricist norms of predictive success, observation independence, and explanatory power are norms for guiding and evaluating the testing of specific hypotheses against the outcomes of specific experiments. These norms give no guidance or evaluation regarding how hypotheses are to be selected in the first place. Although, for reasons already given, feminist political goals can play a significant role in the application of these norms, if feminist goals affect only how these norms are applied in the testing of hypotheses and not how the hypotheses are chosen for testing, these goals cannot resolve the scope problem. Therefore, if feminist empiricism is confined to the context of justification, the scope problem presents a serious objection to its adequacy.

The way to resolve this problem is to point out that the empiricist norms are not confined to those that apply to the context of justification. These norms do constitute, in a very rough way, a methodology for testing hypotheses, but, as I shall argue at length in the next chapter, they presuppose and lend indirect support to a norm that underlies the goal of having hypotheses that are empirically confirmed through testing. This is the norm that requires that hypotheses provide a relatively accurate representation of what the world is like. Assume for the moment that this realist norm can be reasonably included among the empiricist norms. This norm, once it is combined with feminist norms, would provide a basis to select some hypotheses rather than others as being worthy of empirical investigation. Which hypotheses are chosen will depend, of course, on how a researcher interprets past results. But the point is that with this norm included there would be, within feminist empiricism, no restriction to consideration of hypotheses selected on some prior (perhaps androcentric) basis. The potential scope of feminist empiricism would then be wide open, and no aspect of the context of discovery would escape its purview. Contrary to Harding's view, feminist empiricism would not be tied solely to the context of justification.

Why Empiricism?

Before moving on to discuss realism, we should consider why empiricist norms are given a privileged status. It is one thing to show that feminism can be successfully combined with the norms of empiricism; it is another to show that empiricism is necessary or important to feminism. To show the latter, however, we need first to say more about how empiricism is being conceived in this context.

Empiricism is clearly distinct from logical positivism if only because it does not separate the contexts of justification and discovery. Another reason is that it is incompatible with the positivists' twin dogmas of analyticity and verificationism for Quinean reasons to be developed later in chapter 8. What of classical empiricism, though, with its rejection of innate ideas? Does feminist empiricism treat the developing mind as a Lockean tabula rasa? I see no reason to impose this constraint, since it is inconsistent with what we now know about how the mind develops and faces what Louise Antony has called "a massive restriction-of-range problem"—that one's experience is always limited, and thus general judgments based on it alone are invariably suspect and unjustifiable.[36] I take up this problem directly in chapter 5 in which Quine's Darwinian solution to the problem of induction is addressed and the idea of a naturalized empiricist theory of knowledge delineated. Suffice it to say now that the notion that reasoning from nature is driven by experience alone is something that I want to disconnect entirely from the concept of empiricism advanced here. The reasons will come in due course.

It may seem, however, that a vestige of classical empiricism remains in the idea of observation as the cornerstone of experimental testing and that this idea is built into the way that I have identified the empiricist norms of predictive success, observation independence, and explanatory power. Is not this notion itself untenable, since there is good reason to believe that "pure" observation, untainted by any theoretical considerations or influence, is utter fantasy?[37] I want to concede that all observation that is sufficiently regimented to enter into deductive relations with theory has to involve some degree of conceptualization and cognitive control and therefore is at least in this respect "theory laden." But this concession does not in any way undermine the appeal to observation in the minimal sense needed to formulate the empiricist norms mentioned. Take, for example, the norm of observation independence. As we noted earlier (with reference to the insights of Helen Longino and Mary Hesse), all that is necessary to avoid vicious circularity and thus satisfy this norm is that observation be such that it can be verified without relying on the very hypothesis that is being tested against this observation. Its verification is likely to depend on many other theoretical assumptions and be in this sense extremely impure.

A much more serious objection to insisting on observation as a necessary ingredient of experimental testing is raised by Jerry Fodor. Fodor has argued that while all experimental testing involves reference to data, not all data are observed or even observable in an experimental test.[38] He gives an example of his own empirical research in which he tests for differences in the way native speakers respond to the active and passive voice. The experimental situation requires the recording of minute differences in reaction times (differences on the order of fifteen to twenty microseconds) between when a verbal stimulus is presented to a subject and when the subject signals recognition of it. These differences in reaction times—or, more exactly, statistically significant mean differences of this kind—constitute the data that would confirm the hypothesis that people respond differently (finding it harder to identify the passive voice). But, and this is the critical point, such data are not directly observable through the use of sensory organs, such as the eye. The differences in response are so small as to be detectable only through the use of special instruments, not through anything like the "direct" observation that historically has been the focus of empiricism. The latter identifies observation with the having of experiences, and the data "observed" in the experiment through the use of recording devices did not involve any experiences on the part of those devices.

One might attempt to rebut this argument by pointing out that at least the recording instruments themselves must be observed in the old-fashioned way, but Fodor makes it clear that not even that is strictly necessary. Consider his intriguing thought experiment. In a high-tech future science you could "just plug the experimenter's cortex into the computer that collects the experimental data [so that] there aren't any sensory bombardments at all, and nobody ever looks at anything."[39] If everything is hooked up in such a way that it is well understood that the researcher will come to believe the relevant theory if and only if the data are present, we would have a case where belief is rationally constrained by the outcome of the experiment without observation in the classical sense having any role at all to play in confirming the theory.

Though I take Fodor's point that scientific theories need not be constrained by data observed through the use of sensory organs, I am not prepared to say that this shows that the norms governing experimental testing are not in some suitably broad sense empiricist. What is that sense? In formulating the norms for experimental testing, we should speak of "detectable data" rather than observation, and we should allow that the data, like the differences in response intervals described in Fodor's experiments, may not be something that we can notice without the aid of special equipment. Nevertheless, we can say that normally the data are publicly accessible through the use of our senses, where our senses are often aided by devices believed to be reliable. The link with sensory experience is thus indirect, even with respect to our access to data that are themselves only indirectly tied to theory, but it is not normally absent altogether. The only exception would be the kind of science fiction example that Fodor mentions in which sensory experience is bypassed completely, but even here the background theories that allow this shortcut would themselves be confirmed on the basis of sensory evidence.

The upshot is, to be sure, a highly qualified empiricism. It does not treat observation in science as beyond question or as lacking in theoretical commitments or as unaided by technology that must itself be explained by theory. But empiricism so qualified is not vacuous. It does require that theory be tested against experimental data to which we normally have at least indirect access through the use of our senses. That is enough to mark it as empiricist in the suitably broad sense of the term that I am using in this book.

But why should even a highly qualified empiricism be important? Why must a feminist science be empiricist in any respect at all? My answer is based on a realist interpretation of science and scientific norms. This interpretation is defended at some length in the next chapter. For the moment let me assume that a natural world exists, including ourselves and our minds, that obtains independently of our representations of it. I say "obtains independently." What does this mean? It means simply that our representations can be more or less mistaken, individually and collectively, about what the world is like. Let me assume also that we have some knowledge of this world. How do we get this knowledge? From a broad empiricist perspective, this knowledge is based on checking our representations against the results of experiment. Our experiments are, in the familiar phrase, questions asked of nature with the answers given in the results of our experiments. Because of the accidents of our evolution, we normally become acquainted with these answers only through stimulation of our sense organs. There is no metaphysical necessity in this; it is simply how we are. This empiricism is, I contend, the best available account of how we have knowledge, given the assumption of realism. That is my explanation of why it is important.

A feminist might reject realism, but that would be a mistake for reasons I will turn to next. Or a feminist might be a skeptic about knowledge, but that would be also be a mistake, especially for anyone who claims to know that women are in various fundamental ways treated as subordinate to men. Or a feminist might propose a different account of how knowledge of an independently existing world is possible, an account in which testing hypotheses experimentally does not have a central role to play. Feminist standpoint theory may seem to be such an alternative, but, as I shall contend in chapter 4, where standpoint theory rests on solid ground, it is not a real alternative to internal feminist empiricism broadly conceived. Still other feminist accounts of realist-based knowledge may be possible. There is no way, consistent with a thoroughgoing empiricism, to close off alternatives a priori. The best that I can do is to develop one account with some care and argue that it resolves the main problems that face such an approach to knowledge.

Notes

1. Sandra Harding, *The Science Question in Feminism* (Ithaca, N.Y.: Cornell University Press, 1986), 24; see also Harding, "Feminist Justificatory Strategies," in

Women, Knowledge, Reality, Ann Geary and Marilyn Pearsal, eds. (Boston: Unwin
Hyman, 1989), 191; Harding, *Whose Science? Whose Knowledge?* (Ithaca, N.Y.: Cornell University Press, 1991), 111; Sandra Harding, "Rethinking Standpoint Epistemology: What is 'Strong Objectivity'?" in *Feminist Epistemologies,* Linda Alcoff and
Elizabeth Potter, eds. (New York: Routledge, 1993), 51. In her 1993 essay Harding
distinguishes between "spontaneous feminist empiricism" (the position just defined)
and a recent "philosophical" version of feminist empiricism that she attributes to
Helen Longino and Lynn Hankinson Nelson and understands to be a revision of empiricism and hence not subject to her critique. The feminist empiricism defended in this
chapter is not, however, intended to entail a revision of the empiricist norms identified
as operative in current scientific practice. I will assume, therefore, that Harding would
take her original objections to feminist empiricism to apply to the account to be developed here.

2. Harding, *The Science Question,* 25.

3. For a clear statement that Harding thinks that the existing methodological norms
of science are so grounded, see Harding, *Whose Science?* 79.

4. As Harding notes, some natural scientists and many social scientists happily
endorse the norms of positivism, while many others reject them; *Whose Science?* 57.

5. It is a common theme in feminist philosophy of science, for example, that decisions about the weight of evidence are influenced by values embedded in the context
of inquiry even when those making the decisions profess to be guided by norms pre-
scribing value neutrality in such matters. Which are the "existing" norms in a sense
relevant to the proposed definition?

6. Sometimes *empiricist* is used in opposition to *realist* to signify the conservative
epistemic view that we can know only things that are directly observable. As will
become evident, I am not an empiricist in this sense, and neither is Giere. Nor, for that
matter, are most philosophers who are apt to be called *feminist empiricists.* I will use
the term more inclusively. When I speak of the norms to follow as *empiricist,* I mean
that the norms are about the conditions under which sensory evidence would confirm
or disconfirm a theoretical hypothesis. Here I follow Lynn Hankinson Nelson, *Who
Knows: From Quine to Feminist Empiricism* (Philadelphia: Temple University Press,
1990), 9, 20–21, 86, in interpreting empiricism as a theory of sensory evidence. This
way of speaking does not rule out the possibility of giving a realist interpretation to
theoretical hypotheses, nor does it exclude the possibility that sensory evidence is
always theory laden and that no absolute distinction exists between the directly and
indirectly observable.

7. Adapted from Ronald Giere, *Understanding Scientific Reasoning,* 2d ed. (New
York: Holt, Rinehart, & Winston, 1984).

8. The conditions are also implicit in the third (1991) and fourth (1997) editions
of Giere, *Understanding Scientific Reasoning,* but their most explicit formulation is in
the second (1984), 105. Giere's explicit formulation, however, differs from my statement of the conditions in various ways.

Giere's condition corresponding to predictive success stipulates that a statement
describing the outcome be deducible from the hypothesis being tested together with
plausible auxiliary assumptions. The emphasis on deduction with respect to a specific
outcome represents a deliberate oversimplification. Elsewhere in his text and in less

elementary work (Giere, "Causal Systems and Statistical Hypotheses," in *Applications of Inductive Logic*, L. J. Cohen and M. B. Hesse, eds. [Oxford: Oxford Univesity Press, 1980], 251–70), he deals with stochastic theoretical models in which it is not possible to deduce specific outcomes from the corresponding hypotheses (postulating that the models fit various real systems). In these cases what is deduced will be a probability distribution rather than a specific outcome. I have avoided going into these complications, since they are not germane to the argument to follow. What is germane is that auxiliary assumptions are needed to make the connection between hypothesis and evidence, whether what is deduced is a statement describing a specific outcome or a statement describing a probability distribution of possible outcomes.

Giere's condition corresponding to observation independence specifies merely that the existence of the predicted outcome be verifiable by observation in the circumstances of the test. This too is an oversimplification. Observations, as is now generally accepted in postpositivist literature, are theory dependent. For example, astronomical observations of outcomes relevant to confirming astronomical hypotheses depend on the theory of optics. To avoid vicious circularity in testing a hypothesis, the observation of the predicted outcome must not depend on an assumption that the theory or hypothesis being tested is true. I have, therefore, complicated Giere's condition slightly to take this wrinkle into account.

Finally, Giere's condition corresponding to explanatory power was originally stated as requiring that the predicted outcome would be improbable if the hypothesis were not at least approximately true. Here one needs to ask what sort of probability is involved and upon what the probability is conditional. Understandably, Giere avoided entering into these questions in an introductory textbook, since the main point was clear enough: there should be no viable alternative hypothesis that explains the predicted outcome equally well. (If such an alternative existed, then, relative to that background information, the predicted result would not be improbable, even if the hypothesis being tested were false.) Since the point of Giere's third condition is to rule out false positive results and thus bring out the comparative character of confirmation, I have preferred to state the condition directly in comparative terms. For an illuminating discussion of this condition, see Ronald Giere, "Testing Theoretical Hypotheses," in *Testing Scientific Theories*, J. Earman, ed., Minnesota Studies in the Philsophy of Science, vol. 10 (Minneapolis: University of Minnesota Press, 1983), 269–98.

9. Their influence is reflected in the reasons that scientists give when they defend their interpretations of evidence or offer criticisms of the interpretations offered by others. For example, a scientist might criticize her colleague's claim that the evidence of test results supports a certain hypothesis by offering an alternative hypothesis that explains the evidence equally well. Her reasons in this case reflect the importance of explanatory power in evaluating the weight of evidence in support of a hypothesis. It is arguable, moreover, that these standards function as norms for scientists even if some or many of them profess to follow norms incompatible with these. The norm of explanatory power, as I will argue later, is actually incompatible with positivist methodology; nevertheless, scientists who profess to be positivists often reason in accordance with this norm. Explanatory power is an "existing" norm in the sense that it prescribes behavior that scientists implicitly endorse in constructing, defending, and criticizing various experimental tests of theoretical hypotheses. Similar points apply for the norms of predictive success and observation independence.

10. Depending on how one reads her reference to "existing norms," this view may not precisely fit Harding's definition of feminist empiricism, but it is a recognizable form of empiricism (see note 6) and is also feminist in exactly the sense in which what Harding calls "feminist empiricism" is feminist. That is, the view holds that the feminist political ideals of removing sexism and androcentrism from science are achievable through applying empiricist norms.

11. Other forms of internal feminist empiricism are possible. They would involve different empiricist norms, as in the forms of feminist empiricism developed in Helen Longino, *Science as Social Knowledge* (Princeton, N.J.: Princeton University Press, 1990); Nelson, *Who Knows*; Lynn Hankinson Nelson, "Empiricism without Dogmas," in *Feminism, Science, and the Philosophy of Science*, Lynn Hankinson Nelson and Jack Nelson, eds. (Dordrecht: Kluwer, 1996); and Kathleen Okruhlik, "Birth of a New Physics or Death of Nature?" in *Women and Reason*, Elizabeth D. Harvey and Kathleen Okruhlik, eds. (Ann Arbor: University of Michigan Press, 1992), 63–76, which I examine in chapters 3 and 4. I focus on the aforementioned norms because, for reasons given later, I find them to be plausible standards for empirical confirmation. In this respect my defense of feminist empiricism is normative.

12. For the moment, I am understanding feminist standpoint theory to imply that *all* individuals in certain groups are epistemically privileged by virtue of belonging to those groups. Feminist empiricism of the kind defended here is not committed to this sweeping claim, but I would argue that individuals can be in positions of epistemic privilege by virtue of their gender, race, and class (among other categories) and that feminist empiricism can explain why this is so. It may be, then, that a qualified feminist standpoint theory is compatible with feminist empiricism. I take this up in the last section of chapter 4.

13. Harding, *Whose Science?* 115–17.

14. Harding, "Rethinking Standpoint Epistemology," 51.

15. Harding, "Feminist Justificatory Strategies," 190.

16. A principal impetus for this point of view has been the work of Thomas Kuhn; see, for example, Kuhn, *The Essential Tension* (Chicago: University of Chicago Press, 1977), 320–39. The literature, feminist and nonfeminist, on this subject is vast. For references to both before 1989, consult the bibliographic study by Alison Wylie, Kathleen Okruhlik, Sandra Morton, and Leslie Thielen-Wilson, "Philosophical Feminism: A Bibliographical Guide to Critiques of Science," *New Feminist Research* 19 (1989): 2–36. Among more recent feminist studies are Longino, *Science*; Nelson, *Who Knows*; Nancy Tuana, *The Less Noble Sex: Scientific, Religious, and Philosophical Conceptions of Woman's Nature* (Bloomington: Indiana University Press, 1993); and Bonnie B. Spanier, *Im/partial Science: Gender Ideology in Molecular Biology* (Bloomington: Indiana University Press, 1995), which contain detailed examinations of how values enter into current research on sex differences and explanatory models in biological science. See also Harding, *Whose Science?*; Okruhlik, "Birth of a New Physics"; and Alison Wylie, "The Construction of Archaeological Evidence: Gender Politics and Science" in *Disunity and Contextualism: New Direction in the Philosophy of Science Studies*, Peter Galison and David Stump, eds. (Stanford, Calif.: Stanford University Press, 1996).

17. Lorraine Code, *What Can She Know? Feminist Theory and the Construction of Knowledge* (Ithaca, N.Y.: Cornell University Press, 1991), 316.

18. Code, *What Can She Know?* 316.

19. The qualification "in principle" is necessary, since confirming evidence is not always predictable, given what is known at the time. Just prior to 1843, before J. C. Adams and Le Verrier postulated the existence of a planet now known as Neptune, the actual motion of Uranus could have been counted as confirming the hypothesis that the solar system works on Newtonian principles and hence its motion was in principle predictable. In fact, its motion was not correctly predicted on the basis of that hypothesis because the existence and position of Neptune was not even postulated at the time and thus was not included in the calculations.

20. For convenience of exposition, I have assumed that what gets confirmed is the truth of a hypothesis (or its approximate truth). This assumption is not essential in formulating the present norms of empirical confirmation, since we can talk, instead of models, of being confirmed, where models have no truth value. For a helpful exposition and defense of this approach, see Paul Thompson, *The Structure of Biological Theories* (Albany: State University of New York Press, 1989); Ronald Giere, "Constructive Realism," in *Images of Science*, Paul M. Churchland and Clifford A. Hooker, eds. (Chicago: University of Chicago Press, 1985); Giere, "Causal Systems"; for its relevance to feminism, see Helen Longino, "Subjects, Power and Knowledge: Description and Prescription in Feminist Philosophies of Science," in *Feminist Epistemologies*, Linda Alcoff and Elizabeth Potter, eds. (New York: Routledge, 1993), 101–20; and Geoffrey Gorham, "The Concept of Truth in Feminist Sciences," *Hypatia* 10 (1995): 99–116.

21. The philosophical significance of this point is not always appreciated. It means, for example, that (contrary to Karl Popper, *The Logic of Scientific Discovery* [London: Hutchinson, 1959]) it is impossible for there to be disconfirmation in the absence of confirmation, since evidence can disconfirm a theoretical hypothesis only relative to auxiliary assumptions that already have some empirical basis.

22. Longino makes the same point in *Science*, 56, following Mary Hesse, *Revolutions and Reconstructions in the Philosophy of Science* (Bloomington: Indiana University Press, 1980).

23. See, for example, Elizabeth Fee, "Women's Nature and Scientific Objectivity," in *Women's Nature: Rationalizations of Inequality*, M. Lowe and R. Hubbard, eds. (New York: Pergamon, 1981); Alison Jaggar, *Feminist Politics and Human Nature* (Totowa, N.J.: Rowman & Allanheld, 1983), 377–78; and Harding, *The Science Question*, 24–25.

24. The later argument is from my "The Virtues of Feminist Empiricism," *Hypatia* 9 (1994): 90–115. A number of feminist philosophers would agree to reject the link between objectivity and neutrality without wanting to give up on the notions of objectivity and empiricism. See, for example, various articles in Nelson, *Feminism and Science*. Thus, Potter argues in "Good Science and Good Philosophy of Science," 423–39, that the distinction between good and bad science cannot be based on the former involving value neutrality, even with respect to political values. Similarly, Longino argues in "Gender, Politics, and the Theoretical Virtues," 383–97, that certain values that are exemplified in feminist scientific practice and that she earlier classified as contextual rather than constitutive of science are justifiably regarded as being no less cognitive than the traditional values. Nelson and Tuana make points along similar

lines there. My own line of argument emphasizes (1) how political values legitimately function in norms for testing that are traditionally regarded as constitutive of good science and (2) how their legitimate function is best explained by a realist conception of knowledge.

25. More important, large-scale examples can be found in the literature to illustrate the points to follow: the creation of alternatives to the "master molecule" model of cell construction, in Evelyn Fox Keller, *Reflections on Gender and Science* (New Haven, Conn.: Yale University Press, 1985), and Spanier, *Im/partial Science*; the development of gynecentric "woman-the-gatherer" models of human evolution, in Nancy Makepeace Tanner, *On Becoming Human* (New York: Cambridge University Press, 1981); and the attempt to replace the usual linear-hormonal models of higher brain function with selectionist models, in Longino, *Science*, 133–61. I have chosen much simpler examples where the validity of my claims will be easier to assess.

26. Anne Fausto-Sterling, *Myths of Gender: Biological Theories about Women and Men* (New York: Basic Books, 1985).

27. Fausto-Sterling, *Myths*, 30.

28. Eleanor Maccoby and Carol Jacklin, *The Psychology of Sex Difference* (Stanford, Calif.: Stanford University Press, 1974).

29. Fausto-Sterling, *Myths*, 32.

30. Fausto-Sterling, *Myths*, 32.

31. Stephen Jay Gould, "Sociobiology and the Theory of Natural Selection," in *Beyond Nature/Nurture?*, G. W. Barlow and J. Silverberg, eds. (Boulder, Colo.: Westview, 1980). See also Stephen Jay Gould and Richard Lewontin, "The Spandrels of San Marco and the Panglossian Paradigm: A Critique of the Adaptationist Programme," *Proceedings of the Royal Society of London* 205 (1978): 581–98.

32. The information regarding sex differences in the manifestation of CHD is drawn from the Committee on the Ethical and Legal Issues Relating to the Inclusion of Women in Clinical Studies, in *Women and Health Research Vol. 1: Ethical and Legal Issues of Including Women in Clinical Studies*, Anna C. Mastroianni, Ruth Faden, and Daniel Bederman, eds. (Washington, D.C.: National Academy Press, 1994), 64–66.

33. Multiple Risk-Factor Intervention Trial Group, "Statistical Design Considerations in the NHLI Multiple Risk-Factor Trial (MRFIT)," *Journal of Chronic Diseases* 30 (1977): 261–75.

34. Steering Committee of the Physicians' Health Study Research Group, "Final Report on the Aspirin Component of the Ongoing Physicians' Health Study," *New England Journal of Medicine* 321 (1989): 129–35.

35. B. Healy, "The Yentl Syndrome," *New England Journal of Medicine* 325 (1991): 274–76.

36. Lousie Antony, "Quine as Feminist: The Radical Import of Naturalized Epistemology," in *A Mind of One's Own: Feminist Essays on Reason and Objectivity*, Louise Antony and Charlotte Witt, eds. (Boulder, Colo.: Westview, 1993), 197.

37. Although I concede that there is no such thing as pure observation, I still distinguish between observational evidence and background assumptions involved in testing by experiment. Lynn Hankinson Nelson chooses to call both "evidence" on the ground that both function as evidence in deciding whether to accept a hypothesis being tested. See her "A Feminist Naturalized Philosophy of Science," *Synthese* 104 (1995): 399–

421; and "Empiricism without Dogmas." Her motivation is the holistic approach to evidence that I accept. Still, it is convenient to have a term to indicate the outcome of an experiment. I use *evidence* more narrowly for this purpose, recognizing that it is itself theoretically structured and can support a hypothesis only within a context of other assumptions.

38. Jerry Fodor, "The Dogma That Didn't Bark (A Fragment of a Naturalized Epistemology)," in *Naturalizing Epistemology*, 2d ed., Hilary Kornblith, ed. (Cambridge, Mass.: MIT Press, 1991).

39. Fodor, "Dogma That Didn't Bark," 201.

Chapter 3

The Realism Question

Systemic Bias and Explanatory Power

At the core of realism is the view that reality exists independently of our representations of it.[1] Realists generally believe more than this: that sometimes these representations are reliable models of what reality is like and that we can know that they are. But it is the core thesis, about the independence of reality from our representations of it, on which I will focus initially. The term *independence* can be confusing. The idea of independence here amounts to no more than this: that our models of reality—say, of systems or processes found in nature—can be mistaken.[2] People have, for example, represented the solar system as being geocentric, human mental activity as being inherently conscious, and human reasoning as being superior in males. Most people nowadays believe that these models of reality are grossly inaccurate. That some models of reality should turn out to be mistaken is not surprising. Most scientists—indeed, most people—believe that any model *can* misrepresent reality. As such, realism's core thesis appears to be a presupposition of science and indeed common sense.

It is possible, however, to argue otherwise. One can grant the possibility of a mistake but give this an interpretation that does not imply the core thesis. Suppose that there are criteria for choosing among models, and suppose that the criteria are objective in that (given suitable background assumptions) whether the criteria are met does not depend on any particular person's point of view. The norm of predictive success is like this, since whether one model predicts better than another, given the same background assumptions, is an objective matter in the sense specified. These two suppositions thus allow one to speak of being mistaken in an objective sense about how good a model is in the precise sense that one can be objectively mistaken about how accurately a model is able to predict. Note, however, that speaking this way does not, just by logic, commit one to the realist's core thesis. For instance, one need not suppose, just because one can be objectively mistaken about how well a model can predict the results of experiments, that models *themselves* can be mistaken, that they can fail to represent accurately a reality that exists apart from one's representations of it. It seems possible, therefore, to separate the idea of objectively choosing among models from the core thesis of realism.

We can sum up the antirealist's point in somewhat more general terms. Let us speak of *objective confirmation* when the criteria of model choice are objective in some appropriate sense and when a particular model is chosen based on these criteria and the outcomes of experiments. It might seem that the possibility of objective confirmation implies that models can be mistaken about reality and thus constitutes a good reason to accept the core thesis. The antirealist rejoinder is that some ways to understand objective confirmation do not entail this thesis. In particular, one can interpret the criteria of theory choice as involving the three empiricist norms of experimental testing discussed in the last chapter and not be committed, as a matter of logic, to the core thesis. Hence, one can accept internal feminist empiricism, based on these empiricist norms, and therefore the possibility of there being empirical mistakes, without granting the realist thesis.

To move beyond this apparent impass, it will be helpful to ponder the possibility of systemic bias. Consider an argument made by Kathleen Okruhlik to show that objective confirmation can fail to eliminate sexism in science because of the way that theories (or models) in science are generated.[3] Okruhlik notes that the current understanding of scientific method in testing theories is comparative in that we treat a theory as being objectively confirmed only relative to a comparison of alternative theories. This view clearly accords with my own, since the norm of explanatory power can be applied only against a background of potential alternative models for explaining the relevant experimental outcomes. She then points out that no matter how successful the methodological norms are in sorting out the best of a given set of alternatives, the theories that have been generated for testing may all be gender biased. If the available alternative theories "have all been generated by males operating in a deeply sexist culture, all will be contaminated by sexism,"[4] and hence the theories that survive, no matter how good the selection process, will themselves be biased. It follows on her account that "scientific method, by itself, as currently understood, cannot be counted upon to eliminate sexist or androcentric bias from science."[5]

What is particularly significant about her argument in the present context is that it comes immediately after she has tried, first, to discredit two realist interpretations of objectivity—one tied to a seventeenth-century form of physicalism, the other to Kant's metaphysical realism—and, second, to identify feminism with methods of inquiry that are impartial and nonarbitrary but have no realist import. "My claim is that feminist critics should have no qualms about discarding the first two senses of objectivity . . . but that the third (methodological) sense is indispensable to feminist theory and practice."[6] Okruhlik is, in effect, taking the antirealist line of rebuttal just noted, of separating realism from the idea of objective confirmation. Yet, at the same time, and this is the crux, she holds that, within the context of justifying theories against the evidence, it is possible for the theories that are objectively confirmed to be gender *biased* in virtue of the way they are generated. We need to ask here not how such bias is possible—for it surely is on her comparative analysis of scientific methodology—but what it could mean for the justification to be biased *and* objective. Clearly "biased" in this instance cannot signify the absence of objectivity. Nor can it signify a distortion of the truth or reality, given Okruhlik's opposition to realism. But then it is entirely unclear what it could mean.

The problem that Okruhlik faces is a general one for feminist philosophy of science. On the one hand, it is possible that every available model on a certain subject can be gender biased. Each may presuppose, for example, the superiority of male intelligence. It is also possible, on the other hand, for scientists to be impartial and nonarbitrary and hence objective in deciding which among *these* theories is the most acceptable in light of the evidence. The problem is that it is hard to give plausible readings of "biased" and "objective" in this context without bringing realism into the picture.

Being gender biased cannot be simply subordinating women to men without trivializing the charge of "bias" and undermining its moral significance. Nor can being biased boil down to just not being objective in some methodological sense. It cannot on Okruhlik's account, because she makes objectivity relative to choice among a given set of alternative models, and what is biased here is the whole set of options taken collectively. But, more generally, there is a difficulty with any attempt to use methodological norms to limit how models in science are generated, since there exists no "logic of discovery" to ensure the creation of worthwhile models. Though the context of discovery enters into that of justification, the methodological norms that govern the latter context cannot provide a method for discovering beforehand which models will be objectively confirmed in testing. There appears, in short, no way to interpret the kind of systemic bias to which Okruhlik refers.

Realism offers a simple way out of this quandary. Obviously not all possible models of a system or process can be generated for testing. In practice, only a small "sample" will emerge, and this sample can be systematically biased with respect to the system or process that each model is supposed to represent. If each model in the set *misrepresents* reality in the same way, the whole set will contain the same mistake, the same bias, about what the subject is like. Moreover, there is no difficulty in supposing that one of these models may be selected from the set by methods that are impartial and nonarbitrary relative to the set of options, even though the model chosen will be inevitably biased in the different sense of misrepresenting reality.

This solution constitutes an argument for the core thesis of realism. The argument is that the thesis best explains how there can be objective confirmation of a model, within a given set of alternatives, where the method of confirmation is blind to bias that affects the whole set. I will call this *the argument from systemic bias*. Okruhlik is right to recognize the importance of this kind of case. Her error is in failing to see that the case is not fully intelligible apart from the thesis that she rejects.

It will be noted that this solution retains the separation between objective confirmation and the core thesis. But this now requires qualification. We can keep the two separated as long as we relativize objective confirmation to a comparison among a set of known models. The trouble is that this way of understanding the comparative nature of objective confirmation does not do justice to its normative character. Suppose that A and B are the only models being considered in a certain domain and that both are sexist. Further suppose that only one—say, B—successfully predicts some new data. Does that mean that these data justify acceptance of B? Okruhlik implies that it does. For, in her story, the alternative not eliminated in the comparison is confirmed. In a descriptive sense, this seems right. That is, in the context imagined, where no nonsexist alternative has been generated, the rival model not disconfirmed is *taken to be justified*. In her words, "the theory that is selected by the canons of scientific appraisal will simply be the best of the sexist rivals."[7] But from that it does not follow that B will be *justified* by the data. The data justify B only if there is no plausible alternative, C, to explain the data equally well, whether or not C is currently available. This is what the norm of explanatory power implies as I interpret it.[8]

This normative element, which is not visible in Okruhlik's account of the comparative nature of confirmation, is crucial for understanding the motivation of many feminist and profeminism researchers who attempt to develop a nonsexist rival to current models when none is currently available. It is not simply that we happen to prefer a nonsexist explanation of the data. We believe that the sexist explanations are *not justified* by the data. It is hard to make sense of a belief of this kind in a context in which no nonsexist rival has been developed, unless the norm of explanatory power and thus the concept of objective confirmation is interpreted as I am suggesting.

Further, it is precisely this normative element that suggests a realist interpretation of objectivity. Many suppose, for example, that even if a model of human intelligence implying the inferiority of females had some predictive success and no developed alternative model was available, such a model would misrepresent what human intelligence is really like and hence could not be the best explanation of the evidence. In general, we doubt that we have objective confirmation to the extent that we doubt that the model that would be confirmed is accurate. The core thesis is now directly linked to objective confirmation. It is presupposed in the way we think about the norm of explanatory power. This argument from explanatory power fits well the earlier argument from systemic bias. Because systemic bias can give an undermining explanation of apparent confirmation, we are compelled to interpret confirmation as comparative in a deeper sense than Okruhlik allows and thus to be realists about the possibility of being mistaken.

Truth Versus Models

The arguments just given, from bias and explanatory power, have the form of inferences to the best explanation. The core thesis is part of the best explanations of how there can be systematic bias and how the norm of explanatory power functions in those situations. But such inferences are defeasible. If we know that the thesis should explain much more but does not, we will not trust the original inferences. I need then to consider the objections often voiced that realism cannot explain the value of diversity and individuality in feminist theory of knowledge. This section lays the groundwork for considering those objections.

It will not have gone unnoticed that I have used the terms *model* and *theory* interchangeably. This is deliberate. There are currently two rival ways to interpret the concept of theory in science. The most familiar is that a theory is a general statement about what reality is like (or perhaps a set of general statements). So understood, a theory (or the conjunction of statements within it) can be true or false. Sometimes realism is defined with this conception of theory in mind. Thus, it is sometimes said that a realist holds that theories are true or false of an independently existing reality and at least sometimes are true.[9] The other way is to think of a theory as a structure that has no truth value but that may resemble or fail to resemble reality in certain specifiable respects.[10] Such a structure is called a model. I have taken this route and defined realism accordingly.

Nothing has depended on this choice so far. The arguments from bias and explanatory power could have been formulated just as easily in terms of truth. A theory interpreted as a statement misrepresents a system or process (is mistaken about it) when it is false, whereas a model misrepresents a system or process when it fails to resemble it in the relevant respects. Indeed, it may seem that there is nothing much to choose between them. For even with models, we can shift to talking about truth simply by talking about whether it is true that a model *resembles* a certain system or process in the relevant respects. Why then all the fuss? And what is its bearing on feminist epistemology?

An immediate advantage to thinking of a theory as a model concerns the problem of generality. Many philosophers have supposed that any genuine science must postulate universal laws of nature. A difficulty with this received view is that not many theories in the social and biological sciences are able to meet this standard. If theories are models, on the other hand, no temptation exists to suppose that theories must contain propositions that stand for universal laws of nature. Models are structures without truth value. They make no claims at all and hence no universal claims. This feature does not, however, limit their power to represent generality. Take the Newtonian model of particle dynamics formulated mathematically as a set of equations. One can apply this structure just to the solar system as Newton did, or one can follow Laplace in applying it to the universe in general. On the model interpretation, nothing in the nature of what a theory is constrains the scope of its application; at the same time it does not presuppose that there are universal laws.

The liberality of the model interpretation does not, as one might fear, render theories incapable of predicting what would happen to a system or process in a counterfactual situation. The reason is that one can treat a model as representing various possible histories of a specific system, depending on the values of the variables represented in the model. This is indeed how one would test a model for accuracy of fit with some system in nature. One would introduce some change in the system and then see whether the consequences of the change are as the model predicts. To be sure, a kind of generality is operating in this case, for one is supposing that the model applies to the system in a range of possible cases. But, again, one may be dealing with a single, potentially unique system. The theory can accurately fit the case at hand over a large range of counterfactual situations without necessarily representing any other system.

Though models are often formulated in science abstractly as mathematical structures, they can also be constituted physically, as in the case of James Watson's cardboard and wire model of DNA that had the structure of a double helix. Watson's model was accepted as correctly representing the structure of DNA in that it was thought to be *similar* to DNA in the relevant respects. The relation of similarity is crucial to understanding the sense in which a model may be said to "correspond" to reality. It is not supposed that the model is exactly like the system or process that it represents. In fact, we need not suppose that we can give any sense to the notion of perfect likeness. (As long as the representation and the represented are distinct, we can suppose there are respects in which they are not alike.) We only suppose that the model is similar in specific respects and to a certain degree. It is natural, therefore, to speak of a model as giving an approximation of what the system in question is like from a certain point of view.

As such, this approach has a second advantage over its rival, since the alternative is to speak of a theory as being "approximately true" of the system in question. Although efforts have been made to make sense of the notion of approximate truth, it is far from obvious how it should be understood. Truth might be conceived as involving perfect similarity with what it represents, as the limiting case, with approximate truths having various lesser degrees of resemblance. But similarity in this case is no less mysterious than similarity between a model and the system it resembles. Moreover, the idea that truth itself would bear a perfect resemblance to that of which it is true is exceedingly unclear, since what is represented would in most cases not be a proposition and hence would differ in this respect from what does the representing. By contrast, the model approach appeals to similarity directly and need not postulate perfect resemblance even as a limiting case. Examples in the next section should bring this point home.

A third advantage is that by thinking of theories as being nonpropositional representations of reality, one opens the way to supposing that knowledge can be conveyed by nonpropositional structures like emotions.[11] This advantage is critical to being responsive to feminist objections to realism. For example, there is the worry that emotional knowing is incompatible with the realist thesis that reality is independent of its representation. In the next chapter I will explore the view that emotions are a form of nonpropositional knowing and argue that this view is compatible with realism. For now I want to draw on the other advantages of models to defend realism's core thesis against two other feminist objections.

Diversity, Maps, and Individuality

One objection is that realism is difficult to trust as a reasonable basis for epistemology given that it has been used so often as an instrument of power by the elite and the privileged to quiet dissent and to promote consensus when a diversity of opinion is warranted. Anne Seller has expressed this concern. She acknowledges the political appeal of realism:

> The primary appeal of realism is political. If all views are equally valid, so are sexist ones, and relativism appears to disarm me. . . . It is false to say that a woman's womb withers if she uses her brain, irrational to use sexual characteristics rather than economic position as the deciding factor in granting a mortgage, and patently unjust to pay less to a woman than a man for completing identical tasks. A combination of careful observation, willingness to take account of the evidence, and a commitment to consistency will reveal these truths. They are not a matter of perspective, social position or gender.[12]

Granting this, she recognizes a price to be paid for appealing to the scientific-rational epistemology associated with realism.

> First, it is an elitist epistemology. Only some women have the resources . . . to conduct such research, other women will simply have to accept it on authority. . . . Secondly, women have often experienced the scientific-rational approach as oppressive both in its process and in its findings. It has been used to make women

feel foolish because they have been unable to express themselves in its terms, and it has been used to "prove" the inferiority of women.[13]

When questions of group interest and false consciousness are introduced, these problems are made more acute: "At best, some women are telling other women what they are like, what their interests are, and how they might best be served. At worse, some women are imposing their own interests on the movement as a whole."[14]

Seller's worry is complex and manifests a deep ambivalence about realism that is shared by many feminist philosophers. Two quick but unsatisfactory replies need to be noted and set aside. One is that the reasons Seller gives for and against realism are political-instrumental arguments and thus are irrelevant to the truth of realism. (The truth or falsity of realism is entirely independent of whether it is good or bad for feminists.) This reply presupposes the familiar dichotomy between fact and value that we have begun to address already in defending the logical possibility of feminist empiricism. I must postpone a full-dress examination of the dichotomy until Part III, where I will argue in detail against various relevant versions of it. For the moment, let me take for granted the relevance of Seller's "instrumental" concerns. The other quick reply is that Seller has confused realism with a particular theory of evidence. This response is unsatisfactory because it ignores the intimate tie between realism's core thesis and the concept of objective confirmation. I have already argued for this connection and will do so again in the next two sections.

A better way to deal with Seller's concern is to argue that realism permits a diversity of perspectives on a single reality that are equally accurate and reliable. Let me borrow an analogy that Giere has used to make a similar point.[15] Imagine two maps of a single area of land—one showing elevation contours; the other, the layout of streets. The maps function literally as models of reality, a single reality, if you will, involving both streets and changes in elevation. Though each map is better for certain purposes, they may be equally reliable and accurate for their respective uses. One can indeed imagine a large diversity of different kinds of maps of the same area, each one reflecting accurately some relevant aspect of the area mapped.

In this analogy a clear distinction is made between what is being mapped and the map, the reality and its representation. Moreover, some maps of a given kind will be better than others of the same kind in regard to accuracy. (Imagine two topological maps, one showing increase in elevation at a point where the other shows decrease, but otherwise the same.) The analogy is thus consistent with the core thesis of realism. Still, there can be a multiplicity of equally good maps, and it is not implied that a single perfect map exists. In fact, a map showing both elevation and street layout is apt to be unreadable if each aspect is sufficiently detailed. There is no perfect map because the interests involved may be incompatible (representing both elevation and street layout simultaneously). Moreover, there is no fixed set of purposes, contrary to the idea of a perfect map. Since maps constitute an excellent example of models, the analogy illustrates how realism, understood in terms of models, is not only compatible with but explains diversity in perspective. This, we might say to Seller, shows the democratic nature of the realism conceived here. Far from insisting on the importance of an ideally perfect or "God's eye" point of view, it implies that no such view exists.

This reply ignores two important aspects of Seller's concern: the individuality of experience and the fact that knowledge is socially constructed. These concerns are magnified in passages like the following:

> If the violence of a man against a woman is seen as an expression of love, of her desirability and the strength of his desire for her (as it has been seen in so much literature), it cannot be said to be aggressive assault. Rape in the marriage bed is not simply a discovery of a previously unnoticed fact, it is a decision to understand behaviours in a different light, a decision involving men and women in a process of scepticism about what we were really doing and really meant.[16]

The social nature of knowledge is a topic in its own right and will be taken up again in the next chapter. Here I will draw on the map analogy to indicate the sense in which knowledge can be both socially constructed and based on an independently existing reality. Then I will turn to the problem of individuality.

Maps are social constructions, and the same can be said for virtually all models. The only exception would be a natural system taken to be a model of another system—say, where some salient feature of the first is well understood and used to lend insight into the structure of the second. For example, the solar system with planets revolving around the sun was once taken to be a model of the way electrons orbit the nucleus of an atom. Even in such cases the respects in which the one functions as a model of the other would be selected within a social context (in which heliocentrism is taken for granted) for its relevance to current interests (understanding the atom). This granted, it is equally obvious that whether the model fits reality in the relevant respect depends on the nature of reality. We draw a map based on shared interests, and except for the most primitive maps, the construction of the map is a social process depending on complex forms of coordination and cooperation. But the map can be wildly inaccurate, and its inaccuracy is not itself a matter of social construction. If the map indicates a mountain of several thousand feet elevation where there is only a plain, the map misrepresents the terrain, however social the production of the map may be.

Matters are considerably more complex in the case of marital rape, but I maintain that the logic of the situation is parallel. The concept of marital rape is a social construction, as are all concepts, and in this case it contains contested notions, such as the absence of consent. (It is regrettable that in many jurisdictions marriage has been treated as being itself an act of consent on the part of wives.[17]) Still, the fact that models are social inventions, in some cases contested ones, does not entail that there is never a fact of the matter about whether wives have been raped by their husbands. If rape is modeled as unconsented sex, one needs to be clear about what constitutes consent and sex. That clarity, as Seller implies, will be a matter of social decision. But an important reason that we care about making good decisions in this regard is that we want to represent accurately how husbands act toward their wives. We take it for granted that the models we construct may fail to capture the relevant aspects of reality. We may worry, for example, that sex will be defined too narrowly and consent too broadly. In such worries, however, we presuppose realism's core thesis.

Another concern is the individuality of experience, especially as it bears on knowledge of ourselves. This is a frequent theme in feminist writing, and it is reflected in Seller's mistrust of a realist scientific-rational epistemology that emphasizes expert knowledge and discounts impressions based on personal experience. Code, while sympathetic to realism, takes a similar line, calling for a "mitigated relativism" that "takes different perspectives into account" and recognizes the "locateness of knowledge *and* its associations with subjective purposes."[18] On the face of it, there may appear to be no conflict between realism and respect for the individuality of experience. Cannot the unique character of one's experiences be represented accurately to oneself without impugning in the least realism's distinction between what is represented and the representation? A problem arises, however, if one thinks of the representations in a scientific-rational epistemology as being primarily theories and takes theories to be general statements describing universal regularities. Then it would seem that the individuality of experience cannot be adequately represented from a realist perspective.

By now it should be clear that this is not an issue when theories are conceived as models. As we have seen, models can be very particular in their application. (Think of maps.) A model may be of a single system—say, a psychological one—that is not repeated elsewhere in nature. Imagine a system that is a particular, historically located relationship between friends, involving a complex of features unique to itself. Is it not possible for a unique complex of this kind to be represented by a model (say, one in which affection is stable and mutual as long as certain unique features of the persons are present)?[19] And could it not be confirmed by future experience? Such models can, of course, be wrong, but this prospect itself presupposes realism's core thesis. The concern that an epistemology based on realism could fail to respect knowledge of a particular or personal kind can be met, it would seem, by taking models to be structures (which are not propositions) applied to particular systems. We will return to this point when we take up the topic of emotional knowledge.

Finally, I should take note of Seller's complaint that realism is an "elitist epistemology" implying that women who have greater resources can have more authority than others. As I will argue in detail in chapters 4 and 6, the generation of knowledge is social through and through, and inevitably we are dependent on the authority of others if we are to know anything at all. Seller is right to worry that scientific authority can be misused by both women and men, but if the arguments to come are sound, the problem cannot be avoided by giving up realism. We can cope with this problem only by striving to make the institutions that generate scientific knowledge less oppressive, and this is an aim that is consistent with realism.

More Arguments from Norms

I want now to return to the line of argument that we began in the first section: that the core thesis best explains certain important aspects of our thinking about objective confirmation. We considered the arguments from systemic bias and explanatory power. These are arguments that appeal to normative features of objective confirmation. They are based on how we ought to reason when we appeal to empirical evidence to support our theories or models. In this section I want to look at the norm of predictive success and then at the overall point of having norms to guide our reasoning from evidence.

Let us suppose that all we care about in scientific inquiry is how predictively successful theories are overall. In chapter 2, I gave reasons for not accepting this positivist perspective on science. For example, contrary to positivism, we cannot separate caring about whether the norm of predictive success is satisfied from caring about the motivations that lie behind theories and attempts to confirm them. But for argument's sake, let us accept the positivist position and see what would follow. I contend that we should still be interested in realist objectivity as I have characterized it. For accepting theories according to their potential predictive success has no point unless we suppose that there is a difference between them with respect to potential predictive success, and this is *a difference that is itself an independently existing feature of the world.* Moreover, the norm of explanatory power, in the strict sense intended, would still be crucial in testing for potential predictive success. For a given case of predictive success for a hypothesis is not evidence for its potential predictive success *overall* if the predicted outcome is just as probable on the basis an alternative theory. Think again of the successful prediction of women's relatively poor performance on the initial VSA tests. In sum, the core thesis is implicated even in the positivist norm of predictive success.

This argument brings out how the norms of predictive success and explanatory power work together. It is not easy to see this if the norm of predictive success is considered in isolation. Suppose a successful prediction is made on the basis of a certain hypothesis and various auxiliary assumptions. Think of Barash's successful prediction based on his model of aggression in mountain bluebirds discussed earlier or the prediction of women's poor performance on the VSA tests. Although it is often supposed that this evidence counts as confirmation that the hypothesis gives us reliable information about the world, that does not follow according to our norms. For the predicted outcome may be highly probable independent of the hypothesis being tested. There must be an additional constraint to reduce the chances of a misleading positive result (a false positive). For this reason we impose the norm of explanatory power. We want to make sure that no better explanation for the result is possible. But what would be the point of imposing that norm unless we thought there were features of the world, existing apart from our method of testing, about which we could be misled by the outcome of our test? It is hard to see how there would be any rationale for the particular structure of these norms if we believed that the testing process could yield no reliable information about a world existing apart from our views of it.

This last point constitutes a further argument for the core thesis. Suppose we said that objectivity consists simply of heeding the three main empiricist norms for confirmation and disconfirmation discussed in the previous chapter. Inevitably, we must ask, What justifies this definition? Put another way: What is it about these norms that makes them objective? My answer is that the norms are objective because heeding them is the best means we have of learning about the nature of the world, where the world is taken to exist independently of our views about it and our means of investigating it. To the extent that these norms, or any norms of testing, are not a good means to this end, they fail to be objective in this deeper, realist sense of being objective. In my view, then, it is not quite right to say without qualification that objectivity in testing consists of heeding the empiricist norms. This is so only if the norms are objective in the more basic, realist sense of the term.

I am aware how unfashionable this view of objectivity is among feminist philosophers. Not all believe that objectivity in science is possible,[20] and most of those who do choose not to characterize their conception of objectivity in realist terms. Notable among the latter are Helen Longino, Lynn Hankinson Nelson, and Kathleen Okruhlik.[21] These authors defend positions that are, in my terms, forms of internal feminist empiricism. In this respect we are in fundamental agreement. Moreover, each endorses the view that it is possible for methods in science to be objective. But none is prepared to defend a realist conception of objectivity.[22] One wonders whether this is because no adequate defense can be had from a feminist perspective. In this chapter I have offered a number of reasons for feminists to take seriously a realist conception of objective testing. The last and most general is that heeding the norms of testing would lose a natural and robust rationale if we were to give up the idea that heeding them is the best means of learning about the nature of ourselves and the world around us.

Quine's Argument

Nelson, it should be noted, does not explicitly reject the core thesis, but neither does she endorse it. Should she reject it, given that she takes a holistic approach to the evidential relation between observation and theory? Traditionally, realism has been associated with the project of providing an a priori foundation for knowledge. Following Quine, Nelson abjures this project. She argues that any assessment of our methods in science must come from within our evolving empirical knowledge. Thus, when feminists challenge current scientific practices and theories, they must do so, according to her, against a background of their empirically informed beliefs and theories about how science works and how it could change. I accept this view and will defend it in detail in Part II. We might consider now, though, whether a rejection of foundationalism entails a rejection of the realist conception of objectivity.

We have, I suggest, no good reason to think so. For our evolving views of the world, including feminist views about the nature of science, imply that there are important features of the world (e.g., androcentrism in science) that exist whether or not we notice them. Moreover, to the extent that we see our methods of inquiry as tending to make invisible features that we want to know about, we try to adjust our methods accordingly. That is, contained in our evolving understanding of how our methods work and fail to work is the realist presumption that our methods can be adjusted to better reveal features of the world that are not simply artifacts of our methods.

But what about this realist presumption itself? Is it subject to correction also? Nelson would surely suggest so, for in her view no belief, including any belief we might have about objectivity, can escape the test of experience. This seems right. It might be that the theories confirmed by our methods would imply that there is no independently existing world (as some have suggested is implied by modern physics[23]). This should not be excluded as a possibility, nor is it in my view. I have argued for the realist conception of objectivity based on a particular understanding of how hypothesis testing works. That argument is not foundational. The methods and the conception of objectivity they suggest cannot be guaranteed a priori, and nothing in my defense implies they can be. Hence, nothing in it guarantees, independent of experience, that heeding empiricist norms is a good means to gaining understanding of our world.

My efforts here to show the compatibility of realism with Nelson's Quine-inspired, thoroughgoing antifoundationalism can in fact be strengthened to yield another argument in favor of realism if one accepts Quine's contention that epistemology must develop from within our empirical theory of the world. We can call this *Quine's argument*. For Quine, what exists is what our most serious theory of the world posits as existing.[24] We have, he believes, no access to reality that transcends science, no "first" philosophy, no way to establish ontology outside our developing, continually revised, empirical theories of nature. But that very understanding, Quine has noted, posits a world that existed before we did and that is responsible for our evolution through natural selection. By our present lights, therefore, it is a world that is not bounded by our present understanding of it. This is Quine's implicit realism.[25] Since it is empirically based and open to revision or rejection in light of further experience, it is distinct from traditional forms of realism that are held to be demonstrable a priori. But it is realism, nonetheless; it implies access to a world that exists beyond us and is not reducible to what we may desire or believe.

In contrast with the other arguments, this one proceeds not from the content of norms of testing but rather from the results of applying such norms, in particular, from the modern Darwinian theory of evolution through natural selection. The legitimacy of doing epistemology in this fashion—doing what, after Quine, is called naturalized epistemology—and the aptness of pursuing feminist epistemology in particular in this way are matters that will be addressed later in Part II. It is enough at this stage to take note that if this approach to knowledge is justifiable, then there is a direct argument for realism's core thesis based on the kind of theory of evolution that has emerged through the application of the very norms we have been discussing. It will be my contention that feminist empiricism is best interpreted as a form of naturalized epistemology, though one that reveals that some of Quine's own assumptions about epistemology are in conflict with themselves.

The Bias Paradox

In an important essay arguing the relevance of naturalized epistemology for feminism, Louise Antony raises a general problem for feminist critiques of objectivity in science. She calls this problem *the bias paradox*, since it arises from feminist efforts to show that there is a gender bias inherent in the scientific ideal of objectivity as neutrality (i.e., the absence of bias).[26] It would seem that feminists are implicitly appealing to the very ideal that they are attacking and hence defeating themselves in the process. Antony analyzes the nature and source of the ideal and its problems and then proposes what I want to interpret as a plausible realist solution to the paradox. I will begin with the motivation that gives rise to the paradox.

Feminist epistemologists, like Harding and Code, who have taken note of the "locateness" of all knowers, argue that it is impossible to achieve or even approximate the ideal of being absolutely neutral in outlook. Preconceptions or bias of one form or another inevitably enter into all empirical inquiry, but when biases are so deeply embedded in a culture that they affect the point of view of the dominant members of society more or less equally, they become invisible to those affected, and an illusion of neutrality is created. Thus, biases inherent in the perception of women on the part of both sexes can appear to be an objective perception, when there is no alternative perception with the right social standing to serve as a point of comparison. Views of those on the margins of society appear to the dominant members as deviant or "biased."[27]

Antony concedes that this critique of the neutrality ideal has more than a grain of truth in it, but she finds the following difficulty:

> If bias is ubiquitous and ineliminable, then what's the good of exposing it? It seems to me that the whole thrust of feminist scholarship in this area has been to demonstrate that androcentric bias has distorted science and, indeed, distorted the search for knowledge generally. But if biases are distorting, and if we're biased in one way or another, then it seems there could be no such thing as an *undistorted* search for knowledge. So what are we complaining about? Is it just that we want it to be distorted in *our* favor, rather than in theirs? We must say something about the badness of the biases we expose or our critique will carry no normative weight at all.[28]

This statement expresses, in fact, the essence of the bias paradox. If one tries to undermine claims to objectivity by arguing that bias is everywhere, then one serves only to undermine one's own critique of objectivity.

Nevertheless, the way to deal with the paradox is not to insist that objectivity in the sense of neutrality is possible and to be pursued as an ideal. In Antony's view the problem with classical empiricism is that it did not appreciate the need for partiality among human knowers. A completely "open mind"—one completely devoid of any bias whatsoever—would be a mind incapable of knowing anything. There would be simply too many alternatives to sort out for it to cope with the flow of sensory information.

> The problem of paring down the alternatives is the defining feature of the human epistemic condition. The problem is partly solved, I've been arguing, by one form of "bias"—native conceptual structure. But it's important to realize that this problem is absolutely endemic to human knowledge seeking, whether we are talking about the subconscious processes by which we acquire language and compute sensory information, or the more consciously accessible processes by which we explicitly decide what to believe. The everyday process of forming an opinion would be grossly hampered if we were really to consider matters with anything even close to an "open mind."[29]

Of course, not all biases are reliable in leading to knowledge. But once we grant this we are led back again to the bias paradox, for, Antony notes, "if biases are now not simply ineliminable, but downright *good*, how is it that *some* biases are *bad*?"[30] One way or another we must find a basis for distinguishing good from bad biases, or else we lose any normative grounds for rejecting some biases in favor of others. The root of the paradox is the need to hold certain biases to be justified while at the same time treating all biases as if they were normatively indistinguishable.

Antony has a solution: "A naturalistic study of knowledge tells us biases are good when and to the extent that they facilitate the gathering of *knowledge*—that is, when they lead us to the truth. Biases are bad when they lead *away* from the truth."[31] Her solution has two aspects. First, it takes the naturalistic turn in epistemology by looking at how belief-forming mechanisms function to determine whether they are good or bad. Second, it appeals to truth production as a standard of good functioning. The first aspect will occupy us in the middle chapters of the book and need not detain us here. The other takes realism, or its core thesis, as the standard for separating good biases from bad. I want now to make clear that realism has this role in Antony's solution and to argue for its legitimacy, in part on feminist grounds.

Appealing to truth does not automatically commit one to realism. If one takes the truth to be the conclusion that would be reached at the ideal limit of rational inquiry, or something like that, speaking of truth would not imply that there exists a reality separate from our representations of it. One could grant that there are truths but deny the core thesis. We need, then, to interpret Antony's remarks if we are to treat her solution to the bias paradox as realist. A realist reading of her view, on the other hand, seems unavoidable. For if we understand truth purely in terms of the outcome of some ideal method of inquiry, we are left immediately with the problem of determining when biases are an acceptable part of that method.[32] When are biases good biases and when are they bad? This was, of course, the original question that the appeal to truth is supposed to answer. We end up, in effect, simply begging the original question unless we understand Antony's solution to contain a more robust concept of truth—one that entails the core thesis.

We can at this point turn the solution into an argument for the core thesis, provided that we have reason to take the bias paradox seriously. Recall that the paradox stems from the claim that pure neutrality in scientific testing is an impossible and misguided goal. The paradox arises for feminists who reject this concept of objectivity but offer no alternative conception and thus leave no normative room to argue that feminist commitments can have a legitimate place in scientific inquiry. The realist conception offers that alternative.

But is pure neutrality an impossible and misguided goal? Should feminists reject this conception of objectivity? Here we come full circle back to the central arguments of the previous chapter. There I argued against the neutrality ideal based on standard notions of what is involved in the logic of confirmation. Political values, for example, were in that chapter a kind of bias that could augment rather than diminish the objectivity of testing. Given that feminist ground for rejecting the neutrality ideal, we now have an additional reason to favor realism: it provides a way to avoid the bias paradox.

Notes

1. Regrettably, the term *realism* has no single meaning in philosophy. My usage, which is more general than most because it is not formulated with reference to language, is the same as John R. Searle's in chapter 7 of *The Social Construction of Reality* (New York: Free Press, 1995).

2. This is an oversimplification. It is possible to hold that there are cases of incorrigible belief—for example, my belief that I exist or that I am not now in severe pain—and also hold that reality exists independently of our representations of it. For reasons given in chapter 8, I do not believe that any beliefs are incorrigible, but in any case the simplifying assumption will not affect the general points to follow.

3. Kathleen Okruhlik, "Birth of a New Physics or Death of Nature?" in *Women and Reason*, Elizabeth D. Harvey and Kathleen Okruhlik, eds. (Ann Arbor: University of Michigan Press, 1992).

4. Okruhlik, "Birth of a New Physics," 74.

5. Okruhlik, "Birth of a New Physics," 74.

6. Okruhlik, "Birth of a New Physics," 69.

7. Okruhlik, "Birth of a New Physics," 74.

8. A possible objection is that my interpretation commits me to confirmation being a defeasible notion. It does, but, for reasons given in the next paragraph, this seems right. We withdraw the claim that evidence confirms (supports, justifies) a hypothesis when we find a better explanation or when we believe that a better explanation can be found.

9. David O. Brink, for example, takes this position in *Moral Realism and the Foundation of Ethics* (Cambridge: Cambridge University Press, 1989), defining realism about x as the position that there are facts or truths about x that obtain independently of the evidence for them (16). Though authors vary somewhat in how they interpret the independence of the facts or truths (or even whether they refer to independence at all—see Geoffrey Sayre-McCord, "The Many Moral Realisms," in *Essays on Moral Realism*, Geoffrey Sayre-McCord, ed. [Ithaca, N.Y.: Cornell University Press, 1988), they standardly associate realism about x with a commitment to the existence of truths or facts about x. This association, I argue later, reveals an unduly narrow view about how reality, even a robustly independent reality, may be represented.

10. A classic presentation of the model-theoretic conception of scientific theories may be found in Frederick Suppe, "What's Wrong with the Received View on the Structure of Scientific Theories?" *Philosophy of Science* 39 (1972): 1–19. My own approach follows Giere's more recent treatment in Ronald Giere, *Explaining Science* (Chicago: University of Chicago Press, 1988).

11. Whether emotions are propositional in structure is itself a matter of controversy.

For arguments that they are not, see Cheshire Calhoun, "Cognitive Emotions?" in *What Is an Emotion*, Cheshire Calhoun and Robert C. Solomon, eds. (New York: Oxford University Press, 1984); Alan Gibbard, *Wise Choices, Apt Feelings* (Cambridge, Mass.: Harvard University Press, 1990); and John Deigh, "Cognitivism in the Theory of Emotions," *Ethics* 104 (1994): 824–54.

12. Anne Seller, "Realism Versus Relativism: Towards a Politically Adequate Epistemology," in *Feminist Perspectives in Philosophy*, Morwenna Griffiths and Margaret Whitford, eds. (Bloomington: Indiana University Press, 1988), 170.

13. Seller, "Realism Versus Relativism," 171.

14. Seller, "Realism Versus Relativism," 172.

15. Ronald Giere, "Underdetermination, Relativism, and Perspective," paper presented as an Austin-Hempel Lecture, Dalhousie University, 5 August 1993.

16. Seller, "Realism Versus Relativism," 178.

17. Diana E. Russell, *Rape in Marriage* (New York: Macmillan, 1982).

18. Lorraine Code, *What Can She Know? Feminist Theory and the Construction of Knowledge* (Ithaca, N.Y.: Cornell University Press, 1991), 320.

19. Note that the model is not a proposition to the effect that affection between the friends will be stable and mutual as long as certain unique features are present. The model itself is a particular structure (vaguely specified) that could be similar, in some respects and to some degree, to the friends in question; it says nothing about whether it is similar. Instead of using a sentence, I might have given the model by pointing to a short story or to two tightly bonded elephants.

20. For a range of feminist perspectives on the possibility of objectivity of science, see Helen Longino and Evelyn Hammonds, "Conflicts and Tensions in the Feminist Study of Gender and Science," in *Conflicts in Feminism*, Marianne Hirsh and Evelyn Fox Keller, eds. (New York: Routledge, 1990), 164–83.

21. See Helen Longino, *Science as Social Knowledge* (Princeton, N.J.: Princeton University Press, 1990), and "Subjects, Power, and Knowledge: Description and Prescription in Feminist Philosophies of Science," in *Feminist Epistemologies*, Linda Alcoff and Elizabeth Potter, eds. (New York: Routledge, 1993), 101–20; Lynn Hankinson Nelson, *Who Knows: From Quine to Feminist Empiricism* (Philadelphia: Temple University Press, 1990); and Okruhlik, "Birth of a New Physics."

22. Although Longino grants "a minimalist form of realism," this is apparently limited to the independent existence of objects "with which [our] senses interact to produce our sensations"; *Science*, 222. Evidence that she rejects the stronger form of realism that I am defending is clear in her discussion of explanatory power (28–32) and her own account of objectivity as transformative criticism: *Science*, 76–79 and "Subjects, Power, and Knowledge," 112–13. Detailed support for this reading is given in Sharon L. Crasnow, "Can Science be Objective? Longino's *Science as Social Knowledge*," *Hypatia* 8, no. 3 (1993): 194–201. Okruhlik is explicit in rejecting forms of realism implying an independently existing world ("Birth of a New Physics," 69–72) and opts for a "methodological" rather than a "metaphysical" account of objectivity. Nelson endorses the possibility of "an ideal of objectivity that includes self-conscious attention to metaphysical commitments" (*Who Knows*, 311) but stops short of endorsing any form of realism herself. The issue of realism as such is not raised in her book or in her more recent articles cited earlier.

23. For an acute defense of realism that is also feminist in response to the suggestion that quantum physics refutes realism, see Karen Barad, "Meeting the Universe Halfway: Realism and Social Constructivism without Contradiction," in *Feminism, Science, and the Philosophy of Science*, Lynn Hankinson Nelson and Jack Nelson, eds. (Dordrecht: Kluwer, 1996).

24. W. V. Quine, "Posits and Reality," in *The Ways of Paradox and Other Essays* (Cambridge, Mass.: Harvard University Press, 1976), and "On What There Is," in *From a Logical Point of View* (Cambridge, Mass.: Harvard University Press, 1953).

25. Quine's realism is obvious in many passages in "Natural Kinds," in *Ontological Relativity and Other Essays* (New York: Columbia University Press, 1969). For example: "To trust induction as a way of access to the truths of nature, on the other hand, is to suppose, more nearly, that our quality space matches that of the cosmos. The brute irrationality of our sense of similarity, its irrelevance to anything in logic and mathematics, offers little reason to expect that this sense is somehow in tune with the world—a world which, unlike language, we never made" (125–26). But his realism is also evident in more recent writing: "Dispositions to observable behavior are all there is for semantics to be right or wrong about. In the case of systems of the world, on the other hand, one is prepared to believe that reality exceeds the scope of the human apparatus in unspecifiable ways" (*The Pursuit of Truth* [Cambridge, Mass.: Harvard University Press, 1992], 101). In the same work he makes an explicit link between realism (as conceived here) and objective knowledge: "The objectivity of our knowledge of the external world remains rooted in our contact with the external world, hence in our neural intake and the observation sentences that respond to it" (36). For other textual evidence of Quine's realism, see "On the Very Idea of a Third Dogma," 39, and "Five Milestones of Empiricism," 72, both in *Theories and Things* (Cambridge, Mass.: Harvard University Press, 1981).

26. Louise Antony, "Quine as Feminist: The Radical Import of Naturalized Epistemology," in *A Mind of One's Own: Feminist Essays on Reason and Objectivity*, Louise Antony and Charlotte Witt, eds. (Boulder, Colo.: Westview, 1993).

27. A good summary of how the ideal of impartiality can serve to distort reality may be found in Sandra Harding, " 'Strong Objectivity': A Response to the New Objectivity Question," in *Feminism and Science*, Lynn Hankinson Nelson, ed. (Dordrecht: Kluwer, 1995), 329–30.

28. Antony, "Quine as Feminist," 210.

29. Antony, "Quine as Feminist," 211.

30. Antony, "Quine as Feminist," 213.

31. Antony, "Quine as Feminist," 215.

32. I believe that the same problem arises for Linda Alcoff's defense of Hilary Putnam's internal realism; see her *Real Knowing: New Versions of the Coherence Theory* (Ithaca, N.Y.: Cornell University Press, 1996), chapter 6.

Chapter 4

Knowledge as Social and Reflexive

A Case for Social Epistemology

A number of feminist philosophers hold that knowledge is inherently social.[1] Social epistemology, as it has come to be called, is nowadays a familiar position. But in exactly what sense is knowledge inherently social? There is some risk that the position could amount to nothing more than a truism.[2] The burden of this section will be to define the position so that it is precise and controversial enough to be interesting and to show its plausibility on the basis of considerations already developed in the preceding chapters.

Social epistemology might be nothing more than the following position. An individual becomes capable of gaining knowledge only through a process of social training that leads to the acquisition of language, the relevant concepts, and reasoning skills. For example, unless one has learned how to justify one's beliefs, one cannot know that something is true, but it is only through elaborate and lengthy training in a social context that one learns how to justify one's beliefs even to oneself.[3] It is primarily through dialogue that one learns, for instance, how to anticipate objections and to understand what might constitute an adequate response to them. Acquisition of these skills is a social achievement. Without the right kind of social environment the level of one's skills is apt to be very primitive, and one's knowledge (as distinct from right opinion) is apt to be virtually nil.

But surely the inherently social character of knowledge comes to more than this. A philosopher who insists on the individual basis for knowledge could concede the aforementioned points but argue that this shows only that society plays an essential role in developing an epistemic agent. Once such an individual has been formed, she or he can go on to acquire knowledge wholly on her or his own without any further need of fellow humans. While the creation of responsible epistemic agents is a social matter, the acquisition of knowledge by those who have already become epistemic agents, it might be argued, is a thoroughly individual affair, anything but inherently social.

63

It must be conceded that such extreme individualism requires qualification to be even remotely plausible. For although some knowledge may available to the epistemic agent without (further) social assistance (such as knowing that the cat is on the mat), scientific knowledge generally requires cooperation from many others: those whose labors create leisure time for others to pursue research, often human subjects, people who help distribute questionnaires, librarians, the manufacturers of microscopes and computers, and so on. Still, what the individualist might say is this: Though many hands are needed to acquire, organize, and store evidence and to allow the time for others to study it, the actual process of justifying conclusions on the basis of evidence already gathered is an individual matter. At least in principle, this is something that the mature epistemic agent can and perhaps ought to pursue as a single individual, independently of the opinions and assistance of others.

Epistemic individualism of this kind, which we can label *justification individualism*, does not deny the obvious—that people learn through social means to be epistemic agents and need the cooperation of others to acquire and study the evidence on which to justify many important beliefs. But it does deny that knowledge is inherently social in regard to justifying beliefs. This position claims that, though an individual could be assisted by many others in reasoning about the import of evidence, anyone mature enough to be an epistemic agent has the capacity to reason on her or his own about what conclusions are supported by the evidence and (other things being equal) ought to do so. The core idea is that justification of beliefs is an individual responsibility.

Is justification individualism plausible? The conception of objectivity I have developed may appear to support justification individualism, since it is possible for a single individual to apply the empiricist norms of chapter 2 in testing a model. But, in fact, when properly understood, these norms lead in the opposite direction to lend support to social epistemology. The reason is that their application depends on a suitably developed context of auxiliary hypotheses and background information. This context, which forms an essential part of justifying a model relative to a given body of evidence, is socially constructed, socially explored, and shaped by social values. The justification process defended earlier thus transcends the bounds of the individual and cannot be reasonably regarded as merely a single individual's responsibility.

Susan Haack has attempted to refute the claims of feminist epistemologists that the justification process is inherently social by distinguishing between *warrant* for a proposition (a normative notion) and *acceptance* of a proposition by a community (a description notion) and arguing that feminist epistemologists have confused the two.[4] Haack alleges three kinds of mistakes. The first is to argue that, since evidence never obliges us to accept a scientific claim (its truth is always underdetermined by the evidence) and since we have to accept something, acceptance will always be affected by factors besides the evidence, like social values. This is a mistake, she contends, because when the evidence is insufficient to warrant the truth of a claim, we need not accept it; we can say that we do not know. The second mistake is to ignore warrant altogether and conclude that since social values can influence acceptance, they affect justification (where justification is now taken to be purely descriptive). The third mistake is to replace the concept of warrant with some other notion, such as being democratic in inquiry, that is either irrelevant to warrant or else presupposes it. For example, being democratic in inquiry (say, questioning women as well as men) can turn up new evidence, which is epistemically good. But it is good not because knowledge or justification is inherently social but because such inquiry satisfies the demand for evidence to be as comprehensive as possible, a demand that derives from and thus presupposes rather than replaces the concept of warrant.

It should be clear that the argument that I am advancing for the inherently social character of knowledge does not confuse warrant with acceptance or ignore warrant. The argument is that evidence supports (justifies, warrants) a claim only relative to a socially constructed context of auxiliary assumptions and alternative hypotheses. While evidence does not determine the truth of a claim deductively and inductive inference always involves risk, the argument is not that evidence never warrants the truth of a claim. Nor is the argument that those who accept a claim may be moved by social values or that the notion of warrant (I prefer the term *justification*) should be replaced by some other concept. The argument is rather that the normative concept of warrant involves a complex relation whose terms include factors that are inevitably socially created, revised, and maintained. Finally, the argument is not that in virtue of this social construction the justification and resulting knowledge must not be objective. The argument is that the justification can be both social and objective.

An individual can, nevertheless, have an important role to play in the process of justification. A single individual may be able to put the pieces together to show the relevance of the data for a certain model or may devise an alternative explanation of the evidence. A person's epistemic agency is not eliminated by the fact that justification (in the case of either confirmation or disconfirmation) is for the most part a social process that enlists many agents in different tasks. Further, the inherently social aspects of the process of justification do not imply that individuals fail to know anything as individuals. They have knowledge as individuals; only this is made possible in virtue of social processes in which they may or may not have a crucial role to play. Justification includes in this way *both* individual and social dimensions.

At least this is the case for complex examples of scientific knowledge. What of cases from everyday life—for instance, simple perceptual knowledge? Do we want to say that when one sees and therefore knows the water is boiling that one's belief is grounded in a social process of justification? Is not the process of justification in such cases wholly individual? This line of questioning brings out a fundamental ambiguity in the way I have been speaking of social context. One way in which a process of justification can be social is that it involves people exchanging ideas, reasoning together, perhaps dividing up the labor of reasoning where their areas of expertise are sufficiently divergent. In such cases, the process is explicitly social. Another way it can be social is that the steps in the process can tacitly borrow from, and thereby rely on, results or information that has been socially generated without explicitly engaging anyone else in the reasoning. Here it is only tacitly social, though it is still social in the relevant sense. It is social because the individual cannot make the needed connection between the evidence and the conclusion without relying, at least partly, on assumptions that the individual has not and perhaps cannot test for her- or himself.

In light of this distinction, we might ask, Is simple perceptual knowledge at least tacitly social? This is a complex empirical question for which there is no obvious answer. How we see things depends on many stages of unconscious information processing, including not merely sensory stimulation but our readiness to interpret the stimulation in certain specific ways. That readiness is surely shaped to some degree by social training. At least that would seem to be a reasonable assumption given the effect of collateral information on what one may see when presented with highly degraded perceptual input.[5] If that is so, then even primitive forms of perceptual knowledge will qualify as inherently social in the relevant sense. But I do not need to establish this to deny the sweeping thesis of justification individualism. The weaker claim that complex forms of scientific knowledge are inherently social is enough to make the point and to show the bearing of internal feminist empiricism.

Social epistemology might be taken to imply that only social units larger than a single individual are capable of knowledge. The position sketched here allows that groups can know things. A family might know, for example, that there is imminent danger of a flood. That would not mean that every member knows this; an infant in the family would not yet have the concept of a flood, and another member of the family might be in a coma. Still, we speak of groups or institutions having knowledge *only* when most of their members or individuals who are representatives have the knowledge in question. We explain the knowledge of the group or institution by reference to knowledge possessed by specific individuals. In this sense individuals are the primary units of epistemic agency. But—and this is the crucial point—the means by which individuals become justified in their beliefs, enough so to know something, is inherently social. This is so, if not always, then at least in cases of complex scientific knowledge.[6] It is social epistemology in this fundamental but qualified sense that I will take for granted in what follows. (In chapter 6 I will return to this topic to defend a somewhat more radical thesis.)

Longino on Dialogue and Objectivity

Helen Longino provides a carefully developed social model of how objectivity is possible in reasoning from evidence.[7] In her view, objective inquiry is possible only where the method of inquiry permits critical scrutiny of evidential reasoning from multiple alternative perspectives. It is not merely that there be dialogue and hence intersubjective criticism; the context in which the dialogue occurs must have the right social structure. It must permit "transformative" criticism. Longino summarizes the main parts of this structure as follows:

> Scientific communities will be objective to the degree that they satisfy four criteria necessary for achieving the transformative dimension of critical discourse: (1) there must be recognized avenues for the criticism of evidence, of methods, and of assumptions and reasoning; (2) there must exist shared standards that the critics can invoke; (3) the community as a whole must be responsive to such criticism; (4) intellectual authority must be shared equally among qualified practitioners.[8]

Clearly objectivity thus defined is a social property and will vary in degree depending on the social context. Longino's is a clear example of a social epistemology, where the justification of a person's beliefs that is necessary for knowledge is explicitly social.

The idea that objectivity should result from seeing a subject from diverse perspectives and critically comparing the differences has great intuitive appeal. We tend to think that the distortions and biases that might inhere in any one person's perspective will be sifted out through such comparisons if the community is sufficiently diverse, the process of critical discussion is sufficiently free and open, and the participants are disposed to take each other seriously and to accept their own fallibility. The importance of diversity to gaining objective knowledge has already been remarked upon in connection with realism (in chapter 3). It can be seen to be crucial to a successful application of the norm of explanatory power, since one wants to make sure that no alternative explanation for the evidence exists that one might have missed.

Nevertheless, diversity or pluralism in perspectives creates a dilemma of some significance that Longino examines in a more recent work.[9] Objectivity requires pluralism for the reasons just noted, but pluralism appears to make scientific knowledge elusive. Imagine a community whose opinions and points of view are so diverse and contrary that they manage to agree on very little. In that case the process of would-be transformative criticism yields no consistent set of beliefs, no consensus, about the subject and hence, on the present criteria, no process of the required sort needed to justify beliefs about the subject. Without such justification there is presumably no knowledge. Thus, objectivity seems pitted against the possibility of gaining knowledge. On the other hand, if we are able somehow to pursue consensus in the imagined community (say, by leaving some members out of the discussion or embarrassing them), then there is the cost of quieting opposition crucial to objectivity. But how is diversity to be preserved in face of the need for consensus?

Longino's solution is to detach scientific knowledge from consensus of the entire community. This move seems right. It is consistent with the norms of testing defended earlier; none of these tie confirmation or even degree of severity of a test (to be discussed later in the section "Reflectivity and Empiricism") to consensus. Moreover, to suppose that knowledge depends on consensus is contrary to the reasons just marshaled for preserving diversity of viewpoint. Still, it is unclear to me how Longino is able to detach knowledge entirely from consensus and maintain anything intuitively resembling knowledge without embracing some fairly robust form of realism—something that she is loath to do. I want now to explain the nature of this further dilemma and to discuss two suggestions she makes to ameliorate the difficulty.

The problem is that once we refuse to identify knowledge with consensus, even ideally wrought through transformative criticism, we allow the possibility that knowledge can still be achieved when there is only a diverse field of competing points of view. But how? In what will justification consist if not in some actual or potential consensus? And why will some beliefs be sufficiently justified in the circumstances that they qualify as knowledge? It would seem that we need an account of what counts as objective justification that is not tied to consensus, but it is not clear how that is possible without invoking some form of realism.

Longino wants to avoid a realist answer, such as one account of justification is better than another if it is more likely to justify true beliefs. But what is her alternative? She has two suggestions. Theories might be construed as model-theoretic structures so that the question of their being true or false does not arise. But this move does not rule out the possibility of construing knowledge realistically. Indeed, we have already considered a construal of model-based knowledge that implies the core thesis of realism: that models represent an independently existing reality. Longino is perfectly right that we avoid the notion of absolute truth by this move, and she is right that we also avoid the idea of a best or perfect model, since the relevant similarity relation will depend on our interests and there is no one best set of interests. All of this, however, is compatible with realism. More than that, we need realism in any case. For we want to say that some models are better than others, even though there is no best set, and we need norms that will guide us in determining this in the face of disagreement. The appeal to models by itself provides no help in this regard.

The other suggestion is to move to a practice conception of scientific theories.

If we understand science as practice, then we understand science as on-going, that is, we give up the idea that there is a terminus of inquiry that just is the set of truths about the world. . . . Scientific knowledge from this perspective is not the end point of inquiry but a cognitive or intellectual expression of an ongoing interaction with our natural and social environments. . . . Scientific knowledge, then, is a body of diverse theories and their articulations onto the world that changes over time in response to the changing cognitive needs of those who develop and use the theories, in response to the new questions and anomalous empirical data revealed by applying the theories, and in response to changes in associated theories.[10]

But it is not clear how this conception provides a satisfactory solution to our dilemma. Longino writes of knowledge changing over time. In a trivial sense there is nothing objectionable about this; knowledge taken collectively changes as new knowledge is gained. But this cannot be what she means, since the "old" way of thinking of knowledge as composed of justified true beliefs allows us to say the same thing. What Longino seems to mean is that something that was knowledge previously may now no longer be knowledge. If the practice conception of knowledge comes to that, it is at least puzzling.

It is possible, of course, for someone to stop believing what was believed previously. Then, even in the old view, the person would cease to know what had been known, since knowledge that a model is accurate implies belief. There is reason in the passage, however, not to interpret her meaning simply as acknowledging the cessation of belief. Reference to anomalous data, new theories, and changing background assumptions suggests that she is thinking of one theory or part of "knowledge" being replaced by a better theory, better because it fits the data better, coheres with other accepted theories better—in short, is more justified in light of all the evidence. But now a problem arises, because in such situations we are more likely to say that we did not really know what we thought we did. We thought we knew that space is absolute, but now we have strong reason to believe that space is different. It is not simply that our theories have changed or that we have added new knowledge. We normally conclude that we were *mistaken* in our former theories.

If we take this additional step, however, we are led fairly quickly back to the dilemma about consensus and pluralism. What allows us to conclude that some theories in the diverse lot of perspectives before us are mistaken? If we do not identify being justified with having a consensus (and I agree that we should not), we are left without clear guidance. The practice conception of science does not offer any real assistance in this regard.

What is at fault here is not the intuition that the process of justifying viewpoints is inherently social. There is not a problem with thinking of the process as involving a "practice" in the sense of a shared activity guided by norms. The problem is that such a conception of justification goes hand in hand with a realist conception of knowledge. Justification has little chance of succeeding relative to the realist goal of getting a theory that fits well with the system being modeled if the testing proceeds in the absence of diverse points of view. Recall again the norm of explanatory power. That norm, interpreted in accord with the realist's core thesis, is less apt to be satisfied if it is guiding a single individual or a very homogeneous scientific community. A pluralism of perspectives is crucial to the healthy functioning of this norm. But the reason for invoking pluralism is not pluralism for pluralism's sake. It is pluralism for the sake of theories that will not misrepresent how things are.

To recap: The upshot is agreement with Longino about the inherently social dimension of justifying theories and agreement that absolute truth is not the point of justification. Moreover, we agree that the social process must meet the kinds of conditions Longino imposes, such as responsiveness to criticism throughout the community and rough equality of intellectual authority among qualified participants. The difference lies in Longino's failure to come fully to terms with the dilemma she poses regarding the meaning of objectivity. My contention is that the dilemma can be resolved only by interpreting objectivity realistically.

Emotional Knowledge

A further point of agreement with Longino is that in her view knowledge may be nonpropositional. She implies this in her proposal to take scientific knowledge to be expressed through theories but to interpret theories as models rather than as sets of propositions. Talk of nonpropositional knowledge can suggest the traditional alternatives: knowledge as ability (knowing how to add) and knowledge by acquaintance (knowing pain). Neither of these alternatives, however, fits well with knowledge that is expressed through models. Knowing, for example, how something works by having a good model of it does not reduce to knowing how to do something or to knowing something through experiencing it. Model-theoretic knowledge, if I can call it that, is more like knowing things that are true about something, but it is not of propositional knowledge. In this section I want to explore whether emotional knowledge can be interpreted as model-theoretic in this sense and to see in what sense it has an inherently social dimension. (The topic of emotional knowledge will arise again in chapter 6 on self-knowledge and in chapter 9 on moral knowledge.)

Alison Jaggar notes that with a few notable exceptions, the Western philosophical tradition has regarded "reason rather than emotion as the indispensable faculty for acquiring knowledge," and reason "has been associated with the mental, the cultural, the universal, the public, and the male, whereas emotion has been associated with the irrational, the physical, the natural, the particular, the private, and, of course, the female."[11] Needless to say, feminist philosophers writing on emotions have tended to resist this familiar opposition between reason and emotion. One way that they have resisted is to adopt a cognitivist interpretation of emotion. Thus, Elizabeth Spelman has attacked what she labels as the Dumb View of emotions that understands emotions not to be about anything and hence to be inappropriate for rational assessment.[12] On the contrary, she argues, emotions like anger have a cognitive structure and can be evaluated, for example, as warranted or not, depending on the circumstances and what the person is angry about. The idea that emotions are subject to rational appraisal thereby helps to undercut the traditional dichotomy between reason and emotion and at the same time the hierarchial gender structure associated with the dichotomy. It also helps to explain, as Spelman notes, why anger of subordinates toward their superiors, since it conveys with it the implication of justified criticism, is apt to be regarded as an inappropriate emotion.

A problem arises, however, for this attempt to undercut the gendered dichotomy by appeal to a cognitivist theory of emotions. Cognitivist theories have generally portrayed emotions as having two components—a feeling component that is itself devoid of any cognitive structure and a cognition that interprets what the feeling component is really about. For example, if I am afraid that the bear will attack, my emotion has two parts: the pure feeling of fear and the judgment that the bear will attack (and perhaps also that my feeling of fear is aroused by the fact that the bear will attack). But, as Jaggar aptly observes, the two-component approach serves to perpetuate the artifical split between feeling and thought:

> These accounts . . . unwittingly perpetuate the positivist distinction between the shared, public, objective world of verifiable calculations, observations, and facts and the individual, private, subjective world of idiosyncratic feelings and sensations. This sharp distinction breaks any conceptual links between our feelings and the "external" world: if feelings are still conceived as blind or raw or undifferentiated, then we can give no sense to the notion of feelings fitting or failing to fit our perceptual judgments, that is, being appropriate or inappropriate.[13]

While recognizing the inadequacy of the Dumb View, cognitivist accounts typically do not go far enough in showing how emotions embed cognition. In particular, they do not explain how pure feeling, independent of belief or any other propositional structure, can function as a representation of the world.[14]

Can emotion itself—say anger—be knowledge? This is a hard question. Much has been written about how cognition can modify and be modified by emotion. The question here is importantly different. It is about the possibility that an emotion be itself a form of cognition. Emotion is not, let us concede, true or false of anything. My anger cannot be literally true, nor can it be literally false. When I am angry with you for being late again but am mistaken about your being late, my anger is surely misplaced, but it is not literally false. Clearly, then, emotion cannot be itself a form of propositional knowledge. But theories interpreted as models cannot be literally true or false, either. We need to ask whether emotions can function as representations in the same sense that models do. Can emotions be such that they fit or fail to fit how things are in the world?

Consider the case of fear. Normally fear is felt in the face of perceived danger. Can the feeling of fear be treated as a representation of imminent danger? The idea is not that one judges there to be imminent danger and consequently feels fear or that one judges the feeling to be about imminent danger. Rather, the feeling itself represents danger. A reason for treating fear this way is that we take the feeling itself to be irrational when no evidence of danger exists. It is as if the representation embodied in the fear is not justified when no evidence supports it. Furthermore, our intuition in this instance cannot be explained away as simply a case of mistakenly calling the fear irrational when it is one's judgment that there is imminent danger that, properly speaking, lacks rationality; for one may feel fear when one judges oneself to be in no danger.

A feeling of fear is, of course, not merely a device for representing imminent danger. Feelings are conative; they tend to move us to act, in this case to take ourselves from danger. So they function as conative models. Their function in this respect is structured. The feeling that moves us to get away from danger moves us in ways that accord with the specific character of the representation. If one feels afraid of A but not B, one will be moved to avoid A, not B. This is not a matter of judgment that is distinct from emotion, since one may judge both to be harmless. How one is moved to act by one's feelings will depend on what the feelings represent, sometimes independently of one's acknowledged beliefs.

Parallel remarks apply to anger taken as a representation of a perceived wrong (typically, but not necessarily, to oneself). It can be felt when one believes that no one has been wronged. One's anger may be unjustified on the evidence. But it may be justified, even when one is unable to acknowledge, perhaps for ideological reasons, the weight of evidence. It is conative, since one tends to be moved to act aggressively toward the person perceived to be responsible. Again, the impulse to act will be structured by the felt representation of the wrong, sometimes independently of one's acknowledged beliefs about who has wronged whom.

A third relevant feature of emotions is their overtly public or social dimension. Fear and anger are typically felt from without as well as from within, and their public character ties in with their conative and representative character. We learn about danger and wrongs through their public representations in emotions and, to the extent that one shares the representations in one's feelings, are apt to be moved to act in similar ways. It is reasonable to surmise that this kind of direct communication, through arousing shared feelings that serve simultaneously as representations and conations, have some significant evolutionary advantages. The learning is, of course, highly fallible. People get angry without reason and hence can be moved to act in ways that are not justified by the situation. They can also rouse each other to anger without reason and to act unreasonably. In sum, the social function of emotion as communication can go awry; one's feelings can lie even when one does not intend to deceive.

The present suggestion is that, without having truth value, emotions can still serve as forms of knowledge. Though far from infallible, they can be accurate representations of one's situation that are justified by the evidence. (One can know one is in danger in feeling fear and know that one is wronged in feeling anger.) Emotions serve as knowledge, however, in ways that are not easily assimilated to other kinds of cognition. They tend, for example, to move one to act independently of one's beliefs and to be immediately evident to others as much through facial expression and other overt forms of behavior as through word of mouth. They are, nevertheless, cognitive, and directly so, in a way that precludes the separation of thought from feeling.

For this reason the social dimension of justification can apply equally to emotion. Consider applications of the norms of predictive success, observation independence, and explanatory power to the justification of emotions, comparing the points made earlier about the inherently social nature of justification. (1) We test whether our emotions are justified by seeing what would follow if they are based on reality. (We are angry but have we been wronged? We might ask ourselves whether others in the same position would be angry.) (2) We want evidence that can be identified as such without circularity. (We ask whether others similarly placed would be angry, but we should not assume that they would on the ground that they would have been wronged.) (3) We need also to rule out alternative explanations (e.g., that others would be angry because they are mistaken about the facts). In all three instances we are forced to rely on background assumptions that are socially learned and reinforced. We need to assume—for example, in the case of the first point—that people are sufficiently alike to respond to being wronged in much the same way as ourselves (by becoming angry). We learn this not on our own but through living with others and by trusting their testimony.

The cognitive and social dimensions of emotion can be much more complex than I have indicated. Significantly, they can work to reinforce oppression. Based on her experiences as a teacher and on a report by the American Association of Colleges, Sandra Bartky analyzes the intense feelings of shame that women students experience much more frequently than men and that have no evident basis in their academic performance.[15] Although the women often do not believe that they are doing poorly, the feelings persist even in the face of evidence of their superior performance. Since the women appear to have nothing to be ashamed about, is it "false" shame that they are feeling? On the contrary, as Bartky argues, their feelings are revealing of their social situation.

> What gets grasped in the having of such feelings is nothing less than women's subordinate status in a hierarchy of gender, their situation not in ideology but in the social formation as it is actually constituted. Not only does the revelatory character of shame not occur at the level of belief, but the corrosive character of shame and of similar sensings, their undermining effect and the peculiar helplessness women exhibit when in their power, lies in part in the very failure of these feelings to attain to the status of belief.[16]

If the shame were a belief (that one's marks were poor, that one's comments were stupid, etc.), the shame would not survive, given the contrary evidence. Yet we cannot capture the cognitive significance of the shame by simply supposing that the feelings falsely represent the self as being inferior, defective, or in some way diminished, for the feelings reveal one's subordinate, indeed shamed, social status. In Bartky's words, "a pervasive affective attunement to the social environment, . . . women's shame is more than merely an effect of subordination but, within the larger universe of patriarchical social relations, a profound mode of disclosure both of self and situation."[17]

Reflexivity and Empiricism

Bartky's discussion of shame suggests that the cognitive dimension of feeling and emotion is much more complex than I have indicated thus far. In particular, there is the reflexive nature of justification. Let me begin with a simple example. The bare fact of feeling can serve as evidence that the feeling faithfully reflects reality. This may seem circular, but consider an analogy with memory. Do I remember what I had for breakfast? I seem to, but does my memory image accurately represent the past? The fact that I have this memory is in itself evidence that I ate what I remember eating. It is hardly conclusive evidence, but (other things being equal) it counts significantly. This is because normally the hypothesis that my memory is correct is the best explanation of the fact that I have this memory.[18] The circumstances may be such that better explanations are possible. For example, I may have a disease of the brain that causes me to misremember. In that case, the fact of seeming to remember is not reason to believe what I seem to remember. But normally it is. This reasoning is not circular because I am not assuming my memory is correct and then inferring that it is. Rather, I am inferring that it is correct from the fact that I seem to remember and there is no better explanation of this fact.[19]

Notice the parallel. Suppose I feel guilty. Unless I am neurotically prone to feel guilt when there is no reason to or there is some other undermining explanation, the fact that I am feeling this way gives me reason to believe that I have done something I should not have. That I have done wrong may be the best explanation of why I feel guilt. In cases like this, my feeling functions not only to represent my acting badly (and, of course, to move me to make amends); it also serves as evidence that I acted badly. Similar points can be made for countless other emotions: fear, anger, sadness, pride, and so on. Emotions can function simultaneously as representations and as evidence for what they represent.

The dual feature of representations just noted, which is not unique to emotions, reveals an important aspect of justification. This is its reflexivity. We reflect back on the genesis of our models, emotional and otherwise, to see whether their origins do or do not support the model of the world that they present. We are apt to trust only models that are not thereby undermined. As we will see in due course (especially in Part II), the reflexive character of justification underwrites a great deal of feminist theorizing. In Bartky's discussion, for instance, the shame felt by students is understood through an analysis of its origins to represent a shaming and dishonoring social environment. For now I want to relate reflexivity in general terms to the norms of empiricism and then (in the next section) to feminist standpoint theory. I will begin by clarifying what reflexivity is.

In the standard case an emotion is explained by what it is about. We do what we know to be wrong, which *makes* us feel guilt. We face what we know to be dangerous and that causes fear in us. What justifies our guilt or fear is the same as what explains its presence. An analogous situation normally obtains in the case of perception. We believe that there is a candle in front of us because there is. The presence of a candle in front of us that we can clearly see both explains and justifies the belief that this is so. Not all cases of justification, or for that matter explanation, are causal in this way. But many are, and the close tie between justification and explanation is simply that the justification in these cases is a form of what Harman dubbed "inference to the best explanation."[20] In these cases, the origin of the model of what the world is like—whether it has the form of emotion, belief, memory, or something else—plays a crucial role in the justification of the model.

Information about the origin of a model can, by the same token, show that it is not justified or at least undermine the presumption that it is justified. If I know why I feel guilt and know that this has nothing to do with doing anything wrong, then this explanation undermines the ability of my feeling of guilt to give me knowledge of my guilt. I may have indeed done wrong, but feeling guilty is not justified in the absence of any other evidence. Similarly, if I know why I am afraid and know my fear has nothing to do with any imminent danger, this explanation undercuts the ability of my fear to give me knowledge of danger. Whether or not danger is present, my fear is not justified without further evidence.

What is reflexive about this move, both when it succeeds in justifying and when it undermines, is that it places the knower in the same causal plane as what would be known. The potential knower must become in this respect part of the known in order to test the accuracy of the knower's model. We "look back" at how the knower came to have the particular model of the world as a means of checking the model's credibility. The reflexive move can apply, as I will show, not only to the kinds of cases we have been considering, in which the causal explanations may be fairly simple and direct, but also to complex cases of scientific models in which their genesis involves a whole a community of potential knowers and the connection between the evidence and the model is extremely indirect. How models come to exist, as part of the context of discovery, is crucial to their justification even in these more complex cases.

To see how this could be so, I want to show how Harding's conception of reflexivity might be explained by reference to the empiricist norm of explanatory power. Harding has argued in favor of strong reflexivity in science.[21] By this standard science needs to include as part of its evidence not only the social causes of "bad" beliefs and behaviors that scientists have participated in (weak reflexivity) but also the social causes of "good" beliefs and behaviors. In particular, it needs to take into account the kinds of diversity generated within its community and to understand their causes. For the diversities generated may be limited by systematic biases of gender, race, and class (among others) that make invisible many sources of relevant evidence and thereby undermine the objectivity of any conclusions drawn from the present data. In her chapter on strong objectivity (her term) Harding summarizes the argument of feminist standpoint epistemology as follows:

> [I]n a society structured by gender hierarchy, "starting from women's lives" increases the objectivity of the results of research by bringing scientific observation and the perception of the need for explanation to bear on assumptions and practices that appear natural or unremarkable from the perspective of the lives of men in the dominant groups. Thinking from the perspective of women's lives makes strange what had appeared familiar. . . .
>
>   It starts research in the perspective from the lives of the systematically oppressed, exploited, and dominated, those who have fewer interests in ignorance about how the social order actually works.[22]

Can feminist empiricism begin to make sense of this norm of strong reflexivity? Can it make sense of thinking from women's lives as a scientific resource?

It can if we are prepared to take seriously enough the norm of explanatory power. For this norm, when properly understood, implies strong reflexivity. Recall that according to the standard of explanatory power, the predicted outcome of a good test of a model ought to be very improbable if the model is not similar in relevant respects to the system studied, since there is no credible alternative model to explain the success of the prediction. A possible alternative hypothesis that must always be considered is that the agreement between (1) what is predicted by the tested model and (2) what is observed in the test can be explained by the way the test and the model have been generated. To take a simple case, suppose the original model is constructed just to fit the data. Then we cannot say that the agreement between the data and what the model predicts would be very improbable if the model-system similarity were absent, for whether or not the similarity obtained, there would be this deliberately engineered agreement. More generally, we want to know whether any explanation for the agreement is possible other than the explanation that the model postulated is similar in the relevant respects to the system being studied. I suggest that strong reflexivity is implicitly a demand that there be no such alternative explanation, which is exactly what explanatory power demands.

What strong reflexivity demands that makes it distinctive is that social causes of favored beliefs and behaviors be explained. How, one asks, is this implied in the demand that there be no explanation of agreement between prediction and observation other than that the postulated model is relevantly similar to the system to which it is applied? It is implied because a relevant check on whether the fit between model and reality explains the agreement is whether the favored belief (that there is this fit) is explained by causes that count *against* that possibility. For example, if part of the social explanation for the favored belief (and associated behavior) is an insensitivity to certain kinds of contrary evidence or to certain alternative explanations of the evidence—an insensitivity created by an interest in being ignorant of that evidence or those alternatives—then there is good reason to doubt that the fit between model and reality is what explains the agreement between prediction and observation.

A possible source of confusion here is the assumption sometimes made that if the favored belief is correct and it is a response to the agreement between prediction and observation and if, further, that agreement can be explained by the correctness of what is believed, then there is no logical room left for social causes to play any role in generating the favored belief. But this assumption is untenable. There is no logical room only if the belief is generated by the agreement between prediction and observation *alone*. This agreement is normally part of a complex of factors responsible for creating the belief, and it is unrealistic to suppose that the causation of this belief, or for that matter virtually any belief, does not involve multiple social factors. Even the production of simple perceptual beliefs is mediated by social factors. I believe that a table is before me in part because there is one, but many other factors mediate the causal connection. Some are not social, such as events happening at the surface of my skin (touching the table as I type these words); others are social, such as my having the concept of a table and my being able to trust my own experience. In more complex cases—for example, where beliefs about what the world is like are shaped by feminist commitments—the influence of social factors is closer to the focus of Harding's attention, but the point is the same. What explains my beliefs can be my socially generated political commitment *and* what the world is like. That value and fact should function in tandem in this way follows from the main arguments of the second chapter.

Standpoint Theory Compared

If feminist empiricism enjoys anything like the virtues I attribute to it, there is good reason to believe that feminist empiricism overlaps Harding's feminist standpoint theory.[23] This is not surprising. Once one rejects the positivist and external versions of feminist empiricism, one is apt to find it difficult to separate the two epistemologies. Perhaps there is no fundamental difference. But, if not, one may want to know what political agenda lies behind my efforts to praise its virtues under one name rather than the other.[24] I believe, however, that four differences are worth noting, consistent with much overlap.

One obvious difference is that feminist standpoint theory questions the norms that feminist empiricism accepts, since standpoint theory questions any norms implicated in standard scientific practice. Standpoint theory asks whether these norms do not in some way protect perspectives privileged in androcentric science. It is difficult to assess the importance of this difference. Feminist empiricism, as constructed here, begins with some existing norms of scientific inquiry; standpoint theory does not. But both are seen to question these norms. Indeed, the argument is that the self-critical questioning demanded by strong reflexivity is actually implied by a full and consistent application of the norm of explanatory power. Why would this demand then not apply to the empiricist norms themselves, if it is true that they guide scientific inquiry? Feminist empiricism begins with these norms together with a political perspective, but the combination leads to a questioning of the very norms from which it begins. If there is a difference, it is in the starting points, not the reflexive character of the epistemology that emerges.

Yet there is also this difference: while self-questioning appears to sustain the original norms of feminist empiricism, these norms do not receive explicit endorsement in standpoint theory. This difference is politically significant and may go some way toward justifying my point of departure. Unlike standpoint theory, feminist empiricism builds from common ground with those who take seriously existing norms. This gives it subversive power in working for political change in science if resistance to change there can be shown to have no basis in those norms. To start from that common ground forfeits nothing; to ignore it sacrifices a useful avenue for pursuing political change.

A third difference of perhaps deeper significance is an apparent asymmetry in explanatory potential. It is not clear how any form of standpoint theory that does not endorse something like the empiricist norms of predictive success, observation independence, and explanatory power can explain the worth of testing procedures that seem obviously justified and have been used for worthwhile political ends—say, to refute claims about women's natural inferiority to men. On the other hand, unless the foregoing arguments are far off the mark, it appears that such norms when combined with feminist political consciousness have the potential to explain the insight of standpoint theory that those who do not have a vested interest in certain forms of ignorance have an epistemic advantage in that regard. To suggest this asymmetry is hardly to defend it, but it is consistent with the argument that strong reflexivity is internal to feminist empiricism. If this asymmetry exists, it appears to be fundamental and provides a further reason to distinguish defensible forms of feminist empiricism from those that standpoint theorists have rightly rejected and, indeed, to prefer those defensible forms to standpoint theory itself.

Finally, there is a difference in resources for dealing with the problem of essentialism in feminist theory. Harding notes the following dilemma for standpoint epistemology:

> [Postmodernist critics charge that] standpoint epistemology is regressive in assuming some sort of universal feminine condition that can serve as the grounds for feminist claims. And if it does not do so, then just what is feminist about standpoint theories? Don't their grounds deteriorate into views from each of thousands (millions?) of distinctive kinds of social experiences, or perspectives, or activities, or struggles characteristic of different cultural groups of women?[25]

Harding attempts to dissolve this dilemma by emphasizing the power of reflexivity within standpoint theory to combat its essentialist tendencies, which are admittedly there, and concludes that "the subject/agent of feminist knowledge is multiple and contradictory, . . . and women cannot be the unique generators of feminist knowledge."[26] Feminist empiricism concedes the power of reflexivity to generate diversity of outlook, but its pluralism has another source, closer to the surface. What makes it feminist is simply the feminist character of the political perspectives that can guide empirical inquiry, and this character is left undefined. Put another way, in feminist empiricism no single feminist standpoint is put in a position of epistemic privilege relative to any other. Although in both approaches there is ultimately no unitary, coherent subject or agent of feminist knowledge, the path to this conclusion appears shorter from feminist empiricism. This is another of its virtues.

Notes

1. See, for example, Helen Longino, *Science as Social Knowledge* (Princeton, N.J.: Princeton University Press, 1990); Lynn Hankinson Nelson, *Who Knows: From Quine*

to Feminist Empiricism (Philadelphia: Temple University Press, 1990); Lorraine Code, *What Can She Know? Feminist Theory and the Construction of Knowledge* (Ithaca, N.Y.: Cornell University Press, 1991); Sandra Harding, *The Science Question in Feminism* (Ithaca, N.Y.: Cornell University Press, 1986); Jane Duran, *Knowledge in Context: Naturalized Epistemology and Sociolinguistics* (Lanham, Md.: Rowman & Littlefield, 1994); Linda Martin Alcoff, *Real Knowing: New Versions of the Coherence Theory* (Ithaca, N.Y.: Cornell University Press, 1996); and Susan Babbitt, *Impossible Dreams: Rationality, Integrity, and Moral Imagination* (Boulder, Colo.: Westview, 1996).

2. Susan Haack argues that the claim that science is social is either a truism or false in "Science as Social?—Yes and No," in *Feminism, Science, and the Philosophy of Science*, Lynn Hankinson Nelson and Jack Nelson, eds. (Dordrecht: Kluwer, 1996), 79–93.

3. Here I assume without argument that one cannot know something is true unless one is justified in believing it. Note that I am not assuming, as will become clear, that all knowledge is about what is true or that justification must involve such knowledge.

4. "Science as Social?" 82–87.

5. To be convinced, consider the perceptual experiments and discussion of social perception in Paul Churchland, *The Engine of Reason, the Seat of the Soul: A Philosophical Journey into the Brain* (Cambridge, Mass.: MIT Press, 1995), 107–14, 131–32, and 270–94.

6. For examples from recent science that bring this point home dramatically, see John Hardwig, "Epistemic Dependence," *Journal of Philosophy* 82 (1985): 335–49; Hardwig, "The Role of Trust in Knowledge," *Journal of Philosophy* 88 (1991): 693–708.

7. Longino, *Science*, especially chapter 4. For recent refinements see "Cognitive and Non-Cognitive Values in Science: Rethinking the Dichotomy," *Feminism*, Nelson and Nelson, eds., 39–58.

8. Longino, *Science*, 76.

9. Helen Longino, "Subjects, Power, and Knowledge: Description and Prescription in Feminist Philosophies of Science," in *Feminist Epistemologies*, Linda Alcoff and Elizabeth Potter, eds. (New York: Routledge, 1993), 113–17.

10. Longino, "Subjects, Power, and Knowledge," 116.

11. Alison Jaggar, "Love and Knowledge: Emotion in Feminist Epistemology," in *Gender/Body/Knowledge*, Susan Bordo and Alison Jaggar, eds. (New Brunswick, N.J.: Rutgers University Press, 1989), 145.

12. Elizabeth Spelman, "Anger and Insubordination," in *Women, Knowledge and Reality*, Ann Garry and Marilyn Pearsall, eds. (Boston: Unwin Hyman, 1989).

13. Jaggar, "Love and Knowledge," 149–50.

14. For a survey of cognitivist theories of emotion, see John Deigh, "Cognitivism in the Theory of Emotions," *Ethics* 104 (1994): 824–54. Though Deigh is critical of these theories, he appears unaware of the problem Jaggar raises and does not address the possibility of nonpropositional cognitive evaluation.

15. Sandra Lee Bartky, *Femininity and Domination: Studies in the Phenomenology of Oppression* (New York: Routledge, 1990), 83–98.

16. Bartky, *Femininity and Domination*, 95.

17. Bartky, *Femininity and Domination*, 85.

18. The argument derives from Gilbert Harman, *Change in View: Principles of Reasoning* (Cambridge, Mass.: MIT Press, 1986).

19. The style of reasoning here is characteristic of naturalized epistemology, since I am reasoning against a backdrop of models whose adequacy cannot be established independently of reliance on what now seems to be in question. I address the legitimacy of this kind of reasoning in the next chapter.

20. Gilbert Harman, "Inference to the Best Explanation," *Philosophical Review* 74 (1965): 88–95.

21. Sandra Harding, *Whose Science? Whose Knowledge?* (Ithaca, N.Y.: Cornell University Press, 1991), 149–52, 160–62.

22. Harding, *Whose Science?* 150.

23. Feminist standpoint theories hold that women, or at least some women, because their marginalized status in a gender-stratified society gives them experiences and insights that are not possible or are unlikely for the more privileged members of society, are apt to be in a much better position than others to understand the oppression of women and to advance feminist research. Notable examples of feminist standpoint theory besides Harding's work already cited are, Nancy Hartsock, "The Feminist Standpoint: Developing the Ground for a Specifically Feminist Historical Materialism," in *Discovering Reality*, Sandra Harding and Merrill Hintikka, eds. (Dordrecht: Reidel, 1983); Hilary Rose, "Hand, Brain, and Heart: A Feminist Epistemology for the Natural Sciences," *Signs* 9, no. 1 (1983): 73–90; and Dorothy Smith, *The Everyday World as Problematic: A Feminist Sociology* (Boston: Northeastern University Press, 1987). For a recent summary of feminist standpoint theory that takes into account important refinements over the past two decades, see Sandra Harding, " 'Strong Objectivity': A Response to the New Objectivity Question," in *Feminism and Science*, Nelson, ed., especially 341–47.

24. I am grateful to Lorraine Code and Peter Trnka for pressing this question.

25. Harding, *Whose Science?* 175.

26. Harding, *Whose Science?* 180–81.

Part II

Feminism and Naturalized Epistemology

Chapter 5

Normative Naturalized Epistemology

Quine on Induction

Thus far I have sketched a theory of empirical knowledge that allows feminist political values to play a central role in the generation of scientific knowledge. Four general features of knowledge have proved to be important for successfully combining feminism with empiricism.

Objectivity: Knowledge is objective when governed by norms of testing, like predictive success, that (when taken together) place a reality-based constraint on which models of reality turn out to be confirmed by the evidence.

Realism: Reality is independent of the models through which it is known.

Sociality: Knowledge is social due to the way that its empirical support is generated.

Reflexivity: Knowledge is reflexive when it is supported and not undermined by knowledge of how it is generated.

These features are obviously not separate from each other. For example, we have seen how the constraints regarding realism, sociality, and reflexivity are implicit in the norms of testing that define its objectivity. In this chapter I want to look at reflexivity from a more inclusive standpoint. The reflexivity of knowledge turns on how its models are generated, but it also concerns as well how the norms for testing these models are generated. These can be viewed as two aspects of a more general process in which the knowledge generated is reflected back on itself to understand its sources, both in the initial selection of models and in the norms that determine how the models are tested and thus whether they have objective support. It is a pattern called "epistemology naturalized" in Quine's famous essay by that name. The aim of such epistemology is to treat the generation of knowledge as part of the natural world to which we can apply the very knowledge thus generated.

The central question to be addressed in this chapter and the next is whether feminist empiricism of a kind developed thus far can be naturalized in Quine's sense. I will be arguing that it can be, but there is an irony in my invoking Quine's standard for good epistemology. My argument that political motivation and other forms of value judgment naturally and legitimately enter into the application of empiricist norms derives from the Duhem-Quine thesis[1] that empirical tests are holistic, depending on a network of theoretical background assumptions. To introduce the concept of internal feminist empiricism, I have simply pointed out that these background assumptions form part of the context of discovery and hence cannot be insulated from the effects of contextual values. The irony is that Quine himself has maintained that science is free of such effects. In his words, "Scientific theory stands proudly and notoriously aloof from value judgments."[2] Relying implicitly on the Quine-Duhem thesis, I am led, therefore, to a conception of epistemology that Quine thinks is at odds with the nature of science.

To compound this irony, a common criticism of naturalized epistemology is that in turning epistemology into science Quine is destroying the normative content of epistemology. Quine conceives naturalized epistemology as an attempt to understand the link between observation and theoretical science by appeal to (in his words) "the very science whose link with observation we are seeking to understand."[3] A common objection, which has been advanced independently by Hilary Kornblith and Jaegwon Kim,[4] is that epistemology cannot be reduced to science in this way, because epistemology as such (never mind feminist epistemology) is normative through and through. Astonishingly, Quine shares with his critics the assumption that science and hence naturalized epistemology are *not* inherently normative.[5] But if I am right that science is inherently normative, then not only does the objection rest on a false premise, but Quine has in an important way misconceived his own project.

We should, then, look more carefully at what that project is. Quine tells us that naturalized epistemology seeks to understand through science the link between observation and science, but taken in isolation this description is seriously misleading. It makes it sound as if the goal of this epistemology is merely to identify the psychological and perhaps social mechanisms for generating scientific theory on the basis of sensory stimulation. It thus invites the objection that naturalized epistemology answers only the nonnormative question of how we come to have the scientific beliefs we do, without answering the normative question of why we *ought* to have the scientific beliefs we do. Without an answer to the latter question, the issue of justification, which has been central to traditional epistemology, goes unresolved.

In some interpretations, Quine deliberately sets aside the traditional issue of justification as unresolvable and outmoded. This interpretation, however, is not supportable. Quine rejects traditional conceptions of justification, both foundational and coherentist,[6] because they seek to provide an understanding of the nature of knowledge that is prior to and hence not dependent upon science. That understanding, based ultimately on the possibility of a priori knowledge, is not viable in Quine's view.[7] But Quine does not reject the issue of justification itself.[8] Rather, he sees naturalized epistemology (hereafter NE) as explaining how beliefs can be justified by relying on some of the very beliefs whose justification may be called into question. He thus sees NE as addressing the traditional problem of skepticism, but in a new a way.

Is Quine's new way question begging? To see more clearly the logical struc- ture of NE, we need to look at how justification is supposed to work when it is internal to science. A paradigm of explaining science by science is provided in Quine's sketch of how science might explain inductive reasoning. Inductive reasoning is itself a method of justifying beliefs. The traditional problem in- troduced by Hume is to justify this method of justification. How do we know that reasoning inductively, itself a method of justifying beliefs, is reliable? Following Hume, Quine takes inductive reasoning, at least in its primitive stages, to consist in a habit of mind through which we come to expect that similar causes will have similar effects.[9] We project our sense of similarity into the future, expecting that our quality space matches the way things are. The problem of induction is thus "why does our innate subjective spacing of qualities accord so well with the functionally relevant groupings in nature as to make our inductions tend to come out right?"[10] As an example of NE, Quine suggests the following answer:

> If people's innate spacing of qualities is a gene-linked trait, then the spacing that
> has made for the most successful inductions will have tended to predominate
> through natural selection. Creatures inveterately wrong in their inductions have a
> pathetic but praiseworthy tendency to die before reproducing their kind.[11]

Quine appeals famously to science, in particular, Darwin's theory of evolution by natural selection, to explain the inductive basis of science.

But does not this central example in which Quine speculates on how induc- tive patterns of reasoning might have evolved simply highlight the problems of normativity and circularity just broached? How does knowing how we came to think inductively tell us in itself how we ought to think inductively? And if it cannot, how can we honestly take ourselves to be doing epistemology? Once more, to know on the basis of evolutionary theory how we came to think inductively as we do, we must assume that some of our beliefs (e.g., concern- ing evolution) are justified; we are assuming that we have some knowledge to begin with. But if that is so, why have we not just begged the question against the skeptic? Already I have hinted at how these objections might be met. Now it is time to develop my response to these objections more carefully in terms

of the present example and to answer some related concerns about flaws in
our native inference patterns and the difference between reproductive fitness
and truth.

Normativity Forsaken?

The normativity and circularity objections work in tandem, as can be seen in
the following Humean dilemma for anyone who thinks that the facts of evolution can justify induction. Suppose that Quine's story about how we come to
reason inductively is true. Is this a story about how we *ought* to reason "to
make our inductions tend to come out right"? If we assume it is, we commit
the fallacy of inferring what we ought to do from what we do. Worse than
that, we reason in a circle, assuming that we reason the way we ought to,
which is exactly what we were supposed to establish. If, on the other hand,
we do not make this assumption, our story fails to provide a justification for
what we do and of course fails to address the traditional problem. I will address the second horn of the dilemma first, which is the problem of treating
the supposed facts of evolution as having no normative import but thinking at
the same time that they have epistemic significance. The first horn will be
taken up in the next section.

The problem of the second horn is this. How does Quine bridge the gap
between the putative facts of evolution and the "ought" of justification? The
answer resides in a feature of his story that is frequently overlooked. Quine
supposes that there is a point to induction. In his story the understood point
of induction is that our innate subjective spacing of qualities accord so well
with functionally relevant groupings in nature as to make our inductions come
out right. The purpose of our inductions is, in short, that they are reliable.
Since this point is apparently easily missed, let me quote Quine again.

> For me then the problem of induction is a problem about the world: a problem of
> how we, as we now are (by our present scientific lights), in a world we never
> made, should stand better than random or coin-tossing chances of coming out
> right when we predict by inductions which are based on our innate, scientifically
> unjustified similarity standard. Darwin's natural selection is a plausible partial
> explanation.[12]

It is clear that for Quine, standards used in our inductions are good or bad
depending on their usefulness in achieving the aim of "coming out right." In
this respect NE involves normative assessment in a straightforwardly instrumental sense. Inductive methods are explained and indeed *justified* to the extent that they are shown to be a good means to achieving our aim, given how
"we now are . . . in a world we never made." How we are is of course to be

explained by our best science, itself based on induction, but this, as will be argued shortly, does not guarantee that our inductions will be justified as being a good means to achieving our aim having our inductions come out right.

What has emerged is a fairly complex dialectical structure. Let me try now to give a schematic representation of its main elements before going on to the problem of circularity. For the sake of simplicity and generality, I will speak of inductive norms rather than methods, allowing that some may be innate as Quine suggests, while others may evolve socially and be socially maintained.[13] The traditional problem has been to justify the methodological norms of inductive reasoning (be they innate or learned). Quine's story reveals the relevance of another kind of norm, one that gives the aim of applying the methodological norms. Call the norms of *method* "M norms" and norms that specify their purpose or *end* "E norms." In these terms, the traditional problem has been to show that the M norms are a reliable means to fulfilling the E norm of making inductions that come out right. Schematically, NE proposes to solve this problem by seeing whether the body of theory that evolves from applying the M norms can explain how the application of those norms achieves the satisfaction of the E norm in question. Whether this obviously reflexive exercise succeeds is an empirical matter. If it does, there is a clear sense in which the M norms are justified relative to the given E norm. We have thus a procedure that is at once empirical, nontrivial, and plainly normative.

An objection that is bound to arise at this point is that this procedure provides no account of how E norms themselves might be justified. Without such account, it may be contended, NE does not fully succeed in its normative project of justifying the norms that figure in the production of knowledge and hence cannot count as an epistemology that is at once normative and fully naturalized.

A partial answer to this objection is that if NE failed in this way it would not be worse off than traditional theories of justification regarding induction. These theories simply assume that the end of having inductions come out right is appropriate. And why not? The end serves to define the nature of the problem, and thus the question of *its* justification does not arise. What is invariably at issue is not the end but rather the methods of reasoning that are supposed to be adequate for achieving the end. Certainly Hume, when he introduced the problem of justifying induction, did not present it as being in part the problem of justifying the goal of having inductions come out right about the future. For Hume, the goal was simply taken for granted.

But this cannot be a completely satisfactory answer from the standpoint of NE. From this standpoint, science is an activity involving both kinds of norms. If we are to turn science back on itself in an attempt to understand science only through science, then we cannot succeed if we attempt to explain only M norms and ignore E norms. We need to explain and, if possible, vindicate through explanation, all the norms of science, and where some norms cannot be vindicated, we must ask whether they should be revised. To suppose, on the other hand, that some norms, such as E norms, are immune to this procedure is to adopt an external standpoint and hence to surrender to a significant degree the original project of trying to understand science from within. Moreover, it is particularly important not to make an artifical separation between the two kinds of norms, since, as we have already seen, E norms can enter into determining which models of the world are supported by the evidence. If the two kinds of norms function together in producing knowledge of the world, why would the vindication of only one kind of norm be relevant to NE?

My attempt to account for E norms within the general program of NE must be postponed until chapter 7 where I argue that feminist theory suggests a natural extension of the above pattern of reasoning in which the vindication of E norms is possible. Recall that on the present pattern, M norms, such as those involved in inductive reasoning like the norm of predictive success, are vindicated by showing on the basis of the body of knowledge generated from M norms that they serve to satisfy the relevant E norms. The extension will be to see the M norms as functioning together with E norms in producing this body of knowledge (as they are in internal feminist empiricism) and then being vindicated (if possible) in the same way, by reference to the ends implicit in this methodology. This suggestion raises many questions that will be resolved in Part III where the alleged fact-value dichotomy can be addressed head-on.

It should be clear, however, that whether or not I succeed in the further project of naturalizing the ends that are implicit in science, the pattern of reasoning whereby M norms are supposed to be justified is thoroughly normative in the sense relevant to the traditional skeptic. When the antiskeptic claims we ought to follow certain norms to have a reliable representation of reality, the skeptic will challenge this claim but will not, qua skeptic, deny that it is a normative claim. Normativity is not forsaken in the case of Quine's attempt to use science to explain induction; nor, by the same token, does the more general pattern of reasoning that I have identified with NE fail to be normative. There remains, to be sure, the worry that the normativity contained in this reasoning, involving the assumption of ends, cannot be fully naturalized. But this worry only serves to underline the normativity exemplified in Quine's example of naturalizing induction.

Before closing this section, it is worth noting Kornblith's suggestion about how Quine's treatment of induction can be seen as normative. While Kornblith at one time appears to have thought otherwise, he now sees Quine's project as permitting normative questions to be part of empirical inquiry.

Quine has commented that "epistemology, or something like it, simply falls into place as a chapter of psychology and hence of natural science" ["Epistemology Naturalized," 82]. . . . The enterprise described is one which makes room for normative questions, but treats these questions as themselves an important part of empirical inquiry. In examining the process by which we tend to arrive at our beliefs, we are interested to see the extent to which they are well adapted to providing us with an accurate picture of the world.[14]

This view of NE is in line with the picture developed earlier. The "process by which we tend to arrive at beliefs" can be taken from my point of view to be a brain process exemplifying the satisfaction of certain norms of reasoning, or it can be a social process of arriving at beliefs in which norms are self-consciously followed. Either way, the normative issue is whether the process is one that ought to be followed, and, as in my picture, this normative issue is to be resolved ultimately by reference to whether the process leads to an accurate understanding of the world. It is possible, as Kornblith stresses, that empirical inquiry will reveal a respect in which the process is not suitably adapted to the end of accurate understanding. In that case there is reason to modify the process and, I would add, the norms that may be shaping it.

Unfortunately, Kornblith does not make explicit that the normativity of Quine's treatment of induction turns on taking an accurate understanding of the world to be the relevant end of inductive inquiry. As a result, when he discusses the holistic character of belief revision, he ignores the possibility that we might reject our belief that certain ends are appropriate. Let us suppose we have an account of what kind of belief-forming processes we ought to have (given the end of gaining an accurate understanding of the world). Kornblith notes:

> [S]uch accounts, together with a robust antiskepticism, entail that at least a great many of the processes by which we actually arrive at our beliefs meet certain conditions. We may now look to empirical work in psychology to see whether this is, in fact, true. If it is not, then we are mistaken in either (1) our antiskepticism, or (2) our description of the psychological mechanisms which humans embody, or (3) our account of the preferred processes. Traditional holistic considerations suggest that we may not automatically reject the third of these possibilities. The best overall account of the nature of human cognition may require that we modify our account of the processes we ought to instantiate in light of the pressure from the rest of our theory.[15]

Kornblith is perfectly right: we may not assume without argument that our account of the preferred processes is correct if these require psychological mechanisms that empirical studies show is not available to us. The problem is that the web of beliefs that depend one upon the other is wider than he supposes, including beliefs about what ends ought to be pursued, such as gaining an accurate understanding of the world. We may not automatically reject the possibility that we are mistaken in these beliefs, either. This fact will prove to

be of fundamental importance in the chapters to come for explaining how a
naturalized feminist empiricism is possible.

The Circularity Problem

Recall the first horn of the dilemma addressed at the start of the previous
section. It is that if, following Quine's appeal to current science, we assume
that our present norms are the very norms we ought to have, then we commit
the fallacy of inferring "ought" from "is" and reason in a circle, assuming
precisely what we want to establish—that our present norms are justified. The
response just given to the second horn suggests that this might be a false
dilemma, for we have reason to believe that Quine's project is normative. We
are, therefore, not committed to assuming that our present M norms are the
ones we ought to have and hence to reasoning in a circle. But this way of
trying to avoid the charge of circularity faces a problem. When we argue that
our present norms are the ones we ought to have because they serve the end of
gaining an accurate understanding of the world, the specific reason—Darwin's
theory of natural selection—that is given for thinking our current norms do
serve the end of gaining an accurate picture of the world presupposes that we
already have succeeded to some degree in gaining it and hence begs the skeptic's question. At this deeper level, at least, circularity appears to remain a
problem.

That circularity remains is an inevitable consequence if one takes seriously
Quine's reasons for appealing to what we already know through science to
explain the very possibility of knowing. From his perspective there is no "first
philosophy"—that is, no ground external to science and ordinary knowledge
on which we can stand for the purpose of justifying the methods used in
science and in ordinary thinking.

> I shall not be impressed by protests that I am using inductive generalizations,
> Darwin's and others, to justify induction, and thus reasoning in a circle. The
> reason I shall not be impressed by this is that my position is a naturalistic one; I
> see philosophy not as an a priori propaedeutic or groundwork for science, but as
> continuous with science. I see philosophy and science as in the same boat—a
> boat which, to revert to Neurath's figure as I so often do, we can rebuild only at
> sea while staying afloat on it. There is no external vantage point, no first philoso-
> phy. All scientific findings, all scientific conjectures that are at present plausible,
> are therefore in my view as welcome for use in philosophy as elsewhere.[16]

Is such a perspective needed? Are we forever barred from taking an external
standpoint? Later (in chapter 8) I will examine the reasons Quine gives for an
affirmative answer and argue that he is right about this. His reasons, as you
might expect, are empirically based. (It would be foolish to try to come up

with an external reason that there cannot be external knowledge.) But we need not involve ourselves in that debate now. The point here is that NE, as I am conceiving it along Quinean lines, makes circularity of the kind noted unavoidable. That is, NE *assumes* some scientific knowledge to explain the possibility of knowledge.

What we must ask ourselves is whether circularity of this kind constitutes a fatal flaw in Quine's project. Can a circular justification of induction be a genuine justification? Certainly some cases of circular reasoning about induction fail to justify induction. Let us suppose a very narrow conception of inductive reasoning, such as inferring that a pattern of events invariably found in the past will be present in the future, and ask whether this inference can be justified on the ground that *this* pattern has always been found in the past. Hume was right in pointing out that this is not a justification because it consists in simply assuming that the inference pattern will give the right result and then applying it to itself. This move surely begs the question in a way that directly undermines its cogency. But is Quine's appeal to Darwin a fundamentally different kind of circularity? If so, in what ways is it different?

The most significant difference is that Quine offers an empirically based (and empirically defeasible) explanation of why induction has worked as well as it does. Although this does not logically guarantee that induction will continue to work (and, of course, could not do this for reasons Hume made plain), it does offer a broadly based inductive ground for trusting induction. Hume's example in which a simple inductive rule is supposed to be justified by applying it to itself has no such virtue. The problem is not that appealing to the simple rule is more circular somehow; the appeal to Darwin relies on induction at least as much. Rather, the problem is that the inductive inference to the reliability of induction in the case of the simple rule is an inductive inference that has virtually no basis in science whatsoever.

Applying the simple rule to itself appears to appeal to the success of past inductions, but in fact the appeal has no solid foothold in science. The inductive reason for future success in Hume's example is that past patterns of inductive inference have been reliable. Which patterns are these? Not all inductive inferences, surely. At best only the cogent inductions and then only a percentage of those. But we are given no scientifically robust account of what these inductions consist in. The claim that patterns of inductive inferences have been reliable is next to vacuous as an empirical basis for further theorizing. As a result, our faith in induction based on this claim is truly question begging. It has no basis save the vague sense that our reasoning must be reliable. This appeal to induction to justify induction, therefore, has no genuine empirical basis and fails not because of circularity but because of empirical emptiness.

Quine's reliance of the modern synthetic theory of evolution to justify induction is the reverse. This is one of the most broadly based empirical theories in science, combining many diverse, well-developed sciences, including modern genetics. While it has sometimes been claimed that Darwin's theory of natural selection is itself empirically vacuous, there has emerged a consensus that this criticism has been based on misunderstanding the theory and the nature of empirical confirmation. Because it is so broadly based in science, its potential explanatory power is immense. We can understand in terms of the theory why our powers of apprehension, including our inductive ability to track relevant similarities in nature, have been shaped over the course of evolution to be more or less reliable in coping with our immediate environment. A genuine explanation is offered, however defeasible, that implies (in Quine's words) "we . . . should have better than random or coin-tossing chances of coming out right when we predict by induction."[17] It is for that very reason a justification of induction, relative to the end of coming out right.

The robust empirical character of this explanation is evidenced by three features, all of which are absent from the relatively vacuous appeal to "past patterns of successful inductions." First and perhaps most significant, the process of applying induction to vindicate induction in this way can end in failure. Quine's story employs Darwin's theory of natural selection and the auxiliary assumption that people's innate spacing of qualities is a gene-linked trait. Though these are derived from induction, one or both assumptions can be mistaken, and science could arrive at that conclusion based on induction. If it did, then this particular effort at explaining science would fail. It does not, therefore, assume its own success. But the point is general. Nothing in the method of vindicating induction NE-style guarantees that the method will succeed. For science, in applying induction, may not settle on *any* theory that would vindicate induction. Science may never be able to vindicate itself; NE allows that possibility. "Science is," as Quine succinctly puts it, "vulnerable to illusion on its own showing."[18] NE does not imply, therefore, that our methods of inductive reasoning must be the ones we ought to have if we want our inductions to come out right.

Second, the explanation of induction, powerful as it is, does not purport to be the last word. Indeed, it is represented in Quine's program as only the barest of beginnings in our efforts to understand how we interact with the world to come up with representations of it that are variously useful to our needs. It is a program with the potential of immense expansion that is already well under way. Third, the program will reveal definite respects in which our inductions are *un*reliable and can thereby serve to justify norms for inductive reasoning that are contrary to our native inference patterns. (The latter point is discussed further in next the two sections.)

The classically narrow appeal merely to past inductive success has none of these virtues. Its explanatory claim that induction has always or mostly succeeded in the past is for all intents and purposes unfalsifiable. It has also no potential for development and cannot explain how our native inferences can go wrong. Granted, both attempts to justify induction by induction are circular. But only in one case does the circle offer the possibility of a justification for induction that is empirically robust and capable of explaining why induction works as well as it does. This is the relevant difference.

Native Inferential Tendencies

A very different problem for evolutionary justifications of induction has arisen from empirical studies of native inferential tendencies. Let us assume for the sake of argument that our native inferential tendencies have evolved through natural selection and that we can put the problems of normativity and circularity behind us. What if our native inferential tendencies turn out to be relatively bad in relation to "coming out right" over a wide range of cases in which we reason inductively? If what have in fact evolved (by whatever means) are tendencies to reason poorly, then knowing how we got these tendencies hardly serves to justify them. If we know independently that these tendencies are defective with respect to giving us reliable knowledge of the world, their origins are really irrelevant to our normative concerns.

In a series of influential papers produced in the 1970s, Amos Tversky and Daniel Kahneman argued that people tend to reason badly in making inferences from evidence—in fact, so badly that their "intuitive expectations are governed by a consistent misperception of the world."[19] For example, the law of large numbers guarantees that very large random samples will probably be highly representative of the population from which they are drawn. In experiments, however, people's intuitions about random sampling appear to satisfy the law of small numbers, which asserts that the law of large numbers applies to small numbers as well. Many other researchers who have conducted experiments similar to those of Tversky and Kahneman have come to similar conclusions. For instance, if a tiny sample contains especially vivid examples, people will tend to assume that the examples are representative of the population at large. An illustration would be the conviction of the Canadian public that the rate of violent crime has increased, based on the media's reporting of particularly lurid examples, even when the public is confronted time and again with statistics showing a significant decrease in the rate of crime.

It might be supposed that experts reason differently, but Tversky and Kahneman claim that this hope is not borne out in their studies.

> Our thesis is that people have strong intuitions about random sampling; that these intuitions are wrong in fundamental respects; that these intuitions are shared by naive subjects and by trained scientists; and that they are applied with unfortunate consequences in the course of scientific inquiry.[20]

They supported this point by a study done on the American Psychological Association, including those members who were part of a mathematical psychology group. The latter did somewhat better than average but not much so. Numerous other studies have arrived at similar conclusions. It is possible, of course, to resist these tendencies to make bad inferences. Obviously, Tversky and Kahneman and those who devised similar experiments did so in constructing them. The point is that the tendencies are powerful and need resisting. Our "native" tendencies in reasoning, according to the studies, are apt to lead us astray and cannot be relied on simply because they evolved naturally.

In the face of this evidence, Hilary Kornblith has recently mounted a careful defense of Quine's project. He sees the latter as addressed to two questions: (1) What is the world that we may know it? and (2) What are we that we may know the world? He takes Quine to have argued in answer to the first question that the world is divided into natural kinds and in answer to the second that we have been shaped by natural selection to be sensitive to those very kinds. How then is it possible that the naive and expert alike have a tendency to make projections that match up so badly with the world? Kornblith's explanation is elegant and confirmed by the nature of the tests marshaled to show that we are naturally poor reasoners. He argues that in the tests we are given not natural kinds but rather artificial setups to which we tend to react as if we were dealing with natural kinds. Since we did not evolve to cope with these artificial situations, we tend to come up with the wrong answers. But this reaction, he argues, has no more tendency to show that we are by nature defective reasoners than the phenomenon of perceptual illusion shows that we do not normally perceive correctly.

This is a bare thumbnail sketch of Kornblith's general strategy. The details are important. The natural kinds that we might have evolved to be sensitive to involve what Richard Boyd has called "homostatic property clusters" around medium-sized physical objects in environments not too unlike those in which our very distant ancestors lived. It turns out that, despite our relative inability to detect isolated cases of covariation, we are remarkably good at detecting multiple, clustered covariation.[21] Ample evidence from developmental studies also indicates that children tend to divide the world into kinds on the basis of what they believe are the underlying structure of things rather than by their superficial observable features.[22] This means not that children have innate knowledge of natural kinds but that they have a natural tendency to look behind appearance to the causal structure of things. Considerations such as these suggest that we possess an imperfect, but remarkably efficient, innate capacity to learn about natural kinds inductively when they are not too unusual and are encountered in relatively standard settings.

Though Kornblith's hypothesis is exceedingly bold, it has a great deal of intuitive appeal and is supported by a growing body of research on the nature of cognition. It is at least the best explanation currently available of why we are as good as we are at figuring out how to cope with our environment at the day-to-day level and why we often get into trouble in reasoning inductively in nonstandard situations or in the absence of natural kinds. I am prepared, therefore, to accept the hypothesis as a tentative answer to the objection that our native inferential tendencies are radically defective and so cannot be justified on the basis of having been evolved through natural selection.

We should pause a moment, however, to take stock of what this solution means for naturalizing epistemology in general. It implies that modes of inductive reasoning outstrip our innate abilities in coping with unusual natural kinds or with situations in which the relevant properties are not embodied in natural kinds in the first place. How is induction in these cases to be justified naturalistically? Obviously, natural selection does not hold the answer. It is unclear, moreover, how induction more generally would be justified. An answer will have to come from some more inclusive theory regarding our evolution, including cultural evolution, one that explains the social processes that constitute scientific evolution in a way that justifies their continuation. There is no guarantee that such a theory will eventually emerge. In the end, as Quine concedes, the skeptic may be vindicated, not the scientist. The point to remember, though, is that no reason has been given that an empirical theory of this scope will not appear. The objection that our natural inferential tendencies are limited in special ways is, in particular, no such reason.

Truth Versus Fitness

Closely related to the objection that our native inferential tendencies can lead us astray is the objection that natural selection has fashioned us for survival and reproduction, not necessarily for detecting the truth, and has fashioned us to survive and reproduce in a particular kind of environment that may differ in critical ways from the present one. Stephen P. Stich makes both points cogently by a number of striking examples.

A certain species of toad learns on a single trial to avoid eating a noxious species of millipede but "will continue to consume BBs that are rolled past it until it quite literally becomes a living bean bag!"[23] In the original environment where the mechanism for descriminating noxious species from others evolved, there were no BBs, hence no need to make the further distinction between bland-tasting things looking like bugs that are steel balls and bland-tasting bugs. There the process that allows the inference from bland-tasting and buglike in appearance to edible was reliable; but in the new environment, not. Stich notes that a similar problem exists among humans with respect to various inferential strategies. For example, people are apparently very prone to use a "resemblance criterion" to link cause and effect such that great events should have great causes; complex events, complex causes; emotional events, emotional causes; and so on. Though it is speculated that this inferential strategy may have worked well in a hunter-gatherer society, it is completely unreliable in our present circumstances. Stich cites the case of the Azande inferring that the burnt skull of a red bushmonkey was a cure for epilepsy apparently because the jerky, frenetic movements of the bushmonkey resemble the convulsive movements witnessed during an epileptic seizure.

In general, natural selection is relative to environment in that natural selection causes certain features to be preserved in a population where, given the environment, individuals with those features have a reproductive advantage over those without them. Nothing follows, however, about whether that advantage will be sustained in a very different environment. Thus, even if the reproductive advantage of a process for forming beliefs were identical with its reliability for forming true beliefs, we cannot assume that a process will be generally reliable for forming true beliefs just because it has evolved through natural selection.

The other point is that we cannot assume that the fitness of a process for forming beliefs is the same as its reliability for forming true beliefs. Stich cites[24] a case in which rats were caused to develop an aversion to distinctively flavored food and water by giving them radiation sickness after they had consumed the food or water. Although the rats did not develop an aversion to food pellets of the same size or to the area in which the food and water were found, they were strongly averse to consuming any more food or water with the distinctive taste. It was clear that the rats had a mechanism that made them averse to tastes that were followed (within twelve hours or so) by acute sickness. But, as Stich points out, there must be many cases in the wild where sickness caused by sources other than food or water will lead rats via this mechanism to "infer" that food or water with a certain taste should not be consumed. As in the experiment, rats will be misled by a mechanism that has the reproductive advantage of preventing them from getting sick from noxious food or water. The fact that they are often misled will not be a problem as long as there is other food and water available. It follows that a very conservative mechanism for figuring out what might be harmful can have high fitness value, even though it is fairly unreliable as a means of forming true representations of what the world is like. Doubtlessly, there are many analogues of this conservatism among human cognitive mechanisms. We simply cannot assume that a cognitive mechanism that has evolved through natural selection will yield reliable representations of its environment, even when that environment is the one in which the mechanism evolved.

In chapter 3 I argued that truth was not the best way to conceive of the aim of empirical investigation if you wanted to interpret empiricism in realist terms as being about discovering a reality that exists independently of our representations of it. The same objection can be raised, however, whether or not we talk about theories being true or models fitting natural systems. Perhaps processes in the brain that produce representations of the environment are best understood as creating models that may or may not be similar to the environment along certain dimensions and to certain degrees. If so, it is possible that a mechanism that would produce the most accurate models of the environment (along certain dimensions) has lower fitness than some other, more conservative mechanism. (There could be a model in which a distinctively tasting food is always followed by acute sickness whenever it is followed by acute sickness just once.) As before, the fact that a cognitive mechanism is formed through natural selection is no guarantee that it will produce reliable cognition of what the world is like.

The way to handle the present pair of objections is similar to the tack taken by Kornblith regarding the experimental work that purports to show that our native inferential tendencies are deeply untrustworthy. There is no doubt that the tendencies we have evolved for forming beliefs may be less than accurate in situations where survival would favor conservatism and even be wildly wrong in environments greatly unlike the conditions under which those tendencies evolved, but it does not follow that when the demands of reproductive survival would not favor conservatism or when the environment is relevantly similar to that of our distant ancestors, these tendencies will continue to lead us into error. As Quine remarked when he made the appeal to Darwin, natural selection is a partial explanation of our inductive successes, not the whole explanation. It is, nevertheless, some explanation, not none at all. It still allows us to understand why induction succeeds within a large range of cases.

Moreover, in cases in which our tendencies lead us astray, the theory of natural selection appears to explain why we err—for example, why we tend to be more conservative in our tendency to infer than we would be if anciently less had been riding on our inferences, or more hasty than we would be if the costs of gathering evidence needed to make a more accurate inference had not been in ancient times so high. The theory of natural selection decidedly does not imply that we never make mistakes in reasoning inductively—that is, the kind of mistakes that would be called mistakes in statistical reasoning. (Indeed, if it had that implication, we would have independent reason to reject the theory of natural selection.) It justifies, we might cautiously say, only some inductive reasoning and challenges other. In the latter case, it calls it into question in a way that suggests how the reasoning could be improved (by being less conservative or less hasty). This is arguably what we want a good theory of justification to accomplish. It should explain not only why good inferences are good, and bad ones bad, but also how to improve.

In this discussion we have been focused mainly on individual processes or mechanisms of belief formation and inference. It is in these terms that Quine made the original appeal and in these that the objections have been formulated. We must not lose sight, though, of the fact that induction proceeds socially in epistemic communities that are guided by norms of reasoning. We can as easily speak of social mechanisms of belief formation and inference as of individual ones and as easily speak of the norms that they embody. The same

kinds of issues arise, though the evolution of the mechanisms and norms involves culture as well as biology and hence a different theory of evolution.
This is another, larger respect in which the Darwinian story provides at best
a partial explanation of why induction works. We need not speculate about
what a more inclusive theory would be like to see that the type of objections
just considered do not constitute a decisive obstacle to the Quinean program.
The factors that determine the direction of cultural evolution do not have to
be perfectly correlated with the production of good theories in order for the
evolution of inductive norms to generate reliable models in a relevant range
of cases and for the theory to explain why these norms do not when they do
not.

Notes

1. In Quine's words, "our statements about the external world face the tribunal of
sense experience not individually but only as a corporate body"; "Two Dogmas of
Empiricism," in *From a Logical Point of View* (Cambridge, Mass.: Harvard University
Press, 1953), 41. Quine attributes this thesis to Pierre Duhem; see Duhem, *La theorie
physique: son objet et sa structure* (Paris: Chevalier et Rivière, 1906), 132–40.
2. This is the opening sentence of his discussion of values in Quine, *The Roots of
Reference* (La Salle, Ill.: Open Court, 1974), 49. A similar view is expressed in Quine,
"On the Nature of Moral Values," in *Theories and Things* (Cambridge, Mass.: Harvard
University Press, 1981), 55–66. But compare his reference to the normative in viewing
empiricism as a theory of evidence: Quine, "On the Very Idea of a Third Dogma," in
Theories and Things (Cambridge: Harvard University Press, 1981), 39.
3. W. V. Quine, "Natural Kinds," in *Ontological Relativity and Other Essays* (New
York: Columbia University Press, 1969), 76.
4. Hilary Kornblith, ed., *Naturalizing Epistemology*, 2d ed. (Cambridge, Mass.:
The MIT Press, 1994), 1–7; Jaegwon Kim, "What Is 'Naturalized Epistemology'?" in
Philosophical Perspectives 2; *Epistemology*, James E. Tomberlin, ed. (Atascadero,
Calif.: Ridgeview, 1988). It should be noted that this interpretation of Quine, which
appeared in the introduction of the 1985 edition of the anthology and was simply
reprinted in the 1994 edition, does not represent Kornblith's position in his 1993 book
discussed later.
5. See note 2. It seems that more recently Quine has tempered his view: "But
[traditionalists] are wrong in protesting that the normative element, so characteristic of
epistemology, goes by the board. Insofar as theoretical epistemology gets naturalized
into a chapter of theoretical science, so normative epistemology gets naturalized into
a chapter of engineering: the technology of anticipating sensory stimulation"; *The
Pursuit of Truth* (Cambridge, Mass.: Harvard University Press, 1992), 19. Still, this is
a far cry from supposing that political and other contextual values can enter into determining the reliability of theoretical models in science prior to guiding their application.
6. Quine is typically represented as a coherentist, but this is a mistake if coherentism is conceived, as it normally is, to be an epistemology that is prior to science and

hence one that tries to explain the possibility of knowledge without appealing to science. Coherentism, foundationism, and Susan Haack's recent hybrid, foundherentism, all differ from Quine's approach in that they attempt to explain knowledge independently of science; see Susan Haack, *Evidence and Inquiry: Towards Reconstruction in Epistemology* (Cambridge, Mass.: Blackwell, 1993).

7. The attempt to understand knowledge without appeal to science is explicitly rejected in Quine, "Epistemology Naturalized," in *Ontological Relativity and Other Essays* (New York: Columbia University Press, 1969) but the groundwork for this move was already laid in "Two Dogmas of Empiricism." For brilliant exposition of Quine's reasons for rejecting the possibility of a priori knowledge, see Gilbert Harman, "Quine on Meaning and Existence I," *Review of Metaphysics* 21 (1967): 124–51.

8. Quine is explicit in not rejecting the traditional concern of epistemologists to understand how evidence is related to theory. See, for example, Quine, "Epistemology Naturalized," 83, 87; *Roots of Reference*, 1–4; "Five Milestones of Empiricism," in *Theories and Things* (Cambridge, Mass.: Harvard University Press, 1981), 72; *Word and Object* (Cambridge: The MIT Press, 1960), 1–5. Though the term *justification* does not appear in these passages, Quine is best interpreted, for reasons given later, as offering a naturalized understanding of how evidence justifies theory.

9. Quine, "Natural Kinds," 125.

10. Quine, "Natural Kinds," 126.

11. Quine, "Natural Kinds," 126.

12. Quine, "Natural Kinds," 127. It is important to note that Quine says that natural selection provides a *partial* explanation. It can explain our knowledge of middle-sized objects in our immediate vicinity, since getting it roughly right about these would have correlated well with getting on with survival and reproduction when our innate similarity standards evolved. At the same time the theory explains its own limitations; it explains how we are apt to be fooled without special training in an environment that is importantly different. (Critics of evolutionary epistemology often miss this point.) But the foothold gained is a start. On the basis of a rough knowledge of ordinary things, we may be justified in moving beyond our innate "scientifically unjustified similarity standard" to more refined methods of learning about the world. These in turn yield knowledge that both causes us to revise our understanding of ordinary things and calls for a deeper, more inclusive theory of cognitive activity to explain the reliability of our new inductions.

13. Though it receives less emphasis in his writing, Quine allows the possibility of socially evolved standards also. See, for example, W. V. Quine and J. S. Ullian, *The Web of Belief* (New York: Random House, 1970), 47.

14. Hilary Kornblith, *Inductive Inference and Its Natural Ground: An Essay in Naturalistic Epistemology* (Cambridge, Mass.: MIT Press, 1993), 3.

15. Kornblith, *Inductive Inference*, 4–5.

16. Quine, "Natural Kinds," 126–27.

17. Quine, "Natural Kinds," 127.

18. Quine, "Things and Their Place in Theories," in *Theories and Things*, 22.

19. Amos Tversky and Daniel Kahneman, "Belief in the Law of Small Numbers," in *Judgment under Uncertainty*, Daniel Kahneman, Paul Slovic, and Amos Tversky, eds. (Cambridge: Cambridge University Press, 1982), 31.

20. Tversky and Kahneman, "Belief in the Law," 24.

21. John Holland, Keith J. Holyoak, Richard E. Nisbitt, and Paul Thagard, *Induction: Processes of Inference, Learning, and Discovery* (Cambridge, Mass.: MIT Press, 1986), 200–4.

22. Ellen Markman, *Categorization and Naming in Children* (Cambridge, Mass.: MIT Press, 1989).

23. Steven P. Stich, "Could Man Be an Irrational Animal? Some Notes on the Epistemology of Rationality," in *Naturalizing Epistemology*, 2d ed., Hilary Kornblith, ed. (Cambridge, Mass.: MIT Press, 1994), 347.

24. Stich, "Irrational Animal," 146–47.

Chapter 6

Self-Knowledge and Feminist Naturalism

The Genetic Fallacy Fallacy

Reflexivity is central to the project of epistemology naturalized. In large part the project consists of developing a positive conception of reflexivity in which knowledge of nature explains itself as part of nature. The burden of this chapter is to illustrate how the standard of reflexivity works in feminist epistemology when it is focused on self-knowledge. I will explore, in particular, the reflexivity that is found in some feminist discussions of trust, sexual pleasure, self-respect, and autonomy. At the same time I hope to show the relevance of these concepts for self-knowledge and its absence.

To prepare the way, it is necessary to address a general objection against any such reflexive mode of justification. For the sake of argument, allow that knowledge can sometimes explain its own genesis when it is placed in an appropriate theoretical context. The problem is this: How can explaining the origins of a belief add to its justification or evidential support? It may be argued that it cannot, on the ground that to justify a belief through reference to its causal genesis is to confuse causation (an extralogical relation) with justification (a logical relation). Moreover, this mix-up may be said to conflate two kinds of explanation. One can explain a belief by giving its causes, or one can explain it by giving reasons supporting it, but the two kinds of explanation are not the same. It is often claimed that inference based on these alleged mistakes, in which a person infers a belief's justification (or lack of it) from an explanation of its genesis, is an instance of the "genetic fallacy." At least one writer has said, indeed, that the genetic fallacy is particularly prevalent in feminist philosophy.[1]

But is it a fallacy at all? I will examine three reasons for thinking that causation can sometimes be justification conferring. Objections to the first two reasons will provide some rationale for resistance to the idea that causes can have justifying power. In my view, only the third reason is decisive. It shows that the genetic fallacy is itself a fallacy. This reason will set the stage for later discussion because of its bearing on the social nature of self-knowledge.

The first reason that causation can confer justification is to be found in the basis for reflexivity that is contained in the requirement of explanatory power, one of the conditions for an adequate empirical test. For evidence to confirm a hypothesis, there must be no other hypothesis that is able to account for the evidence equally well. Some alternative causal hypothesis may be able to do this and thus may undermine the justification that the evidence appears to confer. Recall the example of testing for visual-spatial ability in which the men in the experiment did better on average than the women. The evidence that these men did better on average fails to justify the hypothesis that men are better on average, since there is an equally credible story in which the test results are caused by special features of the test situation rather than by differences in ability. Here it seems that what determines whether the test data justify a belief that men are superior is the causal process that produces the test results and consequently the belief in male superiority. The belief is justified on the evidence if, but only if, there is an appropriate causal process generating the evidence and belief. If the lack of assertiveness of the women alone in a dark room with a male experimenter causally accounts for the test results and hence the belief, then belief fails to be justified.

The person who doubts that causation can ever justify a belief may concede all this but insist that it is not really causation per se that decides whether the belief in question is justified. What decides whether the belief is justified, it may be said, depends on the *beliefs* that enter into the justification relation. To be sure, beliefs about causation are the relevant beliefs in this case. If one believes that it is the darkness of the room and so forth that causally explains the results, then one will not be justified in believing that men are superior on the basis of evidence presented. But what provides justification or serves to undermine it has to be beliefs about causation, not causation per se. On this view, though causation is relevant, it enters into justification only through beliefs that are held about it.

The general stategy should be clear. Grant whatever is said about the relevance of causation to justification, but insist that the relevance is mediated by the existence of beliefs about the causation. Hilary Kornblith, however, has used a telling example to make it clear that the justification relation cannot be purely logical.[2] Imagine making a list of a person's beliefs. If the justification relation were purely a logical relation among these beliefs, we would have the following anomaly. Let a person have three beliefs of the following form: p; if p, then q; and q. If the "arguments-on-paper-thesis," as he calls it, is true, then the person would be justified in believing q on the basis of his other beliefs. Suppose, however, that the cause of the person's believing q is not the beliefs p and if p, then q, but instead some belief that has no tendency to justify q at all. Then we would not say that he is justified in believing q. We would say that he is justified in believing q given his beliefs p and if p, then q, only if the latter explain why he believes q.

I think that Kornblith's example shows that justification is not purely a logical relation. This is a significant result. A necessary condition for a person's being justified in believing something is that the belief was generated or caused in a way that justifies it. But this does not by itself discredit the idea that another necessary condition is that the belief stands in the right logical relation to other beliefs of the person. It might still be considered a fallacy to infer justification solely by reference to a causal process that is *external* to the person's beliefs. The Kornblith example, therefore, does not by itself dislodge the view that justification, whatever else it might be, is in part a logical relation among a person's beliefs.

What does dislodge this view is the social character of some of our deepest knowledge. John Hardwig gives an example of a team of physicists who measured the life span of a charm particle.[3] There were ninety-nine authors of the paper reporting the results of the experiment, which took 280 person-years to complete. No person could have performed the experiment alone, given just the length of time required. More importantly, no person had the intellectual skills to do all parts of the experiment, even if she or he could live long enough to complete it. Hardwig notes that a similar situation obtains with Louis de Branges's proof of Ludwig Bieberbach's conjecture in complex analysis.[4] The proof required the expertise of a number of mathematicians to complete. Hardwig speculates that it "is quite likely that no one mathematician has or will ever have the logical justification for each step in de Branges's proof."[5] It appears, in short, that for much of our most sophisticated knowledge there is no person whose set of beliefs constitutes the justification for what is claimed to be known. If knowledge exists in these cases and if that entails that a belief in what is known is justified, the justification in these cases must be external to any one person's beliefs.

One might conceivably claim as a fallback position that the justification at least consists in various beliefs, even if not the beliefs of one person. This position will not do either, since, as Hardwig is quick to point out, "it is the interconnection, the structure of these bits of evidence into a unified whole, that enables them to add up to a justified conclusion about charm particles or the Bieberbach conjecture."[6] Knowledge exists in such cases—we have to say unless we are to be skeptics about cases involving the most rigorous organization of evidence—but justification is not wholly contained in people's beliefs, either individually or collectively.[7] A plausible hypothesis is that the justification is contained in the way that the evidence leading to the conclusion is causally structured. It is structured by a process of individual reasoning and social debate that tends to make the outcome of the process—what is said to be known—an accurate representation of reality. At least this is the view of justification that I will assume in the sections to follow.

Hardwig and Baier on Trust

It is clear that in cases like the ones cited by Hardwig, what helps collect the bits of evidence gathered separately into a unified whole is the testimony that one scientist or one mathematician gives to another. Since each is unable, because of lack of time or expertise to verify completely the testimony of the others, they must inevitably rely to some degree on mutual trust. This is one of Hardwig's general conclusions, and it appears to be completely right. But when is trust warranted? This question is particularly difficult to answer from the point of view of an individual but is crucial to understanding the nature of justification.

It seems that justification can exist only when trust is warranted, yet this second-order problem about the justification of trust appears to be no more manageable when it is applied to individuals than the first was. For how is a single individual supposed to determine whether another is trustworthy without having some independent way to verify the claims of the other? And the impossibility of verifying the claims of others for the cases in question is where we began. One can of course check out others' reputations among their colleagues who are experts in the same area, but what grounds are there for trusting the testimony of these others? It appears that there is no way to get around the need for trust. Yet we know that there are those who are not worthy of trust. Thus, the second-order problem of explaining when trust is warranted remains.

How general is this problem? Is it confined merely to abstruse experiments and proofs, or does the problem of knowing when to trust extend to more mundane knowledge? We have reason to believe that the problem is general. All the time we rely on the testimony of others when we claim to know things. In some of these cases we believe that we could, if we had the time and energy, check out the claims of those whose testimony we accept. We accept, for example, a newspaper report that a street is closed for repairs, but we could go to the street and verify it for ourselves. This is not always true, however. It may be physically impossible for us to get to the street. Moreover, even in cases in which we could if we wanted check out any one or even ten of the reports we accept, it would still be physically impossible for us to check out *all* of them. It seems plain that, apart from traditional concerns about direct knowledge in cases of seeing with our own eyes that something obtains, the problem persists that we must rely on the testimony of others for much of our everyday knowledge.

It might seem that self-knowledge is an exception, since in describing the character of my own mind, it might be argued, I do not rely in the least on the testimony of others. But how do I begin to separate out self-knowledge from what I know through others? If others have had a pervasive influence on me in ways that I cannot detach from my current thinking, then it seems that I must trust them to know anything, even things about myself. In a striking passage, Allan Gibbard makes the argument as follows:

> The influence of others has pervaded our thinking since before we could talk. Suppose, then, I reject all fundamental influence from others. Then I have much to correct: my current thought has been shaped in ways I judge distorting. Before I can reasonably think my judgment good, I have to rid it of this distortion. Now if the influence of others on my thought runs deep enough, I shall have to correct my thinking beyond all recognition. Indeed, I shall have no idea how to correct it. If I could reject wholesale the past influence of others, it would carry a prohibitive cost.[8]

To trust my own judgments, even about my own mind, it seems that I must trust others. Their influence on my ways of thinking is too deep and pervasive for me to filter it out. The problem of when trust of others is warranted extends therefore to self-knowledge. I can wonder equally well, When should I trust myself?

Annette Baier provides a criterion for trust between people that is morally worth having.[9] Her criterion is relevant to our epistemic problem, since we expect that a trust that is morally worthwhile is apt, other things being equal, not to lead to error in cases in which a person depends on another for knowledge. It is striking, moreover, that her test is reflexive, asking whether knowledge of the causal basis of the trust would tend to undermine the trust once either party to a relationship of trust comes to understand the factors on which the trust is based. Thus, the truster might rely on his threat advantage to keep the trust relation going, or the trusted might rely on concealment, but once these facts are realized the trust will be weakened. In such cases, Baier notes, "something is morally rotten in the trust relationship."[10] A sense of her general test is conveyed in the following passage:

> More generally, to the extent that what the truster relies on for the continuance of the trust relation is something that, once realized by the truster, is likely to lead to (increased) abuse of trust, and eventually to destruction and destabilization of that relation, the trust is morally corrupt. Should the wife come to realize that the husband relies on her fear of his revenge, or on her stupidity in not realizing her exploitation, or on her servile devotion to him, to keep her more or less trustworthy, that knowledge should be enough to begin to cure these weaknesses and to motivate untrustworthiness. Similarly, should the truster come to realize that the trusted relies on her skill at covering up or on her ability to charm him into forgiveness for breaches of trust, that is, relies on *his* blindness or gullibility, that realization will help cure that blindness and gullibility. A trust relationship is morally bad to the extent that either party relies on qualities in the other which would be weakened by the knowledge that the other relies on them. Where each relies on the other's love, or concern for some common good, or professional pride in competent discharge of responsibility, knowledge of what the other is

relying on in one need not undermine but will more likely strengthen those relied-on features. They survive exposure as what others rely on in one, in a way that some forms of stupidity, fear, blindness, ignorance, and gullibility normally do not.[11]

Can Baier's test be applied to the problem of justifying the trust needed for knowledge?

Applying the test obviously requires knowledge that is not always readily accessible or perhaps not accessible at all. One will likely be forced to trust the testimony of others to some extent to gain insight into the basis of one's trust. One may be able to see one's stupidity, fear, blindness, or ignorance only with the help of others. But if so, is there not a problem of circularity, for then one will need to trust others? The problem of circularity, needing trust worth having to determine what trust is worth having, is not vicious, provided that one is not required to trust the very person whose trustworthiness is in question and one is not calling all trust into question at once. Still, the test would be reflexive. The justification needed for knowledge would be secured in large part by gaining knowledge of the genesis and maintenance of that trust on which the knowledge depends, though gaining this knowledge would depend on trust in turn.

The reflexivity contained in Baier's test is consistent with her naturalism with respect to persons. As Baier has famously remarked, "A person, perhaps, is best seen as one who was long enough dependent upon other persons to acquire the essential arts of personhood. Persons essentially are *second* persons, who grow up with other persons."[12] Contrary to the spirit, if not the letter, of much contemporary epistemology, persons are in their nature, not accidentally and merely contingently, social products who first understand themselves in relation to others, both morally and epistemically, and thus can come to know their world and their place in it as individuals only socially, through the skills and insights developed in interaction with others like themselves. This is a decidedly naturalistic picture not only of what we are but also of how we discover who we are. "Persons are beings who have some sort of personality, and . . . all our *understanding* of personality relates it to its genesis, and, for us, that is in the conditions of biological life, in which one generation nurtures its successor generation, preparing it to take its place."[13] If our self-understanding involves errors, the best clues about their nature are to found in the genesis of our self-understanding. And we can discover this genesis, again, only with the help of others. Baier's naturalistic picture of our capacities as persons is of a piece with the reflexive view that we have to understand the origins of what self-understanding we have in order to understand ourselves more fully. There is no access to ourselves independent of social context.

MacKinnon on Self-Knowledge and Sexual Pleasure

Sexual pleasure is one of the most intimate and profoundly moving sources of self-knowledge. As such, it may appear to be an exception to the claim that there is no access to ourselves that is independent of social context. In moments of sexual pleasure we may experience some of our deepest longings and needs, our sharpest awareness of personal vulnerability, our strongest sense of emotional connection with another. The experience may feel so powerful and primitive as to appear to transcend social value and feel so individual and personal as to appear to lie outside the influence of social convention. Such knowledge through feeling may appear, in fact, to exist beyond the influence of patriarchy, at least when those experiences arise spontaneously through choices that seem uncoerced and unmanipulated. However, there is a feminist line of argument that views the possibility of such knowledge from the standpoint of its genesis—views it, that is, reflexively—and leads to the opposite conclusion.

The argument that I have in mind receives its most trenchant formulation in the work of Catharine A. MacKinnon. In her view, sexuality is socially constructed to reinforce male dominance and gender inequality, and a feminist theory of sexuality must first recognize this fact before it can hope to change it. The mode of reinforcement is that male dominance and gender inequality are sexualized—that is, are themselves sexually arousing and desired as sources of sexual pleasure and satisfaction. Moreover, this reinforcement means that dominance and inequality are sexualized for women as well as men.

> To make a theory feminist, it is not enough that it be authored by a biological female. Nor that it describe female sexuality as different from (if equal to) male sexuality, or as if sexuality in women ineluctably exists in some realm beyond, beneath, above, and behind—in any event, fundamentally untouched and unmoved by—an unequal social order. A theory of sexuality becomes feminist to the extent that it treats sexuality as a social construct of male power: defined by men, forced on women, and constitutive in the meaning of gender. . . . Feminist theory becomes a project of analyzing that situation in order to face it for what it is, in order to change it.[14]

This is obviously a radical thesis regarding sexuality. It implies that any self-knowledge contained in experiences of sexual pleasure would be itself socially constructed and hence not independent of social context or insulated from the influence of patriarchy.

MacKinnon does not directly address the possibility that sexual pleasure could be a form of self-knowledge, and the concept may seem puzzling. Let us take a look at this concept before spelling out the implications of MacKinnon's thesis. I am not talking about knowledge that one is experiencing pleasure or even knowledge of what the pleasure is like. Rather, I am talking about knowledge of oneself in relation to others that could be literally contained in one's pleasure as a mode of apprehending the world. There is a partial analogy in perception. In seeing someone come toward me, I can know that this person is coming toward me. My knowledge that the person is coming toward me is contained in my seeing her do so. Can I know that someone is coming toward me (or responding to me sexually) through taking pleasure in her doing so? The analogy may seem strained, since pleasure, unlike seeing, may not appear to bear an evidential relation to what is supposed to be known. I believe, however, pleasure and other emotions can have an evidential relation to the world.

In chapter 4 I discussed the possibility of emotional knowledge. For example, in fearing something, I can know that it is dangerous to me. In fearing it, I represent it as being dangerous to me, and if my emotion is evidentially based on my response to real danger, then my emotion contains a justified representation of danger that is actually present. I know that there is danger in such cases through fearing it. In other cases my fear can be unwarranted, when, for example, there is no evidence of danger and I respond irrationally. Or, in a more complicated case, my fear may be warranted (ample signs of danger exist) but in fact there is no danger. In the latter case I do not know that there is danger, despite the fact that my fear is justified in the circumstances. This would be analogous to my having a justified false belief.

Before I bring this analysis to bear on sexual pleasure, I should emphasize, as I did earlier, that the emotion need not be accompanied by a belief in what is known through the emotion. I may not believe that there is anything to fear, though I know through my fear that there is danger. In a case in which my fear is a justified response to the evidence when there is real danger, I would know that there is danger, despite the fact that my belief that there is nothing to fear would be unjustified. It would be a mistake, therefore, to require that emotional knowledge be tied necessarily to belief, though normally the two go together. The case with sexual pleasure is no different.

Crucial in all this is that emotion and feeling contain representations of the world, whether they are accompanied by a belief or not, and that as representations they can be justified or unjustified, veridical or not. Characteristically, when I feel sexual pleasure, in feeling this pleasure I represent the object of my pleasure as desirable, attractive, worthwhile. This is so even if for religious or political reasons I may believe that what I am taking pleasure in is not desirable or good. My pleasure can, therefore, be evaluated independently of my beliefs and may succeed or fail to meet cognitive standards that are appropriate to evaluating representations. Moreover, I can be mistaken in my beliefs about what it is that I find pleasurable.

Consider, then, a case in which I find sexually pleasurable my position of dominance and control in relation to my lover, though I do not believe that to be the case. Here what I find desirable and good in the object of my pleasure arguably is not so (e.g., where it simply mirrors a sexist social structure), and my pleasure fails in this respect to contain any self-knowledge. Though in my experience of sexual pleasure I seem to know my loving to be otherwise, I am wrong. I am not simply wrong in my belief that what is pleasurable is not my position of dominance and control. I am wrong also in feeling it as desirable and good when I take pleasure in it. I fail to have self-knowledge at the level of feeling and emotion.

MacKinnon's thesis regarding pleasure under patriarchy is that most, if not absolutely all, sexual pleasure within a sexist culture such as ours can be negatively evaluated in this way, because what is sexual *is* dominance and submission. Notice that her thesis is general. A feminist theory of sexuality like hers that treats sexuality as a construct of male power "centers feminism on the perspective of the subordination of women to men as it identifies sex— that is, the sexuality of dominance and submission—as crucial, as a fundamental, as on some level definitive, in that process."[15] Equally important, hers is a general empirical theory about how and why sexual pleasure is experienced in sexist culture.

> [A] feminist theory of sexuality that seeks to understand women's situation in order to change it, must first identify and criticize the construct "sexuality" as a construct that has circumscribed and defined experience as well as theory. This requires capturing it *in the world*, in its situated social meanings, as it is being constructed in life on a daily basis. It must be studied in its experienced empirical existence.[16]

She recognizes the resistance to this approach:

> To list and analyze what seem to be the essential elements for male arousal, what has to be there for the penis to work, seems faintly blasphemous, like a pornographer doing market research. Sex is supposed to be too individual and too universally transcendent for that. To suggest that the sexual might be continuous with something other than sex itself—something like politics—is seldom done, is treated as detumescent, even by feminists. It is as if sexuality comes from the stork.[17]

Whether or not she is right about where sexuality comes from, her treatment of sexual pleasure can be seen as thoroughly reflexive in its methodology. This is a deeply significant feature of her work. To study empirically the conditions that generate sexual pleasure in our culture and to evaluate the representations of reality that are contained in that experience in light of how we got them is to pursue an understanding of sexual self-knowledge that is reflexive in the sense explained earlier and thus a form of naturalized epistemology.

A source of resistance to her thesis arises, however, that itself has a reflexive basis and needs to be discussed. It is not hard for me to concede that much of my sexual experience is shaped by gender inequality, but it is difficult to believe that in every instance my sexual pleasure derives from a relation of dominance and submission, that my sexuality is entirely bound by sexism. My sexual feelings do not always present themselves that way even after searching reflection. But MacKinnon's thesis does not require that the origins of feelings be open to individual inspection. Moreover, her thesis is intended to apply to females and males, gay and straight, feminists and antifeminists, alike. The fact that I choose to call myself a feminist does not change the social conditions that structure how, when, and with whom I experience sexual pleasure, nor does it automatically give me insight into this causal process.

Still, a puzzle remains. If there is no alternative, from whence does MacKinnon draw her own insight, and why would there be any point in trying to change the norm? Her thesis, it would seem, cannot be entirely general in every respect without being self-defeating. MacKinnon does address this worry. "Audiences want to hear about the design of life after male supremacy. Or, after all this negative, what do I have to say positive[?]"[18] Her answer is that fantasizing about what is *under present conditions* impossible is not useful. It is better to change the present conditions—for example, to stop rape and then see what difference that makes to sexual pleasure. "[T]o consider 'no more rape' as only a negative, no more than an absence, shows a real failure of imagination. Why does 'out now' contain a sufficiently positive vision of the future for Vietnam and Nicaragua but not for women?"[19] Again: "Sex feeling good may mean that one is enjoying one's subordination [or domination]. . . . Or it may mean that one has glimpsed freedom, a rare and valuable and *contradictory* event. Under existing conditions, what else could freedom be?"[20]

MacKinnon implies that the norm for what is erotic can be changed only through changing the social conditions that explain it. Fortunately, in order to understand the causal genesis of the erotic in sexist society, it is not necessary to be able to experience as erotic what is not erotic in a sexist society. On the other hand, if one seeks a society in which nonhierarchical relations are experienced as erotic, one needs first to change the present social conditions— conditions that MacKinnon thinks are not inevitable themselves. This methodology is consistent with naturalized epistemology. Sexual self-knowledge, when it is knowledge rather than mystification, requires understanding the causal basis of one's feelings and having it reflected back into one's feelings. This is true whether the sexual self-knowledge is positive or negative. In the positive case, this knowledge would follow fundamental changes in how power is distributed.

Dillon on Basal Self-Respect

Self-respect is another form of self-knowledge that has received feminist analysis that lends itself to a naturalized interpretation. Following Stephen Darwall, we can distinguish between "appraisal" self-respect, which entails a positive evaluation of oneself, especially of one's merit as a person, and "recognition" self-respect, which entails recognizing and appreciating the worth that one has simply by virtue of being a full and equal member of the moral community.[21] These dimensions of self-respect correspond to importantly different forms of knowledge about oneself. One can fully appreciate one's moral status as a person with all the rights and responsibilities that this entails but have a low regard for one's merit as person, because one knows that one has failed to be a good teacher or mother or friend. Conversely, one can know that one is a good teacher and so forth but not know one's moral worth as a person because one does not take oneself to be equal to others in moral status. The difference has emotional consequences. In the latter case, one can be expected to feel pride rather than shame in reflecting on one's accomplishments yet not to feel resentment when one is treated as if one had fewer basic rights than others; in the former case, the reverse holds true.

While the distinction between two kinds of self-respect and its connections with pride, shame, and resentment seem plausible, Robin Dillon has argued that standard discussions of self-respect along these lines present an oversimple and indeed gender-biased account of its nature. In particular, they do not explain how a person can acquire and maintain self-respect "in the face of institutionalized denial of one's full and equal personhood,"[22] nor do they "allow us to understand certain cases of damaged self-respect, where the damage is played out in the emotional domains of pride, shame, and resentment."[23]

To support her claims, Dillon describes three representative cases. (1) Anne is a successful professional who is highly and overtly admired by her colleagues for her outstanding record of accomplishments. Doing well in her chosen profession is central to her self-conception. She has set reasonable standards for herself and has good grounds for appraisal self-respect. Yet she cannot feel proud of herself or take pleasure in her record of achievements and feels wholly inadequate and undeserving, although she knows that she deserves to take pride in what she has accomplished. (2) Beth is a feminist who is ashamed of her body, although she firmly believes that "women's bodies are fine as they naturally are" and "regards pride as a fitting response to her emobodied being." Even though feminism has changed her concepts, beliefs, and values, these changes "have done nothing to heal her shame about her body."[24] (3) Carissa, since she knows that she has intrinsic worth as a person, would seem to be someone who enjoys recognition self-respect, yet she "routinely feels resentment about things she cannot reasonably regard as

disrespectful."[25] Moreover, because she knows that her feelings of resentment
are ungrounded, she feels "ashamed of herself for being the kind of person
who can't stop feeling that way."[26] Although each woman seems to meet the
standards of recognition and appraisal self-respect, the extreme and persistent
discrepancy between their beliefs and feelings shows that their self-respect is
profoundly damaged and that a richer conception of self-respect is needed to
understand what has gone wrong.

It is possible to resist this conclusion by arguing that the women are irrational. Dillon notes two ways that the claim of irrationality might be pursued in
defense of the standard approach to understanding self-respect. One might
argue that the women have irrational belief sets, believing both that they are
worthwhile persons with intrinsic value and that they are not. Then one could
say that their beliefs do not straightforwardly support the conclusion that they
have self-respect according to the standard analysis. But the premise that the
women believe that they are lacking in worth is gratuitous. Each is able to
give good reasons that they do have worth and expresses no doubt about this
matter. To insist that they must have unconscious beliefs to the contrary, even
though they firmly disavow them, simply because their emotions do not accord with the beliefs they think they have, would reveal an unmotivated lack of
respect for their cognitive capacities. Moreover, it is question begging, since it
provides no independent grounds for rejecting the far simpler view that the
women unambiguously believe that they have worth but are unable to feel that
they have.

The second strategy is to argue that, in accord with the standard analysis,
they do have self-respect after all but their emotions are irrational, since their
emotions fail to track the fact that they are worthwhile in the ways they know
themselves to be. Dillon objects to the imputation of irrationality in this case,
too. While she agrees that the women's feelings of worthlessness fail to reflect
their worth as persons, she holds that their feelings would be a warranted, not
an irrational, response to their experiences of devaluation and subordination
in a society that is hierarchially structured according to (among other things)
gender. Thus, contrary to the standard analysis, the self-respect of the women
has been damaged, as is reflected in their emotions, and their emotions, moreover, have a rational basis, despite the fact that the women are right in believing that they are not worthless and hence are not as they feel.

Still, there is a difficulty with this interpretation of the examples. If, as
Dillon claims, the emotions of worthlessness are a rational response to evidence of worthlessness, how can the women believe rationally, indeed claim
to know, that they are not worthless? On the other hand, if the evidence available to the women is enough to provide rational grounds for their conviction
that they do have genuine worth, then the same evidence should be sufficient
to make their feelings of worthlessness irrational. And if these feelings are
irrational, then, on the plausible assumption that the loss of self-respect must

have a rational basis, we are led back to the view that the self-respect of the women is intact; only their emotions have gone awry.

Although Dillon does not address this objection directly, she answers it implicitly in her conception of basal self-respect, which she distinguishes from the intellectual self-regard found in appraisal and recognition self-respect.

> The heart of basal self-respect is our most profound valuing of ourselves. The worth it grants and takes for granted is intrinsic and unconditional, wholly independent of performance or character and so unlike merit, but simpler, less inferentially constructed, and more intimate than status worth. When secure and positive, basal self-respect involves implicit confidence, an abiding faith in the rightness of my being, the unexpressed and unquestioned (indeed, unquestionable) assumption that it is good that I am. But when damaged and insecure, basal valuing is incessant whispering below the threshold of awareness: "you're not good enough, you're no good, you're nothing." And where basal self-respect is weak or distorted, recognition of personhood is small comfort, cognizance of merit a hollow consolation, for the basal interpretation is uncompromising: this is what *I am* most fundamentally.[27]

Because basal self-respect is not about merit for performance or character and not about recognizing one's moral status in the sense of having dignity or basic rights, it is not sensitive to the evidence relevant to beliefs about one's merits or moral status. It therefore possible for Dillon to hold consistently the view that the women lack self-respect in the basal sense but believe on the evidence that they have the kinds of worth that ground appraisal and recognition self-respect.

The problem still remains of explaining how basal self-respect, and hence the emotions that reflect its presence or its absence, can be sensitive to evidence. How can such a prereflective understanding of the self be rational or irrational? Dillon's answer reveals her implicit naturalism. The self-knowledge that is contained in basal self-understanding grows out of "a natural interpretative response to the experiences of being a valued and valuable, or unvalued and value/less, person among others who are valued and valuable . . . [and] is emotionally-structured because [its] construction begins in the interplay of emotions constituting those early relationships."[28] As a socially cultivated response to the feelings of others, it can be thought of as an instance of someone (mis)learning about her value among others. What is learned is not propositional. She does not learn facts about herself. Rather, she learns to experience herself as valuable among others or not. Later, beginning in chapter 8, I will defend a realist form of naturalism in which representations of value can reflect reality (or not). From this perspective, basal self-understanding develops in response to social evidence that may or may not lead to a reliable nonpropositional understanding of one's value among others. One's

basal understanding thus can be, at least in a sense compatible with naturalized epistemology, a justified or warranted response to one's history of emotional interactions with others.

Conceived in this way, basal frameworks of understanding are not private
matters. They are, as Dillon forcefully puts it, "as much *ours* as mine."[29]
Consequently, they are profoundly shaped by political and social forces and
are apt to reflect the subordination and devaluation of women as a group.
Though not all women will be affected the same way, "other things being
equal, women are more likely than men to have damaged self-respect and . . .
the factors that undermine self-respect, as well as the configuration and meaning of this damage, are likely to be different for women and men."[30] Moreover—and   here   Dillon's   observation   parallels   MacKinnon's   general
observations on pleasure under patriarchy—"Self-respect may be damaged
not because individuals fail to have appropriate thoughts and emotions but
because they fail to have an appropriate situation, one that would support
the construction of a basal framework for positive valuation."[31] If the self-
knowledge contained in sexual pleasure or, more deeply, in basal self-respect,
is to reflect reality in a positive way, it is not the individual, but the gendered
structure of society, that must change.

Sherwin on Autonomy

Must something similar be said for personal autonomy, and, if so, would it
not be a contradiction in terms? Self-knowledge would appear to be an essential part of personal autonomy or self-direction. The problem is that self-direction is generally contrasted with direction from or by others, yet the main
thesis of this chapter has been that self-knowledge is constructed socially and
hence is not primarily an individual matter. It may seem, then, that personal
autonomy is impossible on the present understanding of self-knowledge. But
it would be odd if feminist analysis precluded the possibility of personal autonomy, since feminism as a political movement has been opposed to the
ways in which the autonomy of women is undermined in sexist culture. If the
impossibility of autonomy were the consequence of the present reasoning, it
would seem that the understanding of self-knowledge contained there has
gone deeply wrong.

Susan Sherwin has recently defended a relational view of autonomy that
offers a way out of this dilemma.[32] I will briefly summarize her reasons for
modifying the standard approach to understanding autonomy in health care
ethics and give some of the key elements in the new conception. Then I will
indicate how her conception fits the pattern of naturalized epistemology that I
have applied to the emotional aspects of self-knowledge.

Until very recently doctors have been trained to treat their patients paternalistically on the assumption that doctors would know better than their patients what is in their patient's best interests. This perspective is no longer seen to be defensible, given the importance now placed on treating patients in ways that are compatible with a patient's own value system. As Sherwin puts the argument, "health care may involve such intimate and central aspects of a patient's life—including, for example, matters such as health, illness, reproduction, death, dying, bodily integrity, nutrition, lifestyle, self-image, disability, sexuality, and psychological well-being—that it is difficult for anyone other than the patient to make choices that will be compatible with each patient's personal value system."[33] But if the patient is to make choices that are compatible with her personal value system, she needs to make them under conditions that allow her as much autonomy as is morally and practically possible. Patient autonomy has thus emerged as a key value in the rejection of paternalism as the proper relationship between the health care giver and the patient.

In what does this autonomy consist? Sherwin cites four conditions that are generally considered to be essential to a patient's autonomy in making health care decisions: the patient must (1) be deemed competent (rational) enough for the decision at hand, (2) make choices from a set of available options, (3) have adequate information and understanding about the available choices, and (4) be free from explicit coercion toward (or away from) one of those options. Narrowly interpreted as conditions that apply to single individuals and their immediate circumstances, these conditions define the standard conception of personal autonomy in health care ethics.

Though each condition is important and all too often ignored in practice, Sherwin argues that, so long as they are interpreted in the standard way, these conditions do not define a politically satisfactory conception of personal autonomy. The problem is that, when interpreted narrowly, the conditions separate autonomy from the social and political context of the individual's choice. So construed, this conception of autonomy when put into practice may fail to support or in some cases undermine the patient's ability to give genuine self-direction to her or his health care decisions.

Consider the first condition: that the patient be deemed competent or rational. What should count as rational is in many cases a matter of perspective, and the concept of rationality itself can easily be used by those in power in the medical community to privilege their own perspective. Sherwin points out that women are often considered less rational than men when they demonstate less emotional distance than men from the problems with which they are coping, although it is arguable whether such differences are relevant to judging whether someone is able to think clearly and reasonably. Sometimes emotional distance, far from indicating objectivity, may indicate that the subject fails to understand fully the issue at hand. Though mental competency is clearly relevant to whether one is capable of self-direction, it needs to be carefully interpreted with reference to the social context in which the concept is applied if it is not simply to reflect biases among those who are making the judgment and thus undermine the potential freedom of the person being judged to determine the direction of her treatment.

That the patient should choose among a set of available options to exercise autonomy almost goes without saying. The difficulty is that as long as autonomy is relativized to just those options that happen to be available, we cannot say that a person who has available more options has greater autonomy. In effect, the impact of the social context in which the range of "available" options is determined would be left out of account, and the concept would fail to be responsive to differences that significantly bear on the degree of individual control that a patient can exercise.

> There is a whole series of complex decisions that together shape the choices physicians are even able to offer their patients: These can involve such factors as the forces that structure research programs, the types of results that journals are willing to publish, curriculum priorities in medical schools, and funding policies within the health care system. While all patients will face limited choices by virtue of those sorts of institutional policy decisions, the consequences are especially significant for members of oppressed groups because . . . the sorts of institutional decisions in question tend to reflect the biases of discriminatory values and practices.[34]

A relational conception of autonomy would build in reference to the extent to which medical community and the society through which it is funded is organized to make available options that will improve the health of patients. Autonomy so conceived must be a matter of degree, since some societies will be organized to offer greater ranges of options than others and thus provide more autonomy for those in need of institutional care.

The information made available to patients, referred to in the third condition, is likewise a function of the priorities set by society. As Sherwin points out, what sorts of questions are asked or ignored in the research community depend on factors far beyond the control of the patient, yet the patient's ability to apply information that is relevant to her or his values depends on the type and quality of information that is available as a result of prior research. Autonomy narrowly defined fails to recognize the immense significance of this influence and thus defines autonomy inadequately. *Available information* must be broadly construed to mean available to the community given reasonable and fair priorities that are not biased in favor of the privileged and affluent. Otherwise the concept of autonomy will be skewed so that in its application people who have different ability to control their lives will be falsely judged as equal in autonomy.

Finally, there is the demand for freedom from coercion in choosing medical options. This condition is particularly hard to interpret, since (as I will argue in detail in chapter 9) what should count as coercion ultimately depends on what is to count as a reasonable baseline of options that in a just society should be available. Coercion involves the deliberate restriction of options in the baseline so that the best of those left from the standpoint of the coerced is an option that she or he would not choose except for this interference. Getting someone to give you money by telling them that you will kill him if he does not constitutes coercion for precisely this reason. How then should we regard expensive and risky cosmetic surgery sought by women in a culture in which "they accurately perceive that their opportunities for success in work or love depend on their more closely approximating some externally defined standard of beauty"?[35] How we should see this case depends on how we conceive the relevant baseline of available options. In most cases, no one is forcing the women to seek this treatment in the sense of holding a gun at their heads and threatening them with their lives if they do not. So there is no coercion relative to the baseline understood as the status quo with respect to options for success in work and love. Narrowly conceived, their autonomy is not violated by the presence of coercion. But should we conceive of autonomy so narrowly? Should we, that is, take as the relevant baseline of available options the status quo?

Exactly parallel questions can be asked where women choose dangerous, unproven experiments in reproductive technology to improve their chances of childbirth in a culture that seriously devalues childlessness, or where women choose prenatal diagnosis and selective abortion to avoid having a child with a serious disability in a culture that makes having a seriously disabled child very costly for the would-be parents. Given the status quo, there is no coercion involving the deliberate reduction of options within the norm. Yet one can argue that coercion does exist in these cases if one does not accept the status quo as the relevant baseline. Thus, Sherwin argues that these cases and others are plausibly considered to be instances of indirect coercion and therefore cases in which the patient's autonomy is limited. This move obviously requires understanding autonomy more broadly to include reference to a range of reasonable and fair options that may lie outside the status quo. Sherwin's implication is that these are cases in which, through no fault of her own, the patient will not be able to choose autonomously. This follows because at least one option that the patient would choose were it available has been precluded from the relevant class of options, making her choice indirectly coerced.

Does Sherwin's attempt to interpret autonomy relationally exemplify a naturalized epistemology? Knowledge enters into the present discussion at two levels. First, there is the knowledge needed on the part of the subject in order for her to choose autonomously. The need is implicit in the third condition, which requires that the patient be adequately informed about the relevant options. To make the choice autonomous, it should not be accidentally based on the right information about the option. The person ought to have good reasons for what she believes about the options (whether or not she can articulate them), for otherwise her choice will be less soundly based in her powers of reasoned deliberation than we expect of autonomous choice. From the point of view of naturalized epistemology, however, what constitutes good reasons for the patient will depend on the competency of many others on whom the patient depends to reach adequately supported conclusions. Though these reasons will form part of her reasoned deliberation, the causal process that generates the relevant knowledge will be socially rather than individually based. This coheres with a relational understanding of autonomy but not with a narrowly individualistic account. A failure on the part of experts to develop relevant data would, on Sherwin's relational analysis, undermine the patient's ability to know and hence to act autonomously as much as her being unable to think clearly about the information that is provided to her.

At a second level, there is the question of how we—any of us—determine what constitutes adequate information for someone who chooses autonomously. How do we know about the content of the conditions for autonomy? At this level, too, Sherwin's relational approach coheres with naturalized epistemology. Her interest in the case of personal autonomy is focused on the social and political processes that shape personal decisions. At the same time she is aware that the tendency in health care ethics to view autonomy narrowly, in individual terms, is itself a product of social and political forces that serve the interests of some at the expense of others:

> Here, as elsewhere, feminists are inclined to ask whose interests are served and whose are harmed by the traditional ways of structuring thought and practice. By asking these questions, they are able to see that assumptions of individual-based medicine help to preserve the social and political status quo.[36]

Whether or not she would welcome the term *naturalized*, her reflexive understanding of how knowledge is generated both for the individual patient whose autonomy is in question and for the ethicist who sets about to define the concept of autonomy reflects the methodology contained in naturalized epistemology.

Feminism and Scientism

Granted that reflexivity is an important part of naturalized epistemology, scientism—the view that the methods of science are a paradigm for the justification belief—would seem to be equally important. Witness the role of Darwin's theory for coping with Hume's skepticism about induction. It is therefore striking that the feminist authors just canvassed, however reflexive in their approach to questions of self-knowledge, are not scientistic. While they illustrate an aspect of epistemology naturalized, they do not exemplify the approach as a whole. One could press the objection further. Their reflexivity would lead them to call into question the idea that current scientific methods should constitute a paradigm for epistemology, since the origin of much of science, particularly its methodology in practice, is to be found in the sexist and male-dominated culture out of which it is generated and by which it is sustained. Thinking reflexively about science undercuts rather than supports scientism.

A full reply must await the following chapters in which I develop a more complete conception of naturalized epistemology. I can sketch now, however, the main outlines of my answer. There is an ambiguity in the way scientism has been formulated. Are the methods of science *all* those that are currently in practice, or are they only some of them, such as the ones cited earlier as being a core feature of objective hypothesis testing? If the term *scientism* is taken to refer indiscriminately to all or even most aspects of current practice, then I want to concede that reflexivity stands in tension with scientism and that either naturalized epistemology must disavow scientism or else feminism must disavow naturalized epistemology. In short, I concede the objection when the term is understood this broadly.

What if *scientism* is interpreted much more narrowly to include the methodological ideals that are part of internal feminist empiricism? Then I am prepared to argue that (1) scientism, so conceived, is part of an adequate epistemology naturalized, and that (2) there is no principled basis for excluding scientism from the study of such topics as trust within a community of knowledge seekers, sexual pleasure under existing social structures, basal self-respect, and the degree of autonomy that is currently possible for patients in certain choice situations. Resistance to this combination of claims lies either in the view that feminist empiricism is itself incoherent or in the sense that values, though perhaps an inevitable dimension of scientific inquiry, have no objective status themselves and hence cannot be part of what is studied scientifically. I have replied to the first view already at some length and will simply assume here that internal feminist empiricism is a coherent position. I therefore assume that there is nothing incoherent or logically suspect about including feminist political goals as an integral part of any scientific investigation. It is only scientism in which these goals are integral to the paradigm that is to be included in naturalized epistemology.

The second source of resistance is much deeper and requires a different tack. The idea that feminist values, such as might be presupposed in MacKinnon's discussion of sexuality, have no objective status threatens to undermine the idea of a feminist naturalized epistemology, because if the latter is to be turned reflexively back on itself, the values contained there—the ends contained within internal feminist empiricism—must be explained in a way that is consistent with the values being objective. I shall try now to explain how such objectivity is possible.

Notes

1. Ellen R. Klein, *Feminism under Fire* (Amherst, N.Y.: Prometheus, 1996), 29, 61–63, 191.

2. Hilary Kornblith, "Beyond Foundationalism and the Coherence Theory," *Journal of Philosophy* 72 (1980): 597–612.

3. John Hardwig, "Epistemic Dependence," *Journal of Philosophy* 82 (1985): 335–49.

4. John Hardwig, "The Role of Trust in Knowledge," *Journal of Philosophy* 88 (1991): 693–708.

5. Hardwig, "Trust in Knowledge," 696.

6. Hardwig, "Trust in Knoweldge," 697.

7. If most knowledge in science is like this, the result would go some distance toward supporting Lynn Hankinson Nelson's view that knowledge is to be located primarily in communities of scientists rather than individuals. I would still contend that individuals have knowledge, but since the justification of their beliefs that makes possible that knowledge would be social, there is a sense in which communities of knowers would be the primary epistemic units. In the next section, I argue that the need for trust and hence the reliance on communities to create knowledge is, in fact, very general.

8. Alan Gibbard, *Wise Choices, Apt Feelings* (Cambridge, Mass.: Harvard University Press, 1990), 179.

9. Annette Baier, "Trust and Anti-Trust," *Ethics* 96 (1986): 231–60.

10. Baier, "Trust and Anti-Trust," 255.

11. Baier, "Trust and Anti-Trust," 250–51.

12. Annette Baier, *Postures of the Mind: Essays on Mind and Morals* (Minneapolis: University of Minnesota Press, 1985), 84.

13. Baier, *Postures of the Mind*, 85.

14. Catharine MacKinnon, "Sexuality, Pornography, and Method: 'Pleasure under Patriarchy,' " *Ethics* 99 (1989): 316.

15. MacKinnon, "Sexuality, Pornography, and Method," 316.

16. MacKinnon, "Sexuality, Pornography, and Method," 317.

17. MacKinnon, "Sexuality, Pornography, and Method," 317–18.

18. Catharine MacKinnon, *Feminism Unmodified: Discourses on Life and Law* (Cambridge, Mass.: Harvard University Press, 1987), 219.

19. MacKinnon, *Feminism Unmodified*, 219.

20. MacKinnon, *Feminism Unmodified*, 218; my emphasis.

21. Stephen Darwall, "Two Kinds of Self-Respect," *Ethics* 88 (1977): 34–49.

22. Robin Dillon, "Toward a Feminist Conception of Self-Respect," *Hypatia* 7 (1992): 38.

23. Robin Dillon, "Self-Respect: Moral, Emotional, and Political," *Ethics* 107 (1997): 232.

24. Dillon, "Self-Respect," 233.

25. Dillon, "Self-Respect," 233.

26. Dillon, "Self-Respect," 233.

27. Dillon, "Self-Respect," 242.

28. Dillon, "Self-Respect," 245.

29. Dillon, "Self-Respect," 245.

30. Dillon, "Self-Respect," 236.

31. Dillon, "Self-Respect," 243.

32. Susan Sherwin, "A Relational Approach to Autonomy in Health Care," in The Feminist Health Care Ethics Research Network, Susan Sherwin, Coordinator, *The Politics of Woman's Health: Exploring Agency and Autonomy* (Philadelphia: Temple University Press, 1998), now in press; citations to follow are to the manuscript.

33. Sherwin, "Relational Approach," 21.

34. Sherwin, "Relational Approach," 26–27.

35. Sherwin, "Relational Approach," 28.

36. Sherwin, "Relational Approach," 31.

Part III

Feminism, Meaning, and Value

Chapter 7

Fact-Value Holism

Can Ends Be Objective?

We must now address an objection that threatens the core of naturalized epis-temology. This is the objection raised two chapters ago that this approach (NE), while it can explain how its methodological (M) norms are justified relative to its end (E) norms, does not explain how the E norms themselves might be justified. Among E norms, at least for a feminist NE, are the political norms that define the aims of feminists. Without such an explanation, NE cannot fully succeed in its normative project of justifying the norms that it counts as epistemic.

It might be suggested that if NE failed in this way, it would not be worse off than traditional theories of justification regarding induction. These theories simply assume to be relevant to the end of having inductions come out right. Indeed, this end serves to define the nature of the problem. The question of *its* justification, therefore, does not arise. We have already noted in chapter 5 the inadequacy of this suggestion. Science is an activity involving both M and E norms. If we are to understand science through applying science to itself, we cannot succeed if we attempt to explain only M norms and ignore E norms. We need to explain and, if possible, vindicate through explanation all the norms of science.

It is worth noting that NE has within it the resources to call into question its E norms. Suppose that the M norms fail to yield a body of theory that is capable of explaining how the M norms are a good means to E. Then the justification project fails for those particular M norms. Now suppose that there is good reason to believe that it will fail for other sets of M norms as well, given the same E norms. In this case, what may need to change is the E norms, on the purely pragmatic ground that there is not much hope of satisfying them. Consider a nonfeminist example: The goal of having inductions come out right might be interpreted in realist terms initially and then modified in light of arguments that the norm cannot be satisfied when it is construed this way.

Feminist norms too can be modified in light of an evolving body of theory about the causes of women's subordinate position. As conceptions of sexism change, so does the content of norms prohibiting it. Contrary to some persistent misconceptions of feminist epistemology,[1] in feminist NE, both M and E norms are subject to revision in light of the theory that they generate.

The revisability of E norms has a striking consequence. For a naturalized epistemology to be feminist, it must contain a norm or norms that oppose the subordination of women to men.[2] Yet, for reasons just given, even norms that oppose the subordination of women to men are subject to possible revision or rejection. Were this not so, feminist empiricism could guarantee its own success. In that case, feminist NE would entail a standpoint or foundation that is logically prior to and separate from any evolving theory of the natural world and would cease to be a naturalized theory of knowledge. Hence, for the same reason that the skeptic about induction cannot be rendered incoherent or dismissable a priori by NE, a skeptic about the legitimacy of gender equality cannot be dismissed out of hand for reasons that are external to empirically grounded theory.

But we must ask, What would the grounds for revision be? Granted that there can be a pragmatic basis for norm revision, is there any firmer ground for maintaining a norm than the absence of pragmatic reasons for change? Can there be an *objective* basis for feminist norms? Indeed, can there be an objective basis for *any* norms that lie within NE? Such questions are not easy to answer. A large part of the difficulty is that it is not clear what we are asking when we inquire about the objectivity of norms in the context of NE. We need a suitable way to interpret the concept of objectivity within this context.

The question of objectivity arose earlier. In chapter 2, I suggested that objectivity in testing consists in being guided by certain empiricist norms (such as predictive success and explanatory power). That suggestion, on reflection, appears to be incomplete for two reasons. First, we can ask, Why should *these* norms determine objectivity and not others? Second, how could such norms ever explain the objectivity of *end* norms? For example, feminist norms that oppose the subordination of women to men are among the E norms of any NE that is feminist. How could an empiricist standard of objectivity for testing hypotheses about the world be relevant to determining the objectivity of such norms? We have dealt with the first question at some length in the third chapter and provided a realist answer. The second question, however, has not been directly addressed, and it is by far the most difficult.

In our present interpretation of what it is for M norms to be objective within the context of NE, M norms are objective when they are seen to be a good means to satisfying the E ends in light of our understanding of the world that has been generated by applying both kinds of norms. Clearly this account of how we might determine the objectivity of M norms does not dissolve the thorny issue of how to determine the objectivity of E norms. For suppose that empiricist M norms of the kind indicated are by present lights the right ones for objective testing and that NE determines this through the process just described. This process of vindication is relative to, of course, the goal of arriving at reasonably accurate models of what the world is like. That goal embodies a particular E norm, and we should now ask whether this norm has any objective basis itself. Indeed, we can ask this question of any E norm contained within NE. The problem is, How is NE to answer this kind of question? The empiricist M norms would seem to be irrelevant to answering it, and presumably we cannot appeal to some further E norm without inviting the same question all over again. When it comes to finding an objective basis for E norms, we seem to be left tugging at our bootstraps.

The Fact-Value Dichotomy

The present difficulty is generated, I think, by a nest of connected confusions. To get at them, let us take seriously the commonly acknowledged difference between making a merely descriptive statement that is devoid of normative content and making a statement that has normative content. Of course, it is controversial how to draw this distinction, but I will assume that there is an important difference between, for example, saying that women earn on average less than men and saying that this is unjust. The latter claim is clearly normative in a way that the former is not. Allowing borderline cases, I will assume that in general statements can be divided between those with explicit normative content and those without it.[3] Call this *the weak normative/descriptive thesis* or simply *the weak thesis.*

It is important to recognize just how weak this thesis is. In particular, it does *not* express a dichotomy between fact and value. The weak thesis does not rule out the possibility that a statement with normative content, such as the claim that women are paid unjustly, describes something that is true or, in other words, is a fact. The weak thesis allows a statement to be both normative and descriptive and allows the possibility of normative or value facts. The weak thesis merely implies that there is a difference between normative claims and nonnormative ("merely descriptive") claims. Someone who maintains that some normative claims are true and thus report facts about the world can still grant that some claims are not normative. Nothing more is implied by the weak thesis. It is a thesis so uncontroversial as to be held by both camps: those who distinguish factual claims from normative ones and those who do not.

What is philosophically interesting, of course, is the issue of what distinguishes normative from nonnormative claims, and on this point no consensus prevails. One thesis is that with claims that have normative content there is an internal or conceptual tie between making such a claim and being motivated (or having a reason) to act in accord with the claim, whereas no such link exists in the case of a nonnormative claim. This view, known in the literature as internalism, is often embraced by those who hold that no normative claims can be factual, but it has also been held by moral realists who believe that moral claims are factual. A recent thesis is that normative claims make implicit reference to the currency or justification of standards, while nonnormative claims do not.[4] There are numerous other ways of trying to explain the difference. For my immediate purposes it is not critical just why we make the distinction. I assume it is obvious that there is a difference, whatever its explanation, and I will not pursue this question further until the next chapter.

Much more controversial and constituting a genuine dichotomy between fact and value is noncognitivism, the thesis that normative statements have no truth value while nonnormative ones do. Later I will offer reasons to reject noncognitivism, but for the moment I will assume this strong thesis too, for the sake of argument. As will become clear, the arguments to follow do not depend on either the weak thesis or noncognitivism. If anything, these theses make it more difficult to explain how E norms can have an objective basis. It will not be question begging, then, to let these theses stand for the moment. It appears to be but a short step from noncognitivism to concluding that E norms can have no objective basis in reality, but I will argue that this step is a mistake.

Given noncognitivism, it is tempting to say the following. Purely descriptive statements can have an objective basis in how the world is because they can be known to be true, but normative statements, since they cannot be true, cannot have an objective basis. Since normative statements expressing the content of norms cannot have an objective basis, neither can norms. Why is this? M norms tell us what procedures we ought to follow. Such norms, it may seem, cannot have an objective basis unless there are corresponding true statements asserting that these procedures ought to be followed. Similarly, E norms tell us what ends ought to be pursued, and they too cannot have an objective basis unless there are corresponding true statements asserting that these ends ought to be followed. In short, given noncognitivism, both M and E norms would seem to be devoid of any objective basis.

But this is too fast. Although M norms could not be matched with true statements about what ought to be done, they could still have an objective basis in the following sense. They can generate a body of theory consisting of true, merely descriptive statements that would have an objective basis just in the sense of being true. Thus, M norms can acquire an objective basis *indirectly* by generating a true theory, even supposing the truth of noncognitivism. They can be a reliable guide to what is true and thus have a basis in what the world is like. It appears, on the other hand, that E norms cannot have an objective basis even indirectly, since they have no truth value themselves and do not provide a method to generate statements that do have truth value.

At this point we arrive at just the impasse suggested at the end of the last section. The norms of testing in science, the M norms in terms of which we understand what it is to be objective in deciding strength of evidence, can be objective as a reliable guide to discovering statements that describe what nature is really like. But the norms that specify our ends—like the norm that tells us to invent reliable models of what nature is like—have no similar function and hence lack this kind of indirect objective basis. Our most basic E norms, those that cannot be justified by appeal to further ends, must float unsupported in the justification network. Though many other norms may derive their justification indirectly through them, the most basic E norms are not tied to anything further and correspond to nothing in reality directly. They are, therefore, without objective basis and mark in their justificatory isolation an absolute separation of fact from value.

Fact and Value as Interdependent

Something like this picture seems to underlie the resistance to regarding E norms as having an objective basis. But this picture cannot be right, even assuming that noncognitivism is true. The picture supposes that M norms are capable of guiding us to true theory independently of the influence of any E norms. This supposition is manifestly false. Our interests play a fundamental role in developing research agendas and fueling our imaginations in the construction of theories, and these interests are significantly shaped by norms regarding the goals we ought to be pursuing—that is, by E norms. Moreover, as we have seen, E norms can enter into the application of M norms in the context of justifying theories on the basis of data. We have already seen this to be true when M norms are empiricist. It follows that M norms cannot acquire an objective basis indirectly unless E norms do so likewise. The two kinds of norm work together in generating and empirically confirming theories. One is as tied into reality as the other, and this is so whether or not noncognitivism is true.[5]

The reasoning that leads to the illusion that E norms have no objective basis in empirical reality contains a fundamental error. This is the assumption that we can know the truth of descriptive claims about the world independently of relying on a combination of M and E norms to guide us in testing these claims against experience. In fact, true descriptive claims stand in a reciprocal relationship with justified normative claims. On the one hand, normative claims about specific things can be justified only against a background of descriptive claims that are held to be true. If something x is judged good or bad, right or wrong, and so on, we cannot support this claim, even by appeal to further normative claims, except on the basis of some descriptive account of x. Conversely, for the reasons already marshaled, support for a descriptive claim will ultimately depend explicitly or implicitly on norms.

I call this reciprocal relationship *fact-value holism.*[6] Thus defined, fact-value holism presupposes the distinction between merely descriptive claims and normative ones (the weak thesis). Note, however, if the weak thesis is false, the spirit of fact-value holism would be preserved, since there would be no way to identify facts independently of values. This would be a trivial consequence of fact that there would be no "purely" descriptive claims. Let us, therefore, extend our use of *fact-value holism* to cover this case too. In the case in which the weak thesis is true but noncognitivism is false, the spirit and the letter of fact-value holism would be intact. Indeed, even if both the weak thesis and noncognitivism are true, fact-value holism remains defensible. Fact-value holism is a remarkably robust thesis that is unaffected by conventional ways of drawing or rejecting a distinction between facts and values.

Interestingly, fact-value holism undermines two of the most influential arguments in favor of noncognitivism. One of these arguments derives from internalism.[7] This is the view that values have a direct or "internal" connection with our reasons or motives for action. If facts are by themselves inert in this regard, values cannot be facts. This is the same reasoning used by Hume to claim that morals are based on sentiment rather than reason. Hume reasoned that, because facts in themselves cannot move us or give us reason to act while morals can, there are no moral facts to be discovered by reason.[8] To see the relevance of fact-value holism, consider the premise that, by themselves, values move us and give us reason to act. To be at all plausible, this premise must mean that acceptance of a value or norm (i.e., acceptance of something expressed by a normative claim) by itself moves us and gives us reason to act. But then, for the logic to work, the premise that facts are inert must be read to mean that the *acceptance* of a fact and thus acceptance of a purely descriptive statement cannot by itself move us or give us reason to act. But this premise flies in the face of fact-value holism, which implies that acceptance of a fact, at least when it is a reasoned acceptance, directly involves motives and reasons for action and therefore can by itself move us and give us reason to act. If fact-value holism is true, a premise of the argument from internalism has to be false.

The other influential argument is (1) values play no essential role in explaining facts that are accessible to direct observation; hence, (2) there is no need to posit values or "normative facts" as part of the natural world. But (3) if normative claims are not about normative facts, they are best construed as having a purely noncognitive function, such as to express commitment to norms or to exhort people to action.[9] As with internalism, this argument has inspired a large and tangled literature. We need not engage this literature, however, to see that fact-value holism is in conflict with the first step—that values play no essential role in explaining observable facts. It may be that there is no need to posit normative facts as part of the natural world. (I will dispute this second step later.) But the reason behind the second step, contained in (1), that we can produce relevant explanations of observable facts independently of appeal to norms is not supportable. Even if the weak thesis is true and, further, we can describe our explanations only in nonnormative descriptive terms, these factual explanations will not be accessible without appeal to norms.

Noncognitivism does not thereby stand refuted. But in undermining the arguments from internalism and explanation, fact-value holism blocks two prominent reasons for believing noncognitivism. In the next chapter, I will examine the assumptions underlying these arguments and give reasons for rejecting noncognitivism outright. For the present, it is enough to have shown that the philosophical picture that seems to make plausible the idea that E norms can have no objective basis in the facts rests on a failure to notice the thoroughgoing interdependence of fact and value, quite independently of the truth of noncognitivism.

Models and Norms in Okin's Theory

In this section, I want to consider how fact-value holism bears on a specific example of feminist moral and political theory. To do this I need first to clarify the relation of models to norms. Fact-value holism has the consequence that the models and norms of science have distinct *functions*. Indeed, their distinctness reflects a very weak fact-value dichotomy, but one I believe we should respect. The primary function of models is to represent the structure of actual systems in nature. At least that is the view I have defended earlier in the form of naturalized realism. The function of norms, however, is not to represent the structure of things as they are but to set a standard for how things ought to be.

This difference in function between models and norms is implied in the prior account of how norms enter into the practice of science. For example, the empiricist M norms cited earlier set a standard for testing theoretical hypotheses. These norms do not necessarily represent the practice of science as it is, nor are they designed to do so. They are not models of science in that sense. Rather, they are designed to represent how testing ought to be carried out. E norms set a standard of another kind. They set the goals that ought to be achieved—for example, goals to be achieved in scientific testing.

It is easy to suppose that the difference between models and norms plays into the hands of noncognitivists who hold that the descriptive and normative functions of language are independent. But this independence does not follow, for reasons that are (ironically) Quine's. Though models and norms serve distinct functions, there is no reason to suppose that the linguistic functions of description and of normative expression cannot be simultaneously exemplified.[10] Nor do the distinct functions of models and norms call into question the fact that these functions are interdependent. Successful representation still depends on the guidance of M and E norms, since they play a critical role in the production and assessment of models. Conversely, application of such norms depends on representing in some suitable fashion the situation to which the norms are to apply. The norm of predictive success, for example, depends on the reliability of auxiliary models to make a testable prediction.[11]

The distinct but complementary character of these functions permits a richer conception of justification than we have allowed until now. Recall the general structure of NE. The central question in NE is whether the models of nature generated by the M and E norms can explain how the M norms satisfy the E norms and thus can vindicate themselves. Thus, the Darwinian model of evolution explains how innate standards of similarity spacing used in inductive reasoning are reliable, thereby partly vindicating our methods of arriving at that model. The direction of justification, if I can call it that, is from models to norms and back to models. That is, the norms are justified by the models they yield, which in turn partly vindicates the models themselves. It is, in effect, how the natural world is—or at least how it appears through the lens of our best models—that ultimately explains the representational and normative aspects of the science. But might not the direction of justification go in the other direction as well? Might not our best norms explain why the natural world is (or appears) as it is and this fact in turn explain why we have the norms we do? Of course, neither mode of justification need succeed in any given case. The question is whether the second direction makes sense.

Susan Moller Okin's revision of Rawls's theory of social justice provides a striking illustration of how the direction of justification can be from norms to models and back to norms.[12] Okin argues that Rawls's use of an "original position" to justify certain principles of justice is gender biased. In the original position, free and rational representative members of society who are motivated to increase their individual shares of primary goods are to choose principles for determining the structure of the major social institutions and to do so behind a veil of ignorance that keeps them from knowing their individual identities. The veil of ignorance is supposed to eliminate bias, regarding such matters as race, religion, class, and perhaps even sex. But, as Okin convincingly argues, the fact that Rawls has selected "heads of households" for the representative persons in the original position significantly skews the outcome of the choice problem. Not only are those who would count as being heads of households likely to be males, but there is a tacit assumption that what transpires within the family and how it is affected by what goes on in the public realm are matters beyond the reach of the principles of justice. The principles would be chosen to govern relations between heads of households and hence relations that exist mostly in the public realm rather than to govern as well relations that exist *within* families.

The inevitable effect of structuring the choice situation in this way is to make gender inequalities largely invisible to the principles of justice, since such inequalities are rooted in the domestic-public dichotomy itself. It makes invisible, for example, the injustices that arise from the fact the care and nurturance of preschool children is largely the responsibility of women. To correct this bias, Okin restructures the original position so that the choice of principles there is to be made by all members of society and to apply to relations within the family and to the way that those relations are affected by institutions in the public realm. Moreover, the choice is to be made in light of information about the nature of the gender inequalities that now exist and their causes.

Note the direction of justification in Okin's discussion. Her point of departure is normative: that an adequate theory of social justice ought to have the power to discern injustice with respect to gender. In this respect the situation is not parallel to the case of justifying norms for testing scientific models. One begins there by assuming certain models of the world (e.g., of natural selection). But another important difference exists as well. The initial norms do not exist for the purpose of generating models of what the world is like, which may then be used to justify these norms and finally themselves. Rather, the norms serve, when coupled with views about gender inequality and Rawls's norm of justice as fairness, to generate a new, much more complex normative structure for justifying principles of social justice. Norms exist in this instance to generate more refined normative structures. Norms serve other norms rather than models.

In this instance norms are not invoked to identify reliable models. Instead, it is the other way around: reliable models—say, regarding the causes and consequences of gender inequalities—are needed by the parties to the original position to make a fair choice of principles for social justice. Reliable models are deemed worthy of notice only in respect to their usefulness in applying the norm in question. Their existence is justified because of their relevance to certain norms. The reversal goes even deeper. If the justification project succeeds, so that the norms of social justice with which we began or a refined version of them is vindicated through this process, these norms will have been justified ultimately by reference to themselves, much as models were in the previous case. Though models and norms remain interdependent for justification, norms occupy here the central point of reference.

Does this mean that E norms can explain what the world is like? To a significant extent they can, at two levels. They determine what models are relevant and hence can determine how we see the world. That this is true in general is an implicit consequence of fact-value holism. But in feminist theory the determination is apt to be explicit. Compare Rawls unrevised. Contractors in the original position, though ignorant of their identities, have general knowledge of economics, psychology, and social theory. But which general knowledge? General facts about gender inequality will not come to light in a relevant way apart from a normative structure that renders their importance visible. In Rawls's original normative structure, such information is not important. Indeed, even in Rawls's latest work, the relevance of models of gender inequality is obscure.[13] It is only in Okin's radical restructuring of the normative standard for justifying principles of social justice that the relevance of such models to the original position becomes clear.

This is to say that norms of social justice can explain what the world is like to us—that is, how we see it. But norms can also explain the shape of the world more directly: they can guide actions that effect change in the world and in this way play a direct role in making the world conform more closely to their standards. Consider, for example, the norm of men sharing equally with women in child care—a norm Okin thinks would be chosen behind the veil of ignorance in her revision of the original position. If it were to be widely internalized, present society would be changed in a fundamental way. Suppose that happened. Then to the question "Why have things changed in this regard?" we could answer that the new arrangement for child care is fairer. Reversing the earlier direction of justification, we would be justifying how the world is by appeal to a normative standard, one justified in turn by appeal to another standard: choice in an original position of equality. This direction of justification is no less basic or explanatory than the other.

Can Norms Explain the World?

It will be objected that what would explain the change in society would be the fact that the new child care norm is widely internalized, not the content of the norm itself. It must be conceded that the currency of the norm in society, or its coming to have currency, could explain many aspects of the changed society. For example, it could explain why there are different expectations about how men and women plan their lives. But the objection implies that such an explanation rules out the norm itself as having any power to explain change. That men ought to share equally with women in child care has in itself no power to explain what happens. Is this implication justified?

There may seem to be reason to think so, if one takes the aim of explanation in this case to be to explain why the change in question did occur, not why it should have occurred. To explain why the change did occur requires a causal explanation. Any causal explanation must refer to another event or state of affairs that can be a causal factor in bringing about the event to be explained. Since the content of a norm is in no sense an event or state of affairs, it is not the kind of thing that could possibly serve in a causal explanation of the kind envisioned.

A direct rebuttal of this objection would be an argument to show that the reference to the norm in this case is reference to an existing state of affairs that can stand in causal relations to events like the one in question. This is, in fact, the line that some moral realists have taken.[14] They would argue that it can be true that men ought to share equally in child rearing and that this is a fact whose existence can explain causally why it is believed that men ought to share equally in this work. They conclude that such normative facts can enter into causal explanations of social change.

This line of defense does not require that such facts provide the only causal explanation of social change. There would be reason to think that more immediate, particular events, involving people's motives and beliefs, combine to issue in social change, but that view is compatible with reference to normative facts having a role to play in causal explanation and being in some contexts more relevant than other facts in explaining why events have transpired in one way rather than another. Such facts may provide, moreover, the most complete and relevant account of change.

Let me give a mundane analogy. Suppose the question is, Why did John go into room A instead of B? Let the background be that John wants a desk on which to work, that he can easily find out which room has a desk, and that he is more or less rational in his behavior. Then the fact that A has a desk and B does not can explain causally why John went into room A instead of B. This explanation allows us to see a larger causal structure that includes the fact that John formed the belief that A has a desk *because* A has a desk and the fact that this belief together with his wanting a desk led him to go into A. It is true, of course, that the fact that John had this belief (together with our background assumptions that he wants a desk and functions rationally) would be enough to explain his behavior, without reference to the fact that A and not B has a desk. Nevertheless, the first explanation is adequate, and, more than that, it gives a somewhat fuller story of how John came to go into room A instead of B.

The moral realist who takes moral facts to be part of the natural world can make a move that is exactly parallel. She can argue that facts about fairness (together with background facts about people's motivational states and the social surroundings) can explain social change, even when a more particular account referring to the immediate causal antecedents of the event to be explained would also suffice. Although both explanations can give a true and adequate account of why the event occurred, the story that includes facts about fairness, she would argue, gives a more complete causal picture. This moral realist point of view, unfortunately, is directly opposed to noncognitivism. I cannot, therefore, appeal to it here without first defending cognitivism. I will defend cognitivism in the next chapter,[15] but is there another way to meet the objection? I want to conclude this section by showing how the objection can be defused by appeal to fact-value holism alone. I have suggested that norms themselves can help explain how the social world comes to be what it is, first by determining which models of the world are relevant to guiding our social interactions in it, and second, more directly, through actions that are pre-scribed or proscribed by the norms. The objection is that there is an asymme-try between norms and models. Models fit facts; norms do not. Hence, norms alone cannot be used appropriately to explain causally what happens, unless in speaking of norms being able to explain why an event occurs, one means that the acceptance or currency of norms in society is able to explain it.

Now I have already conceded that there is an asymmetry in function be-tween models and norms and argued that it is consistent with fact-value ho-lism. We need to consider what significance this asymmetry has in the present context given fact-value holism. Suppose we concede that norms alone cannot explain events. Might it also be true that models *alone* cannot, either? To answer this question fairly, we need to allow that there is a use of *explain* such that only events or states explain other events or states. In this use we cannot say that norms themselves explain events or states unless, as some realists have thought, there are norms that can be identified with certain events or states. But if we talking about models of the world providing insights into the causal structure of events, they do so only in conjunction with norms and never alone. The reason is just that we cannot explain via models unless we have reason to believe that the models fit the world more or less well, and we cannot do that—gaining empirical confirmation that they do—without the influence of norms, as is implied in fact-value holism. We can thus say that norms themselves enter into the explanation of events, even without taking the step all the way to normative realism and claiming that norms can enter directly into causal relations with events to be explained. Norms can explain on a par with models, in virtue of the holistic character of empirical investiga-tion on which explanation depends.

What Are Epistemic Norms?

Fact-value holism implies that E norms enter into the confirmation of models of the world and thus guide the production of empirical knowledge. At one level this fact is commonplace. Many would readily concede that a relevant E norm is having reliable models of the world. They might say that this end is constitutive of scientific practice, for someone who was not in any sense seek-ing to come up with reliable models of the world—seeking the truth, if we think of theories as sentences—is not really engaging in scientific practice beyond perhaps mimicking the moves. In this view, the end of having reliable or true theories is an essential or constitutive element of knowledge seeking. The end is by its nature epistemic. Certain other E norms might qualify as essential as well, such as seeking theoretical simplicity, breadth of scope, fruitfulness in generating new, empirically confirmed theories, self-consis-tency and consistency with theories in other domains, and maybe still others.

One wants to ask, What determines membership on this list? And if there is a criterion for membership, how would this standard for being an epistemic E norm be justified?

In the picture of knowledge that I am defending there is no legitimate way to mark off certain ends as essential to knowledge seeking. Which ends are to be called *epistemic* will depend on which ones regularly arise in the successful pursuit of knowledge. There will be nothing hard and fast, and certainly nothing permanent, about which ends tend to have a normative function in guiding the generation and testing of theories or models of the world. Any of the ends mentioned have been called into question by someone and at times for good reason. None are beyond challenge or necessarily defining of empirical inquiry. By the same token, no end is necessarily excluded from being relevant to learning about the world. If, in a context in which facts about gender inequality are camouflaged, the end of seeking gender inequality continually plays a critical role in gaining access to those facts, then it has epistemic significance in that context. It can be usefully described as an epistemic E norm. It is not essentially epistemic, but then perhaps nothing else is, either.

It will be objected that to be an epistemic end norm there must be something about its content that shows it to be directly relevant to knowledge seeking. Truth is like that; gender equality is not. But is this objection telling? It is possible to reject the concept of truth as lacking scientific integrity, as Paul Churchland has done, without rejecting the possibility of empirical knowledge.[16] I have argued for model reliability as being a legitimate end, where reliability is given a realist interpretation. But that argument was itself based on the assumption of empirical knowledge. Thus, I argued that it was plausible on Quinean grounds to assume an independently existing world based on modern evolutionary theory. This way of reasoning, however, cannot be used to support an essentialist conception of epistemic ends, grounded as it is in the putative facts of empirical theory. There are no essential epistemic E norms in any sense that places them beyond revision based on evolving scientific theory. Model reliability interpreted realistically is not one. But similar remarks apply equally well to simplicity, breadth, fruitfulness, and so on. Nothing about their content makes them necessarily epistemic.

Helen Longino distinguishes between constitutive and contextual values within science.

> I will call the values generated from an understanding of the goals of science *constitutive* values to indicate that they are the source of the rules determining what constitutes acceptable scientific practice or scientific method. The personal, social, and cultural values, those group or individual preferences about what ought to be, I will call *contextual* values to indicate that they belong to the social and cultural environment in which science is done.[17]

Longino rejects the view based on the traditional interpretation of the role of values in modern science "that its constitutive and contextual values are clearly distinct from and independent from one another."[18] Part of her argument is that contextual values have often been transformed into constitutive values, so that there is no firm, unbridgeable boundary between the two kinds of values. She cites the economic conditions of seventeenth century Europe as giving rise to a preference for a controllable world conceived as "a mechanically organized collection of machines decomposable into quantitatively describable and manipulable parts"[19] that was eventually translated into a standard for good theories of nature and thus a constitutive value in guiding scientific practice. The two kinds of values are interdependent in her account.

This much is completely consistent with, and indeed follows from, fact-value holism. But two parts of Longino's account are not compatible with the theory of knowledge developed here. Late in her book she says:

> The notion of intrinsic value neutrality of the sciences is, therefore, built on inadequate notions of experience, of inference, and of the inquiring subject. As I argued in Chapter Four, however, it doesn't follow that the sciences are completely determined by contextual values. Constitutive values provide a check on the role of contextual values and cultural assumptions.[20]

The first two sentences present no problem, but in the third Longino attempts to explain why contextual values do not tell the whole story by giving, surely unintentionally, a foundational role to constitutive values.[21] This move is, unfortunately, entirely consistent with her understanding objectivity as social criticism guided by constitutive values that is presented earlier in her book. One wants to ask how the constitutive values are themselves justified, but the only answer that makes sense within her antirealist view of objectivity is that they are somehow self-supporting. While it seems obvious that the sciences are not completely determined by contextual values, the reason must surely be that science is guided in significant part by the interactions created in experiments run in the laboratory and field. It is, I suggest, inputs from controlled experiments that "provide a check on the role of contextual values and cultural assumptions." The check is imperfect, to be sure, and a check that is inevitably mediated by further theory and values, as we have seen. But it is a check, nonetheless, and a check that must ultimately help to determine which constitutive and contextual values are good guides to knowledge.

The second part where we differ is closely related. With reference to the contextual origins of seventeenth century mechanistic philosophy, Longino says:

> That such a story *can* be told of early modern science frees us from supposing that the pragmatic successes of physics and chemistry are proof that the theories

involved are *true* in the sense of being accurate representations of an underlying or fundamental reality, or that these models of what science is are achieved through value-free inquiry.[22]

There should be no doubt that models of what science is as well as those within science are not arrived at through value-free inquiry. But from this, for all the reasons we have seen in earlier chapters, it does not follow that the notion that there can be accurate representations of systems in nature will go by the board. It may be that by *underlying* and *fundamental* reality Longino means something other than the aspects of natural systems that explain what we observe about them in experiment. If so, I am puzzled about the import of this passage. But if she means the basic structural properties of a system that explain our experience of it, properties that exist independently of our knowledge of them, then her conclusion seems insufficiently unmotivated and is at odds with the position that has been developed here.

I want to conclude with Longino that there is no fundamental distinction to be drawn between E norms which are constitutive of science and those that are contextual. Both can serve as epistemic norms, but neither can be essentially epistemic. The broad interdependence of fact and value undermines any strict division between epistemic or constitutive norms and other kinds of norms. At the same time, this interdependence of fact and value does not undermine the possibility of objective knowledge, since the basis of the latter is to be found in the structure of our interactions within nature, not in a set of intrinsically objective norms.

Notes

1. See, for example, Ellen R. Klein, *Feminism under Fire* (Amherst, N.Y.: Prometheus, 1996).
2. It seems clear that it is not sufficient. An epistemology that incorporated a norm against the subordination of women to men but that implied that none were in fact subordinated would not be judged feminist by most of those who apply the label to themselves.
3. For an excellent defense of this distinction, see David Copp, *Morality, Normativity, and Society* (Oxford: Clarendon, 1995), 11–15.
4. This thesis is advanced in Copp, *Morality*.
5. The argument made here for the interdependence of fact and value is contained in my "The Virtues of Feminist Empiricism," *Hypatia* 9 (1994): 90–115. There are, however, different routes to a similar conclusion, all beginning with a version of Quine's holism. See, for example, Nicholas Sturgeon, "Moral Explanations," in *Morality, Reason, and Truth* (Totowa, N.J.: Roman and Allanheld, 1985), 49–78; Morton White, "Normative Ethics, Normative Epistemology, and Quine's Holism," in *The Philosophy of W. V. Quine* (La Salle, Ill.: Open Court, 1986), 649–62; Hilary Kornblith, *Inductive Inference and Its Natural Ground: An Essay in Naturalistic Epistemol-*

ogy (Cambridge, Mass.: MIT Press, 1993); and Jack Nelson, "The Last Dogma of Empiricism?" in *Feminism, Science, and the Philosophy of Science*, Lynn Hankinson Nelson and Jack Nelson, eds. (Dordrecht: Kluwer, 1996), 59–78. For an argument not based on Quine's holism, see Hilary Putnam, *Reason, Truth, and History* (Cambridge: Cambridge University Press, 1981), 127–49.

6. The name is appropriate if we allow that facts are what true descriptions are about and values are what are expressed by normative claims. But the name should not be taken to imply that an ontology of facts and values is presupposed by this doctrine. The reader will observe that the doctrine has been explained without reference to facts or values.

7. For recent critical discussion of whether internalism supports the fact-value dichotomy, see David McNaughton, *Moral Vision* (New York: Blackwell, 1988), 20–24, 46–50; Jeffrey Goldsworthy, "Externalism, Internalism, and Moral Skepticism," *Australasian Journal of Philosophy* 70 (1992): 40–60; and Richmond Campbell, "Critical Notice of Allan Gibbard, *Wise Choices, Apt Feelings*," *Canadian Journal of Philosophy* 23 (1993): 299–323.

8. David Hume, *A Treatise on Human Nature*, L. A. Selby-Bigg, ed. (Oxford: Clarendon, 1978), 457.

9. An excellent discussion of this argument with copious references to the relevant literature is Geoffrey Sayre-McCord, "Moral Theory and Explanatory Impotence," *Midwest Studies* 12 (1988): 433–57.

10. I elaborate this point in the next chapter.

11. One might worry that talk of functions is inconsistent with naturalism. Whether that concern is valid depends, of course, on how functions are conceived. I subscribe to Larry Wright's conception in Wright, "Functions," *Philosophical Review* 82 (1973): 139–68. His view, which has gained some currency in its application to biological functions, is roughly this: Doing y is x's function if x's doing y is what explains why things of kind x exist. For example, circulating blood is the function of the heart, since natural selection favored organs that did this, and hence their doing this explains why hearts exist today. So conceived, functions are hardly incompatible with naturalism. Allan Gibbard has developed conceptions of representation and normative commitment along these lines, understanding them to be biological adaptations with distinct functions; Gibbard, *Wise Choices*. For reasons given later, I disagree with Gibbard's noncognitivism. Nevertheless, his view that the functions of models and norms are distinct biological adaptations is fully consistent with feminist NE as I am conceiving it.

12. Susan Moller Okin, *Justice, Gender, and the Family* (New York: Basic Books, 1989).

13. Susan Moller Okin, "*Political Liberalism*, Justice, and Gender." *Ethics* 105 (1994): 23–43.

14. See Sayre-McCord, "Moral Theory."

15. This oversimplifies: I will defend the view that a normative judgment, indeed a moral judgment, can be true, but for reasons developed in chapter 9, I also allow that moral judgments can at times lack truth value. In the end, I defend moral realism but reject the dichotomy that implies that moral claims are either all cognitive or all noncognitive.

16. Paul M. Churchland, "The Ontological Status of Observables: In Praise of Superempirical Virtues," in *Images of Science*, Paul M. Churchland and Clifford A. Hooker, eds. (Chicago: University of Chicago Press, 1985).

17. Helen Longino, *Science as Social Knowledge* (Princeton, N.J.: Princeton University Press, 1990), 4.

18. Longino, *Science*, 4.

19. Longino, *Science*, 97.

20. Longino, *Science*, 223.

21. Helen Longino recently corrects this move in her "Cognitive and Non-cognitive Values in Science: Rethinking the Dichotomy," in *Feminism, Science, and the Philosophy of Science*, Nelson and Nelson, eds., 39–58. The problem remains, however, of explaining why some values that guide the practice of science are better than others without appealing to realism, both normative and otherwise.

22. Longino, *Science*, 98.

Chapter 8

Meaning-Value Holism

Analyticity and the A Priori

In developing these implications of fact-value holism, I have not assumed that there is any fact of the matter about whether something is fair or just. I have not assumed, for example, that gender equality in child care being just could be a fact about the world that obtains independently of whether anyone now thinks it is a fact. I have thus steered clear of normative realism, the doctrine that implies that there are such normative facts. This is consistent with Quine's well-known antirealism regarding moral value.[1] But it is not obvious how antirealism about value is consistent with Quine's views about the nature of definition and meaning. Given his holism about meaning, I shall argue, Quine should accept rather than reject the possibility that a statement might function both as a representation of the world and as an expression of normative commitment. Using his views on analyticity, I shall defend a form of meaning-value holism and from there argue for the possibility of feminist normative realism. I begin with Quine's attack on analyticity.

Traditionally, analytic truths have been regarded as truths that can be known a priori. This is because they are, as a matter of definition, truths that can be known in virtue of their meanings *alone* and hence truths that can be known independently of sense experience. Quine has attacked this idea at more than one level. At the most familiar he calls into question whether there is a satisfactory explanation of the notion of meaning on which the concept of analytic truth depends. How can an analytic truth be known from meaning alone? Quine suggests that such knowledge is thought to be possible because, when synonyms are substituted for synonyms, analytic truths can be transformed into logical truths and logical truths are true just in virtue of their logical form. But, Quine contends, the notion of synonymy presupposed here cannot be explained without appealing sooner or later to the concept of analyticity itself and thus reasoning in a circle.[2]

Take the standard example: "All bachelors are unmarried." If for "bache-

lors" the synonym "unmarried males" is substituted, the result is the logical
truth, "All unmarried males are unmarried." Quine asks, What constitutes
synonymy in such cases? The answer cannot be just that the terms have the
same extension, for that would mean that the sentence "All animals with
hearts are animals with kidneys" turns out to be an analytic truth when it is
not, at least not according to those who claim to have a clear understanding
of analyticity. The answer, Quine suggests, is that the synonymous terms must
be not merely coextensive but such that they *necessarily* have the same extension. But, as he points out, the notion of necessary coextension seems no
clearer in this example than the notion of analyticity itself. Quine considers a
number of attempts to get around the difficulty by defining synonymy in other
ways, but in each case either some new difficulty arises, or the discussion
presupposes the very notion that we want explained.

Quine's attack on the concept of analyticity has generated much discussion
since the original publication of "Two Dogmas of Empiricism" in 1953, including many rebuttals. One of the most significant of these is the reply that
Paul Grice and Peter Strawson published in 1956. Their reply is important
because it reveals a failure to understand the depth of Quine's attack that still
persists today. Grice and Strawson suppose that if they appeal to our ordinary,
rough-and-ready sense of when terms are synonymous, they can succeed in
explicating a tolerably precise notion of analyticity that is sufficiently clear to
demarcate a real, though not absolutely precise, boundary between analytic
and synthetic truths. Indeed, they suggest that Quine is caught in a contradiction at those points where he seems to grant that synonymy is possible. For if
synonymy is possible, never mind whether we can define it with absolute
precision, then analytic truths must also be possible. This is because Quine
has himself defined the notion of an analytic truth as one that can be transformed into a logical truth by substituting synonyms for synonyms.

The difficulty with their reply is that Quine's attack is not merely about the
lack of clarity in the notion of meaning invoked by defenders of analyticity—a
notion that he believes is philosophically untenable. He is also arguing at a
deeper level that meaning, insofar as we can make sense of it, cannot sustain
the concept of a priori knowledge. It is this second level of argument that is
frequently ignored and that we need to pursue to understand the relation between meaning and value and to get at the heart of the moral realism debate.[3]

Quine's argument is in essence simple. Meanings cannot be grasped apart
from making assumptions about which truths obtain, and these include truths
that virtually everyone concedes are known partly in virtue of sense experience.[4] Meanings, in short, stand in a reciprocal relationship with empirical
truths; we cannot know one without some knowledge of the other. Hence,
there cannot be knowledge based on meanings alone, at least not in the strong
sense that requires meanings to be identified independently of knowledge
based on sense experience. Since the concepts of analyticity and a prioricity

both presuppose that meanings can be identified independently of knowledge based on sense experience, the argument against analyticity is at the same time an argument against a priori knowledge.

It is worth dwelling on this point for a moment. It is often remarked that Quine himself invokes a notion of analyticity at various places in his writing. It is then concluded that he cannot without contradiction be maintaining that no notion of analytic truth makes sense or is worth preserving. The inference is valid. Quine's precise target is the traditional concept of analyticity. What Quine is arguing against is the idea that it is possible to know some truths without relying at all on sense experience—that is, to know them a priori. While analytic truths have been considered by some philosophers, famously by Kant, to be just one kind of truth that can be known a priori, the notion of a synthetic a priori truth has been notoriously problematic. By attacking the notion of analyticity, thought by most people to be the most intelligible and defensible conception of a priori knowledge, Quine is calling into question the very idea of a priori knowledge. This means, however, that Quine is not opposed to notions of analyticity that do not pretend to serve as a basis for a priori knowledge. I shall argue, in fact, that the concept of analyticity that people implicitly rely on to identify examples of analytic truths is just such a notion. In sum: Quine's attack is focused on the traditional concept of analyticity and behind it the concept of a priori knowledge and the understanding of meaning on which both concepts depend.

Quine's general argument, as we noted, turns on there being a reciprocal relationship between meaning and empirical truth. This is in essence why truth cannot be learned independently of sense experience. His argument why the reciprocal relationship holds between meaning and empirical truths is, however, subtle and easily misunderstood. In outline, his argument has two major steps. First, there are no language-independent meanings (i.e., no meanings that can be known apart from knowing a particular language).[5] Quine's argument for this step is his thesis of the indeterminacy of translation, but there is another reason to accept this step, which I will come to shortly. Second, we learn meanings either firsthand in conjunction with learning truths about things with which we have more or less direct sensory experience or else through translation into a language whose meanings are already known. In the latter case, discovering the best translation depends on what we believe is empirically true, including what we believe (other) native speakers believe is empirically true. Either way meanings cannot be understood a priori.

The upshot is that ordinary meaning—that is, language-dependent, empirically grounded meaning—is reciprocally tied to our empirical understanding of the world. Each plays a role in fixing the identity of the other. In Quine's words:

[I]t is nonsense, and the root of much nonsense, to speak of a linguistic component and a factual component in the truth of any individual statement. Taken

collectively, science has its double dependence upon language and experience;
but this duality is not significantly traceable into statements of science taken one
by one.[6]

We could call this fact-meaning holism, understanding the terms *fact* and
meaning loosely and informally. Quine's argument against analyticity and the
doctrine of a priori truth generally is that they require a language-independent
conception of meaning. We can talk about synonymy, but language-dependent
synonymy will be always inexact and empirically grounded, and our talk will
not imply that there is any fundamental difference between dictionaries and
encyclopedias. Such meaning is of no use to those who believe that we can
understand the content of truths without any recourse to empirical knowledge.

We can even construct a notion of analyticity based on language-dependent
meaning. We might say that a sentence is analytic, relative to a certain empirically based specification of its meaning, if given that meaning (together with
the relevant synonyms) the sentence can be seen to be true. But this notion of
analyticity would obviously have no interest to believers in a priori truth. It
may be that students internalize just such a relativized notion of analyticity
when they learn to distinguish analytic from synthetic truths. How else do
they learn to apply the distinction more or less consistently to an open class
of cases? The difficulty is that any construction of this kind, being compatible
with fact-meaning holism, can add nothing to the credibility of analyticity as
traditionally understood.

The possibility of analyticity based on language-dependent meaning provides an answer to an objection from Grice and Strawson that the traditional
notion of analyticity must be a viable concept since independent speakers can
learn to apply the term *analytic* consistently to an open class of cases.[7] Their
argument is that unless the term marks a definite distinction, there would be
no explanation of how independent speakers can fairly consistently arrive at
the same conclusion. The problem with this objection is that consistent application shows only that there is *some* difference among cases that speakers are
responding to. For example, they might be picking out the truths that are
analytic in the language-dependent sense identified in the last paragraph. It
does not follow that there exists anything that fits the theory of language-
independent analyticity.

To give an analogy relevant to feminism, speakers can be trained to identify
independently examples of "female nature" for an open class of cases without
there being anything corresponding to the theory about female nature. Speakers can learn to classify persons according to their "femaleness" by responding to social differences between males and females in a given culture and
then project this classification onto a potentially infinite set. But there need
not be any essence of femaleness. Having learned a theory about why they
classify as they do, people will interpret the instances that they classify as

"having a female nature" as confirmation of their theory, but it may be false. Cases of females judged independently not to fit the type would be said to lack a female nature, but the presupposition that there is such a thing may be utterly groundless. Constancy in classification is confirmation of the theory that explains it only if there is no alternative theory that explains it equally well.

Kitcher on A Priori Knowledge

Philip Kitcher has presented a defense of the a priori that is important for Quine's argument in four respects.[8] First, it allows a minimal role for experience in a priori knowledge and thus appears to circumvent the main thrust of Quine's attack as I have presented it. Second, it implies that there are meanings or concepts that are language independent in the sense required by the traditional notion of analyticity, and we have not directly addressed this issue in developing Quine's attack. Third, it is embedded in a naturalistic epistemology. Finally, the defense is arguably the most carefully developed of any in recent literature and therefore provides an interesting test for measuring the depth of Quine's critique.

Kitcher begins with a quote from Kant that appears not to allow any role for experience in a priori knowledge: "we shall understand by a priori knowledge, not knowledge which is independent of this or that experience, but knowledge absolutely independent of all experience."[9] Quine's reason for rejecting such a conception in the case of a sentence claimed to be known to be true on the basis of the sentence's meaning is that our knowledge of meaning is not "absolutely independent of all experience." Kitcher anticipates this difficulty. He retains Kant's idea that a priori knowledge is knowledge that is independent of experience but defines independence in a way that appears to get around the Quinean objection:

> Many philosophers (Kant included) contend both that analytic truths can be known a priori and that some analytic truths involve concepts which could only be acquired if we were to have particular kinds of experience. If we are to defend their doctrines against immediate rejection, we must allow a minimal role to experience, even in a priori knowledge. Experience may be needed to provide some concepts. So we might modify our proposal: knowledge is independent of experience if any experience which would enable us to acquire the concepts involved would enable us to have the knowledge.[10]

To make this suggestion precise, Kitcher introduces a number of technical terms and then provides an account of the natural processes that might lead to knowledge that is independent of experience in the relevant sense.

An "experience" at a particular time is a person's sensory state at that time.

The total sequence of experiences a person has had up to a given time is that person's "life" at that time. A person's life in this sense is said to be *sufficient* for that person for a given proposition that p, just in case that person "could have had that life and gained sufficient understanding to believe that p." Next Kitcher introduces the concept of an *a priori warrant* for a belief by appealing to the terms just defined. A psychological process in X is an a priori warrant for X's belief that p just in case it is a process such that, given any life sufficient for X for p: (1) some process of the same type could produce in X a belief that p; (2) if a process of the same type were to produce in X a belief that p, then it would warrant X in believing that p; (3) if a process of the same type were to produce in X a belief that p, then p. Finally, we can say that X *knows a priori* that p if and only if X knows that p and X's belief that p was produced by a process that is an a priori warrant for it. Put more simply: "if a person knows a priori that p then she could know that p whatever (sufficiently rich) experience she had had."[11] This is the sense in which a priori knowledge is independent of experience without being absolutely independent of experience.

We have here a fairly precise account of how psychological processes can yield a priori knowledge that seems to avoid the idea that knowledge can be absolutely independent of experience yet still manages to incorporate in the notion of sufficiently rich experience the traditional concept of language-independent meaning. It has the virtue of being a psychologistic account of a priori knowledge in that whether there is knowledge of the right kind depends on the psychological process through which the knowledge arises. Thus, it would be a mistake to speak of an analytic truth *simpliciter* as constituting a priori knowledge in the relevant sense, since one could come to believe an analytic truth by a process that is not an a priori warrant for the belief (say by accepting the truth merely on the basis of authority). If an analytic truth is known a priori, it would be known through a sound process of reasoning based on the concepts involved.

Kitcher points out many further interesting features of his account—for example, that it does not count knowledge of one's mental states as a priori yet allows the possibility of a priori knowledge of some contingent truths, such as that one exists. He also defends his analysis against various objections. Neither these additional virtues nor the objections need detain us, since none bear directly on the question whether Kitcher's analysis is immune to Quine's original reasons for rejecting analyticity and with it the possibility of a priori knowledge. Let us turn now to that question.

The notion of an a priori warrant contains within it the idea that it is possible for one to grasp certain concepts, given a sufficiently rich life, and to hold their content constant over time, whatever *further* experiences one might have. It is exactly this idea that implies the existence of language-independent meanings. For if, given certain experiences, the content of some concepts can be grasped and held constant in one's mind, whatever further experiences one may have, these concepts have the status of meanings that the mind can hold constant without having to check the constancy of translation of words or sentences found in any language. Whether certain words or sentences retain the *same* meaning over time depends on whether the identity translation (where the unit translates as itself) remains the most plausible translation, and that depends in turn on whether (other things being equal) the identity translation preserves truth. Since new experiences can change what we count as true, translations can never be immune to change whatever experiences may come our way. The idea that the content of concepts can sometimes be immune to change in the face of new experience must mean, therefore, that such content is language independent. Such content would have the status required of meanings in the traditional notion of an analytic truth.

The problem that Quine's attack on analyticity presents for Kitcher's revised notion of a priori knowledge should now be evident. Although the revised notion allows experience to have a role in fixing the content of concepts and thus blocks Quine's objection on one front, the revised notion implies that this content can be held constant over time whatever new experiences arise and thus is open to Quine's objection on another front. We can now ask, What constitutes identity of a concept over time? Kitcher's analysis of a priori warrant provides no answer to this question. Yet without an answer the notion of a priori warrant is no more clear than the traditional notion of analytic truth.

Suppose for the sake of argument that we can give sense to the idea of a concept retaining exactly the same content over time. Then one ought to be able to use a symbol to stand for this content such that the symbol retains the same meaning—represents the same thing—over time. In Quine's parlance, the symbol would have the identity translation over time. But, of course, the revised notion of a priori warrant implies that this identity translation can be preserved over time for at least some concepts whatever new experiences arise. Is this plausible? That depends on what we mean by "can be preserved." We might arbitrarily insist on the identity translation, independent of any other considerations, but then we would be giving up on appealing to meaning as an explanation of truth. It would be like saying that a statement is true not because of its content but because we say it is true. Since truth is supposed to be explained by meaning according to the traditional notion of analyticity, we cannot arbitrarily declare that the translation over time has to be that of identity. If, on the other hand, we mean "can be preserved and still be a translation that is consistent with all our evidence," then it should be clear that it is not at all plausible to think that the identity translation can be preserved in the relevant sense whatever new experiences arise. The revised notion of a priori knowledge implies a conception of meaning that does not cohere with the ways in which we understand sameness of meaning.

How should we understand sameness of meaning if meaning is language dependent? Gilbert Harman has suggested that we mean that expressions are *roughly* the same in meaning when we say their meaning is the same.[12] This would be like saying that two books have the same color, knowing that for certain purposes their color is not exactly the same. For language-dependent meaning to be exactly the same would be for a translation to preserve in every respect the elements relevant to identifying meaning through translation, such as truth and similarity of usage. Since in every case goodness of translation is a matter of degree and context, there is never exact sameness of meaning, only similarity in meaning. A direct consequence is that the relation of sameness in meaning is not transitive, contrary to what it would have to be in the conception of language-independent meaning that is appropriate to the traditional notion of analytic truth. Grice and Strawson were right that Quine is committed to the existence of synonymy, but synonymy of the kind that Quine allows involves close similarity of language-dependent meaning. The latter does nothing to support the possibility of analytic or a priori truth.

Quine has another reason for rejecting language-independent meaning. He believes that meaning is radically underdetermined by experience. In this view, no matter how extensive our sensory stimulation may be, the translation of language will not be uniquely determined. This thesis, known as the radical indeterminancy of translation, obviously cuts at the heart of the idea that sensory experience can be "sufficiently rich" and thus might be used by itself to argue that there is no language-independent meaning. The indeterminancy thesis, however, is extremely controversial. The above argument has the advantage of being independent of Quine's indeterminancy thesis. Even if, contrary to Quine, translation were not radically indeterminant, there would still be good Quinean reasons for rejecting the possibility of holding meaning constant come what may and hence for rejecting Kitcher's defense of a priori knowledge.

Adding Fact-Meaning Holism

The Quinean argument developed thus far against the traditional notion of analytic truth and against a priori knowledge has been an argument for fact-meaning holism. This is the thesis that it is impossible to separate out the linguistic from the factual in the truth of any individual statement. I have argued that the identification of meaning depends on identifying the facts of the world through experience, since locating meaning entails that one makes assumptions about what is true based on experience. The reverse is, of course, also true: one cannot formulate what is true based on experience without attention to meaning. Meaning and fact—that is, fact that is established through experience—are interdependent. To quote Quine again: "Taken collectively, science has its double dependence upon language and experience; but this duality is not significantly traceable into statements of science taken one by one."

When fact-value holism is combined with fact-meaning holism, they have the important consequence that meaning and value are reciprocally related to each other. Meanings are based on empirically grounded facts that are in turn shaped by various normative commitments; the latter are based in part on empirical truths that are in their turn understood in relation to the meaning of sentences through which the truths are expressed. *Meaning-value holism*, though implicit in Quine's understanding of meaning and evidence, suggests a broader web of belief than he officially allows.

Might this web not have within it definitions linking normative and nonnormative expressions? And if so, would this not allow for expressions that function both to represent the world and to express normative commitment? Return for a moment to Okin's Rawlsian theory of justice. In this theory, for a major social institution like the family to be just *is* for it to conform to principles that would be chosen in the original position (structured in the new way that Okin suggests). Question: What is the force of "is" in this claim? Could it be construed as conveying identity? Suppose for the sake of argument that whether a social institution conforms to principles that would be chosen in Okin's original position is a matter that is, at least in principle, empirically decidable. (I take it that the issue of which among alternative options would be chosen by someone under specified assumptions about the person's information and motivation regarding those options need not be in principle empirically undecidable, nor need it be empirically undecidable whether a social institution conforms to certain principles regarding the distribution of benefits and burdens.) For brevity we can speak of whether *Okin's model* fits a given institution. On the other hand, whether an institution is just is surely a normative issue if anything is. If, then, the *is* above is that of identity, the question whether Okin's model fits a given social institution would be both a normative issue and one that is empirically decidable.

There is, I contend, no way to close off this possibility on grounds of meaning alone, once we concede meaning-value holism. Suppose we regard the identity claim as a definition offered within Okin's theory of justice. It is perfectly legitimate to dispute this definition on any number of grounds. For example, one might argue that the definition produces unacceptable conclusions about what is just. What one cannot do is argue that the definition is mistaken on the ground that the words used to specify Okin's model, since they have cognitive meaning and can be true or false, are by their intrinsic nature devoid of any normative meaning. Such reasoning would imply that there is a class of meanings that can be specified completely apart from any normative commitments, but this is just what meaning-value holism denies. The cognitive and normative import of any terms is to be determined holistically by reference to their place within an evolving theory that is itself embedded within an evolving language. For this reason there can be no intrinsic barrier to terms acquiring normative force in virtue of their position within a theory of justice. Even if the terms function there to convey an empirically testable representation of social institutions, they are not thereby barred from the role of expressing normative commitment.

An immediate objection might be that this result is contrary to the weak thesis offered earlier that, allowing for borderline cases, uses of language to express normative commitment can be distinguished from nonnormative uses. Thus, the observation that women in our society do vastly more than men do in the day-to-day care of children does not itself express a commitment to any norms. This I have been willing to concede, but it is not a thesis about intrinsic meaning. The weak thesis does not preclude the possibility that some terms function both to express normative commitment and to convey a representation of how things are and play these roles simultaneously. Potentially, this is true of the following open sentence: "x is an institution that conforms to principles that would be selected in Okin's reconstruction of the original position." In effect, meaning-value holism opens the possibility of a normative realism in which moral claims can be true and, like many other empirical claims, true independently of their being recognized to be true.

Is Feminist Metaethics Possible?

Before turning directly to normative realism, it would be well to discuss the kind of worry that many feminists have raised about realism in general. While recognizing its political advantages (the subordination of women can be claimed to be objectively wrong), it has the political disadvantage that moral truth is conceived as being potentially divorced from individual experience and may thus be used as an instrument of patriarchy to devalue women's personal experience. Anne Seller expresses this concern as follows:

> So the political problems of the rational-scientific epistemology are made more acute when questions of ideology and false consciousness are introduced. At best, the use of this epistemology appears to be profoundly undemocratic. At worst, it is an exercise in domination. . . . How do we know when we are not simply being sold someone else's ideology if we cannot rely on our own judgment?[13]

The objection is important for a number of related reasons. The most significant of these is that it is a *political* objection. A brand of metaethics is called into question on feminist grounds. In fact, it is not unusual for feminists to attack and defend realism for political reasons.[14]

Anyone who is familiar with the literature on moral realism will know that political objections to a metaethical position are seldom raised outside feminist philosophy.[15] There is in most of this literature the presumption that meta-ethics is a politically *neutral* inquiry into the meaning and logic of ethical discourse.[16] The very idea of bringing political considerations to bear on meta-ethical issues would be regarded in many quarters as based on a misunderstanding of the issues, if not a case of intellectual dishonesty. But it would be a profound mistake to answer the feminist worry on these grounds. Indeed, I want to argue that both the worry and the charge of irrelevance have their source in the same mistake.

The mistake is to suppose that our understanding of meaning and our normative commitments are not interdependent. It is to deny meaning-value holism. Quine has argued against the twin dogmas of verificationism and analyticity on grounds that the factual and meaning components of language are inextricably intertwined. I have extended this holism with respect to evidence and meaning to apply to normative commitments as well. In this extended view, the value components are no more separable from the web of belief than those of fact and meaning.

This undermines the charge that metaethics is necessarily value neutral. But it also, at least potentially, undermines the charge that normative realism necessarily devalues personal experience and other sources of normative commitment. Whether it does or not depends on how normative realism is conceived. Here I urge it as part of a feminist naturalized epistemology in which diverse feminist political commitments are internal to inquiry about models and norms. To suppose that realism about norms precludes the relevance of personal normative commitments to determining what really has value is of a piece with supposing that feminist political commitments are necessarily external to empiricist methods for testing the validity of models of nature. It is exactly in opposition to this form of fact-value dichotomy that I am advocating a feminist normative realism.

Feminist Moral Realism?

Before we leave this chapter, however, we must be much clearer than we have been so far about what is meant by *realism* in the realm of moral norms. Confusion on this subject abounds. I will attempt to achieve some clarity by reviewing five ideas about moral realism that appear in the literature. I will use Okin's revision of Rawls as an illustration of a theory of justice that could provide "background" for interpreting the metaethical import of normative claims about justice. Utilitarianism, when suitably interpreted, provides another illustration. In what sense these theories could serve as background will become clear as we proceed.

Truth

Moral realism is generally used to distinguish moral theories that accord moral claims realistic import. What exactly that import is depends on how the term is understood. In the simplest version, a theory is realist if it implies that at least some moral claims are literally true. Notice that this version does not merely say that a realist theory implies that moral claims are literally true or false. Though the present version says this much, it says more; if it did not, realism would be compatible with "error theory," and in that view moral claims are all literally false. By contrast, moral claims are not merely true or false according to moral realism; some at least are literally true. Indeed, most theories that qualify as realist in this sense provide guidance for determining which moral claims are literally true. Realist theories need not be, therefore, merely theories about moral language or moral reasoning—"metaethical theories"—but can be normative theories that support specific normative claims.

What does the adverb *literally* add if we say that moral realism implies that some moral claims are literally true? This is the term that Geoffrey Sayre-McCord uses in defining moral realism.[17] Though he never explains just what makes a claim literally true, it is clear why the qualification is needed. Some authors suppose that normative claims cannot be true in the same sense that other claims can be. For example, a noncognitivist would hold that when a person claims that it is "true" that it would be wrong to do such and such, the person is not claiming that this is true in the same sense as when a person makes a claim that has no normative import. In normative contexts "true" would perform a different function (e.g., to recommend, express an attitude, make a commitment) from that of reporting something that is simply or literally true. The moral realist, however, takes the position that some moral claims are true in exactly the *same* sense that it is true that words appear on this page or that Earth is nearer to the sun than Mars is.

The realist import that a theory accords to some moral claims may not be immediately evident and may require interpretation and analysis. Utilitarianism, for example, can be interpreted in a way that makes a particular version of it noncognitivist and hence antirealist, but it can also be given a realist reading. Suppose one interprets maximizing aggregate utility in a way that makes it literally true that some actions (in a given context) maximize aggregate utility. Then, a theory that identifies the property of maximizing aggregate utility with the moral property of being a morally permissible action would be a utilitarian theory that is realist in the aforementioned sense. Similarly, the Okin-Rawls theory discussed earlier would be a moral realist theory in this sense if the property (applied to social institutions) of conforming to principles selected in the way prescribed earlier were literally true of some institutions and the theory was interpreted so that this property is identified with the property of being socially just. These theories, so interpreted, provide the theoretical background for ascribing realist import to specific moral claims. The moral claims themselves are not instances of moral realism, but they can be seen to have realist import if they are supported by a credible background theory that is realist.

This seems to be the clearest and most useful way to understand what moral realism is. Other approaches are possible, as we will see, but they are inferior to the present one for reasons to be given shortly. Two qualifications must be added, however. What has been said so far does not imply anything about whether moral knowledge is possible according to moral realism. I have noted that theories that are realist in the above sense usually do provide some guidance for determining which moral claims are true, but this guidance is not part of moral realism as defined. We might distinguish then between two grades of moral realism in the literature: one implying that some moral claims are literally true; another, stronger version, implying that some moral claims are *known* to be literally true. As it turns out, reasons given for thinking that some moral claims are literally true are almost always intended to be reasons for thinking that some can be known to be, so the difference may not be important. I shall, however, intend the stronger position, unless otherwise indicated.

The second qualification concerns truth itself. In chapter 3 we compared versions of realism concerned with models that fit the system being studied instead of true statements about the system. One virtue of formulating realism by reference to models and the similarity of a model to an actual system is that indefinitely many models can be equally similar to a given system. This gets us away from the idea that there is a single true perspective—One True Theory—about any part of reality, without lapsing into antirealism. While there can be indefinitely many equally good models of a system (each responding to somewhat different interests), there will be indefinitely many bad models that are not at all similar to the system in the respects that are relevant to a given set of interests. Would it be possible to formulate a moral realism with respect to models rather than truth?

This possibility has not been explored in the literature. An immediate difficulty in doing so is that it is unclear what is to take the place of the "real system" that in the nonnormative case a model is supposed to be similar to. For example, one can speak of a Newtonian model being similar along certain dimensions to the actual system of planets orbiting around our sun. But in the moral case what kind of entity would serve as a real system in the actual world? It is perhaps tempting to say that we do not want to limit the reference to any real system, since in making moral claims we would be talking about how the world ought to be, not necessarily how it is. This direction of thinking, though, leads to incoherence, for the realist takes us to be making moral claims about how the world *is*. The answer lies rather in how the realist background theory interprets successful moral claims. If they are interpreted with reference to the similarity of models to moral structures in the world, the background theory would have to make clear what features of the world are supposed to be tracked by the competing models. I will postpone until the next chapter my proposal for how this might be accomplished without reference to truth. I note for now only that moral realism put in terms of truth about the world may have an analogue put in terms of models that could be of particular relevance to a feminist theory of justice.

Mind Independence

Traditionally, realism has been contrasted with idealism in which reality is, in one form or another, an aspect of the mental. Thus, in a recent book on the advancement of science, Philip Kitcher takes realism in its strongest form to imply the existence of a "mind-independent causal structure."[18] In this passage, however, he is defining what scientific realism is; it is not clear that this notion of realism can be successfully extended to moral realism. Though it is not difficult to imagine causal structures existing outside the mind when we are thinking of physical reality, can we do the same for moral reality? Whatever we take moral reality to be, is it not necessarily mind-dependent? And, if so, is not moral realism a nonstarter when realism is so conceived?

The answer depends on how we understand mind independence. Suppose that the realist thesis is made out to be that moral properties themselves are not defined or constituted in any part by what is mental. Then, surely, we have understood mind independence too narrowly. Perhaps G. E. Moore was a moral realist of this kind, for he held that an action is wrong if it does not maximize the good but maintained also that the property of being good is indefinable (much less definable by reference to the mental).[19] But, while this conception of moral realism may not be so narrow as to exclude Moore and maybe a few other theorists, it seems far too stringent to capture what is often intended in the recent debates around moral realism. For example, in these debates it is frequently assumed that some forms of naturalistic utilitarianism would be realist if the property of maximizing aggregate utility is conceived as being no less a natural property than some of the complex, empirically confirmable properties studied in science. Yet this apparent paradigm of moral realism would be disqualified on the understanding that is proposed, since utility is defined with respect to preferences, and hence being wrong (not maximizing aggregate utility) would not be mind independent.

But, however we define mind independence, it is misguided to look to idealism as the opposite of realism in the sense relevant to morals. Those who want not to be realist about morals do not generally shy from being realist about mental states, such as pain. They hold that mental properties, such as being in pain, exist as part of the world in a way that moral properties, such as being wrong or bad, do not. They are, in other words, realists about mental properties and antirealist about moral properties. On the proposed understanding of realism, however, they would be barred from being realist about mental properties, since the latter are obviously not mind independent. The possibility of mind-independent moral properties is not, it would appear, what most realists and antirealists are debating regarding morals.

Evidence Independence

Instrumentalism is another doctrine that has been traditionally contrasted with realism. For example, in an instrumentalist view of science, theories are instruments for manipulating experience, whereas in a realist view theories are about a reality that explains our experience. Our experience, on the realist view, is our evidence for the truth of the theory. Or, in other words, truth, according to realism, is distinct from our evidence for it. This conception of realism is advanced by David Brink, who defines moral realism as entailing that (1) there are moral facts or truths, and (2) these facts or truths are independent of the evidence for them.[20] A view can be antirealist either by denying that there are moral facts or truths or by claiming that moral facts or truths are not independent of the evidence for them. The first option is embraced by noncognitivism and the second by what Brink calls *moral constructivism.* The moral constructivist agrees with the realist that there are moral facts or truths but denies that they obtain independently of the evidence for them.

To assess this definition of moral realism, we need to understand what would count as evidence in this context and what is intended by the notion of evidence independence. Brink tells us that he has in mind not causal independence but conceptual or metaphysical independence. Thus, the moral realist would hold that moral facts or truths are evidence independent if they are not constituted by the evidence for them, such as beliefs about what is right or wrong. The constructivist, by contrast, would hold that moral facts or truths are *constituted* by such moral beliefs. In the latter case, moral facts or truths might consist, for example, in an appropriate kind of coherence among our moral beliefs. Or they might consist in the moral facts or truths that would be reached in some ideal limit of inquiry.

One difficulty in construing evidence independence and evidence in this fashion is that constructivism so conceived appears to lapse into nonsense. This is because there appears to be no way to give a coherent account of the content of moral beliefs. The content of the belief, say, that capital punishment is wrong will be constituted by other moral beliefs, while these in turn will be constituted by still other moral beliefs, and so on. Even if we postulate an infinite set of moral beliefs, there appears not to be in principle any way to specify by their content which set of beliefs we mean. A consequence of this vicious regress is that Brink's condition (2) for moral realism, that the moral facts or truths be evidence independent, adds nothing to his condition (1), that there be moral facts or truths.

We might try to avoid this difficulty by restricting what may count as evidence—for example, by excluding moral beliefs as evidence. But this restriction would appear to be unreasonable. We would certainly not think it reasonable to impose a parallel restriction in the case of a nonmoral claim—that is, to exclude nonmoral beliefs from providing some evidence for the truth of nonmoral claims. (That I believe that you spoke to me yesterday is some evidence that you did.) On the other hand, if we take evidence independence to be causal rather than conceptual or metaphysical, another difficulty emerges. This move would have the consequence that the naturalistic form of utilitarianism referred to earlier would not count as realist. This is because the truth of a moral claim about what is right would depend on people's preferences and in turn the latter would depend causally to some degree on their moral beliefs.

Stance Independence

Is there another way to capture the form of antirealism that Brink has in mind? We may be able to get some help from Ronald Milo's conception of stance independence. He defines moral constructivism as the type of theory that implies that there are moral facts but construes moral facts in a way that makes them dependent on an intentional psychological state:

> A fact will be said to be stance *dependent* just in case it consists in the instantiation of some property that exists only if some thing or state of affairs is made the object of an intentional psychological state (stance) such as a belief or a conative or affective attitude. Conversely, a fact will be said to be stance *independent* just in case it is not dependent in this way on some psychological attitude.[21]

Ideal observer theories and contractarian theories would qualify as forms of moral constructivism in this sense. A virtue of this way of understanding moral constructivism is that it avoids the circularity difficulty that faced Brink's formulation. A theory can make moral claims stance dependent without making them evidence dependent in the objectionable way just examined.

Unfortunately, this formulation will not do as it stands. It is plain that psychological theories about mental facts would have to be forms of constructivism and hence not realist as long as mental facts were intentional in the sense indicated. We want to allow the possibility that a theory about mental events could be realist in exactly the same sense that a moral theory could be realist. There is, however, a way to repair the conception of stance independence so that it will not simply reduce to mind independence. Suppose that we restrict the object of the stance to the thing that would have the property in question. Let us say that a fact will be said to be stance dependent just in case it consists in the instantiation of some property that exists only if the thing or state of affairs *that would have that property* is made the object of an intentional psychological state (stance). When stance dependence is understood this way, the property of being in a mental state, such as being in pain or having a desire, is not necessarily stance dependent. For example, when I have the property of being in pain, it is not true that this property exists only if I am the object of some particular intentional stance.

On the other hand, the property of being wrong applied to actions is stance dependent if an action has that property only if the action is the object of some intentional state, such as being an action of which an ideal observer would disapprove or being an action that rational contractors would agree to prohibit in their society. These are for many philosophers the theories that intuitively qualify as forms of moral constructivism rather than moral realism. It seems, in short, that realist theories are precisely the ones that imply that there are moral facts or truths that are stance independent in the special sense just defined.

Is this a suitable way to make the realist, antirealist distinction? That depends on what kind of contrast we want to draw. Marking off stance-independent facts or truths as having a special relation to what is "real" associates the real with what is mostly beyond the control of our will or choice and unaffected by our feelings. Why is this association appropriate? Note that, even when the choice, feeling, or will is that of a highly idealized agent or community (as in ideal observer theory and Rawls's contractarianism) or is necessitated for all possible rational agents (as with Kant), the resulting stance-dependent conception of morality is regarded in this vein as less anchored in the structure of reality just because of its association with will, feeling, and choice. I suggest that this way of thinking about realism derives from a false view of the nature of science.

Compare, for example, the way Milo describes the objectivity of scientific truths as imposing itself on us independently of our will:

> [T]he objectivity of scientific truths derives from the fact that they describe a stance-independent reality. This reality imposes itself on us through the causal control it exercises over our experiences and beliefs. We feel compelled to recognize certain truths about it because we find it necessary (insofar as we choose to be guided by reason and evidence) to postulate these truths in order to provide the most plausible explanations of our experiences and observations (which are also largely independent of our will). This is how the objectivity of scientific reality manifests itself.[22]

This way of characterizing scientific objectivity is incompatible with fact-value holism. In the latter view, personal factors, such as will, feeling, and choice, play an active role in creating an accurate represention of reality. Yet the reality thus uncovered has an existence that is not simply a function of these factors; it will be what it is whether or not we are able to represent it accurately.

Let it be granted that no realism worthy of the name can allow that reality is simply what we happen to think it is or what we happen to prefer, either individually or collectively. But the forms of constructivism designated as stance dependent do not allow that implication or at least not obviously so. If what is morally required of me is determined by the feelings or choice of an ideal agent who is utterly distinct from me and perhaps from anything I will ever become, it can hardly be said that what is morally required of me is a matter simply of what I think is right or would like to be right. Similarly, if what is morally required of all of us is determined by the feelings or choice of an ideal community that is utterly distinct from what we now are and perhaps from anything that we will ever become, again it can hardly be said that what is morally required of us is a matter simply of what we think is right or would like to be right. Morality, in sum, may be both constructed and reality based, in that, although constructed, its demands are considerably beyond the control of our present individual or collective preferences.

I believe, therefore, that the stance-independent contrast mislocates the distinction we are looking for, if the question is whether morality involves facts or truths that are on a par with those found in the best of science. Morality may be about us because it is about the stances that we would take under special conditions. Thus, the facts or truths of morality may not be stance independent. But those facts or truths may yet be part of reality and hence every bit as objective and rooted in the nature of things as any nonmoral truths revealed in science.

Social Manipulation Independence

What is legitimate and also of particular interest to feminists in the worry about stance independence is the concern that moral reality not be conceived in such a way that it reflects gender-biased or other oppressive social feelings and preferences. Morality must be independent of morally corrupt stances. One strategy for excluding such stances is to stipulate that moral reality be stance independent. But another feminist worry that is equally legitimate is that, by conceiving of ideal morality as insulated from social influence, we simply mask the social influences that are inevitably shaping how we think of ideal morality. Arguably, we would also disconnect ideal morality from anything like the actual socially generated morality that works within us. How can something inherently social emulate something inherently nonsocial? What we want, it can be plausibly argued, is a conception of moral reality by which morality is independent of wrong stances—but not of all stances.

This seems right. This is, however, a moral criterion, not a criterion that we can call upon as a morally neutral means of classifying moral theories. There is no need, of course, for our metaethics to be morally neutral, but without a theory of morals that will enable us to discriminate among stances, we are apt not to make any significant progress in developing a general account of moral realism along these lines. I propose, then, to return to the account of moral realism with which we began: that a moral theory is realist if it implies that some moral claims are literally true. Given the considerations just raised, some such theories will be objectionable because they will imply that some moral claims are literally true when there are moral reasons for believing otherwise. For example, a contractarian moral theory might imply that actions are not wrong when they meet tests that do not exclude the influence of sexist assumptions. These theories will give a false account of moral reality. But it should not surprise us that some moral realisms are implausible from a moral standpoint. It is not their being realist that is at fault. What we need to turn to is the problem of developing an adequate feminist theory of morals. If it implies that some moral claims are literally true, it will be realist in a sense that is congenial to meaning-value holism.

Notes

1. W. V. Quine, "On the Nature of Moral Values," in *Theories and Things* (Cambridge, Mass.: Harvard University Press, 1981).

2. This is the essence of Quine's critique of the first dogma in Quine, "Two Dogmas of Empiricism," in *From a Logical Point of View* (Cambridge, Mass.: Harvard University Press, 1953).

3. In much of the interpretation to follow, I am indebted to Gilbert Harman's discussion of Quine in Harman, "Quine on Meaning and Existence, I," *Review of Metaphysics* 21 (1967): 124–51.

4. This view closely resembles Donald Davidson's Principle of Charity that we must assume the general truthfulness of a majority of any coherent set of beliefs; see Donald Davidson, *Inquiries into Truth and Interpretation* (Oxford: Clarendon, 1984). But, as Davidson acknowledges, the basic idea may be found in Quine's discussion of translation in W. V. Quine, *Word and Object* (Cambridge, Mass.: MIT Press, 1960), 26–79.

5. The primary argument for this step is to be found in Quine's indeterminacy of translation thesis; see Quine, *Word and Object*, 27, 54, 72, 206, 221; and Quine, "Ontological Relativity," in *Ontological Relativity and Other Essays* (New York: Columbia University Press, 1969).

6. Quine, "Two Dogmas," 42.

7. H. P. Grice and P. F. Strawson, "In Defense of a Dogma," *Philosophical Review* 65 (1956): 141–58.

8. Philip Kitcher, "A Priori Knowledge," in *Philosophical Review* 86 (1980): 3–23; reprint in Hilary Kornblith, ed., *Naturalizing Epistemology*, 2d ed. (Cambridge, Mass.: MIT Press, 1994). Hereafter, page references for Kitcher are to Kornblith's collection.

9. Immanuel Kant, *Immanuel Kant's Critique of Pure Reason*, Norman Kemp Smith, tr. (New York: St. Martin's, 1961), 43.

10. Kitcher, "A Priori Knowledge," 148.

11. Kitcher, "A Priori Knowledge," 152.

12. Harman, "Quine on Meaning and Existence," 142.

13. Anne Seller, "Realism Versus Relativism: Towards a Politically Adequate Epistemology," in *Feminist Perspectives in Philosophy*, Morwenna Griffiths and Margaret Whitford, eds. (Bloomington: Indiana University Press, 1988), 172.

14. Lorraine Code, for example, defends a qualified realism (which she prefers to call a "mitigated relativism"), but her position, too, is based largely on political grounds: "Politically, feminists could not opt for an absolute relativism that recognized no facts of the matter—no objective, external reality—but only my, your, or our negotiated reality" Code, *What Can She Know? Feminist Theory and the Construction of Knowledge* (Ithaca, N.Y.: Cornell University Press, 1991), 319. Lisa Helke rejects both sides of the traditional debate, offering an alternative that she calls *the Corresponsible Option*; Helke, "Recipes for Theory Making," *Hypatia* 3 (1988): 15–29. In this case, too, the rationale is political: "to construct epistemologies that are respectful and representative of the differences in women's experiences, without being glib, unreflective or uncritical about those differences" (17).

15. For an excellent introduction to the literature on metaethics and moral realism, see Geoffrey Sayre-McCord, "The Many Moral Realisms," in *Essays on Moral Realism*, G. Sayre-McCord, ed. (Ithaca, N.Y.: Cornell University Press, 1988), and Stephen Darwall, Allan Gibbard, and Peter Railton, "Toward *Fin de siècle* Ethics: Some Trends," *Philosophical Review* 101 (1992): 115–89.

16. This presumption is challenged in Susan Sherwin, "Theory Vs. Practice in Ethics: The Case Study of a Feminist Perspective on Health Care," in *Philosophical Perspectives on Bioethics*, Wayne Sumner, ed. (Toronto: University of Toronto Press, 1996).

17. Sayre-McCord, "The Many Moral Realisms."

18. Philip Kitcher, *The Advancement of Science: Science without Legend, Objectivity without Illusions* (New York: Oxford University Press, 1993), 169–70.

19. G. E. Moore, *Principia Ethica* (Cambridge: Cambridge University Press, 1903).

20. David Brink, *Moral Realism and the Foundations of Ethics* (Cambridge: Cambridge University Press, 1989), 17.

21. Ronald Milo, "Contractarian Constructivism," *Journal of Philosophy* 92, no. 4 (1995): 192.

22. Milo, "Contractarian Constructivism," 194.

Part IV

Feminism and Moral Knowledge

Chapter 9

Feminist Contractarianism

Feminist Motivations in Conflict

In the last two chapters, I have defended the possibility of a feminist moral realism. In this view, moral judgments about how we ought to be, including feminist ones, can be literally true in the same sense that judgments in science—say, about the relative size of the sun and Earth—can be literally true. Put without reference to truth: models or representations of how we ought to be can adequately represent a moral reality that obtains apart from whether we represent it adequately. My argument thus far, however, has not been specific to morality. Much less have I developed a particular theory about how we ought to be from a feminist standpoint. It is time to be more specific. This chapter and the next develop a contractarian theory of moral knowledge that is at once feminist, realist, and naturalized.

Feminist philosophers have subjected contractarian theory to considerable criticism. I hope to understand contractarianism in a way that will enable me to meet the standard objections and still retain its basic insight. There is, however, an important objection that has not been raised before and lies at the heart of recent efforts to defend the contractarian project as worthy of endorsement by feminists. The objection is the main subject of the present chapter and touches on important topics in feminist moral theory, such as the supposed opposition between justice and care and the importance of political context in moral theorizing. Resolution of the objection requires, in my view, an explanation of how a feminist contractarianism can be naturalized. This account, which comes in the next chapter, answers feminist worries about the individualism implicit in the idea of a social contract and also about the merely hypothetical character of the consent it implies. To begin, here is the objection in summary form.

Feminists have two important reasons to found a society's morals on the mutual agreement of its members. First, such a foundation, at least in its Kantian interpretation, implies that each member has equal intrinsic worth. In particular, women have no less intrinsic worth than men and are therefore equally worthy of being treated with dignity and respect. This implication would seem sufficient by itself to make women's subordination to men morally unacceptable, assuming a Kantian contractarian foundation for morals. Second, this foundation entails that conventional morals, which are shaped by their political context and may be gender biased, would be subject to evaluation and potential rejection by appeal to a position of equality that is external and prior to conventional morality. Jean Hampton[1] has recently appealed to the first reason to defend feminist contractarianism against its feminist critics; Susan Moller Okin[2] has appealed to the second reason to show the inadequacy of the contractarian views of Nozick[3] and Rawls,[4] which, she argues, incorporate certain sexist features of conventional morality.

Unfortunately, these two motivations are in tension with each other. Mutual agreement about the morals that members of society should impose on themselves cannot serve to be a foundation for morality unless that agreement is formed autonomously—that is, without any coercion and with full knowledge of the nature of the choice. Indeed, autonomous self-legislation is part and parcel of the Kantian idea of equal intrinsic worth among people who treat each other as ends in themselves. A dilemma arises from trying to find a conception of autonomous agreement that is at once credible and compatible with Okin's requirement that the agreement at issue will be formed from a position of equality that is external and prior to conventional morality. There are good reasons to think that what should count as uncoerced, informed choice depends on what should count as justice. At least so I will argue, drawing on some recent developments in feminist theory. But then the feminist contractarian is faced with the following dilemma. If justice is understood conventionally, perhaps in ways that are biased against women, the promise of appealing to a position of equality that is external and prior to conventional morality is undermined, thus violating the important constraint that Okin places on feminist theories of justice. If, on the other hand, it is understood otherwise, the feminist contractarian must give up, on pain of circularity, the project of basing morality, including justice, on an independent foundation of autonomously formed mutual agreement, which is the important constraint imposed by Hampton. A contractarian conception of justice would have to be used that is neither conventional nor derived from autonomous mutual agreement.

The Hobbesian tradition of social contract theory might be supposed to provide a way out of this dilemma, since it appeals to mutual agreement that is grounded in people's preferences more or less as given rather than in their autonomous choice. This alternative is not viable from a standpoint that understands sexist preferences to be entrenched in the status quo, since sexist preferences will then be reflected in the moral norms that are chosen by mutual agreement. Why should those aspects of the status quo be privileged in determining which social arrangements should be morally acceptable? The reason for appealing to autonomous choice is to have a basis for assessing moral norms that is independent of sexist and other objectionable preferences. Without such independence Okin's constraint would be violated.

The way out of the dilemma, I will argue, is to distinguish between two ways that a feminist contractarian can appeal to autonomous agreement as a basis for evaluating conventional morality. One way, foundationalism, does lead to paradox, but the other, a form of naturalized epistemology, does not; yet the latter contractarianism, as I will attempt to show, preserves both of the feminist motivations that are expressed in Okin's and Hampton's constraints.

Before moving to this solution, though, I need to explain the underlying realist framework presupposed in my exposition of the problem and in the solution that I offer. To prepare this ground, I will use the next two sections to sketch a realist theory of moral judgment that embeds a contractarian view of moral reasoning. (Readers may choose to skip these somewhat technical sections without losing the main thread of the argument.) I need also to motivate the problem. Why should a feminist care about morality having a foundation in autonomous choice? I will elaborate the reasons given earlier, defending the importance of autonomy in Hampton's contractarianism and arguing that the centrality of autonomy there is compatible with an ethic of care ("Reconciling Justice with Care"). I will also defend the importance that Okin places on justice being external to and independent of conventional morality ("The Need for an Archimedean Point"). Then in the last three sections I show why these values present a paradox.

A Hybrid Theory of Moral Judgment

Recall that two schools of thought prevail regarding the content of moral judgments. Cognitivists maintain that moral judgments are factual claims and thus are true or false, while noncognitivists deny this and hold instead that moral judgments have a "noncognitive" function, such as to express commitment to a normative ideal. Given this dichotomy, moral realists must be cognitivists, since they hold that at least some moral judgments are true; antirealists must be either noncognitivists or error theorists, believing that moral judgments are systematically in error. J. L. Mackie, who believes that no moral judgment is true (since he thinks that each falsely implies that moral properties exist), would be an example of the latter.

Notice that this way of conceiving the debate supposes that moral judgments must be either all one way or all the other. Is this supposition really necessary? It is natural to think so if one assumes that moral judgments are linguistic entities, either in the form of statements that have truth value (cognitivism) or in the form of commands or exclamations with no truth value (noncognitivism). It is possible, however, that moral judgments are mental states that normally perform two functions and are open to two kinds of linguistic expression. One of these functions is to dispose the appraiser to act, feel, and generally be motivated in a morally appropriate way. Another is that of representing this dispositional state, along with the norms that it embodies, as being justified or warranted.[5] I contend that this hybrid understanding of moral judgment has most of the advantages of each of the standard alternatives yet none of their defects and fits better what we know of human evolution. Contractarianism, given this conception of moral judgment, will fall into place as a theory of reasoning about which moral dispositions and corresponding norms are genuinely justified for a given society.

Consider the hybrid character of moral judgments. Setting aside for a moment how the two functions are to be understood exactly, we might say that one is representational or cognitive while the other is not. The hybrid theory thus agrees with the cognitivism regarding the normal cases of moral judgment. Such a judgment purports to represent how things are in a certain moral respect. The theory therefore shares many of the advantages of cognitivism. It is able to claim that its interpretation of moral judgments comports well with (1) the commonsense view that moral judgments are about how things are morally, (2) the declarative language of moral judgments, and (3) the simplest interpretation of the logic of moral reasoning—namely, that such reasoning is no different in its logic from any other reasoning involving claims with truth value. At the same time, the hybrid theory agrees with noncognitivism regarding normal cases of moral judgment—namely, that the motivational element of being disposed to act or feel is embodied in the judgment itself. The theory is thus easily able to explain the practical and emotional character of most moral judgments. Suppose that someone says that a certain type of act is morally wrong but *feels* no inclination not to do it, no guilt after doing it, no indignation when others do it—in short, no opposition of any kind to this type of act. Then we are apt to question whether this person judges it to be wrong. Our reaction makes perfect sense if normally moral judgments have this hybrid structure.

Unfortunately, matters are far more complicated than I have indicated. A major complication derives from my view (defended in chapter 4) that emotional knowledge is possible in which feeling can serve to represent reality without any corresponding belief. An implication of this view is that in the hybrid theory of moral judgment the so-called noncognitive element of moral judgment (e.g., the feeling of indignation that moves one to act) can have a representational or *cognitive* function, even though it may not be accompanied by a moral belief. Feelings devoid of propositional content can thus represent the wrongness of an action just as well as a belief that the action is wrong. This result is consistent with the hybrid view that moral judgments have a dual function, roughly to represent and to motivate, but it is inconsistent with the standard assumption of cognitivists that a moral judgment represents only through its propositional content. One advantage of this complication is that it makes clear that the hybrid theory is thoroughly realist in its conception of moral judgment, implying that both the belief and the feeling normally contained in a moral judgment can serve to represent moral reality. A second advantage is that when moral belief does not accompany moral feeling it is still appropriate to speak of a moral *judgment*, since the feeling itself purports to represent how things are. The disadvantage is, of course, that this way of thinking runs counter to the common assumption that the distinction between cognitive and noncognitive matches that between belief and feeling.

To make matters yet more confusing, cognitivists recognize that a close connection of some kind exits between making a moral judgment and being disposed to act or feel in an appropriate way, but they believe that they can explain this connection without giving up their view that moral judgments are nothing more than propositional representations of how the world is. Two strategies for accomplishing this task are possible. Those who are externalists argue that the content of moral judgments is such that we are moved appropriately in virtue of a purely contingent relation between the content of our judgment and our antecedent desires and interests. For example, a cognitivist who maintains that the content of moral judgments is utilitarian (so that to judge an act morally right is to judge it as creating at least as much happiness or as little unhappiness among those affected by the act as any alternative act) might hold that human nature is such that we are normally favorably disposed to some degree toward an act that we judge to maximize happiness over unhappiness. This connection between judgment and disposition to act or feel would be "external" in that if our natures were such that none of us ever cared about the happiness of others, we might make the same moral judgments but not be at all favorably disposed toward doing what is morally right. A good externalist, of course, must have a plausible account of the content of moral judgments and a plausible account of human nature that explains moral motivation by reference to the content of moral judgments.

Cognitivists who are internalists, on the other hand, maintain that the content of moral judgments is such that we are necessarily moved to act and feel appropriately just in virtue of making such a judgment. For internalists, the connection between seeing an act as morally right and being disposed to respond to it appropriately is a necessary or "internal" relation, so that one cannot represent an act as being morally required without at the same time recognizing that one has a reason or motive to do it. Though this view contradicts Hume's dictum that recognition of facts cannot motivate us independently of prior desires, the view provides a much more solid, and some think more intuitively plausible, link between moral judgments and reasons or motives to act and feel.

Though each kind of cognitivism has its own virtues, they share a common problem. Each understands the motivational part of moral judgment as *always* tied to its propositional content—the content of a moral belief. In the externalist case the tie is contingent and indirect, mediated by human nature; in the internalist case the tie is immediate and necessary. In neither case, however, is there any explanation of why one would be disposed to behave and feel in a morally appropriate way in the absence of having a corresponding moral belief about the thing in question. For example, neither view explains how one could fail to believe that something is morally wrong when one responds to it emotionally exactly as if it one believed that it were morally wrong. Yet this situation does occur. At times, though for most people not that often, one feels that something is morally wrong (or right) and is strongly disposed to avoid (or embrace) it, even though intellectually one believes just the opposite. Due to one's upbringing, for example, one may experience feelings of disapproval toward certain sexual practices without believing that they are wrong. An adequate theory of moral judgment needs to explain how this is possible.

Can the hybrid theory explain this possibility? I take the theory to postulate that "moral judgment" normally involves the operation of two coordinated systems of social control, one that is much older in evolutionary terms and more primitive than the other and can function independently of it.[6] This system is an adaptation that allows us to internalize social norms so that we are disposed to act and feel in harmony with them without making any assessment of their purpose or ultimate worth. If such a mechanism of social control did not exist, it would be impossible for the very young to learn the morals of their social group or, for that matter, for anyone to learn them in the relevant sense. Morality in the form that we know it would not have evolved, and we would not internalize moral norms of our society as we do. Though this process of socialization goes hand in hand with learning to express moral approval and disapproval, learning such expression does not presuppose cognitive capacities beyond those needed to tell how a norm applies (e.g., to know whether something is forbidden in one's social group).

Grafted on to this system is another that makes possible the adjudication of norms in deciding whether they apply to strange cases, how to resolve cases of conflicting norms, and when norms no longer have validity. This more cognitively advanced system of social control presupposes language and rides piggyback on the former, without which the latter would have no evolutionary function. Though the systems work in tandem, their distinctness is evident in those cases in which one's internalized norms and thus moral feelings and attitude are at odds with one's assessment of the moral facts. The hybrid theory of moral judgment accounts for these important anomalies, while narrowly cognitivist theories do not.

It might be objected that, contrary to the hybrid theory, moral dispositions to act or feel cannot be properly classified as "moral" unless there exists already a moral belief that such and such is so morally. In other words, one cannot simply feel that something is wrong without at the same time judging it to be wrong. If, as in the cases imagined, one also believes that the action in question is *not* wrong, these cases are best described, it might be argued, as instances in which one has conflicting beliefs, only one of which is the object of moral feeling. In this way cognitivism would be equally able to account for the apparent split between belief and feeling.

The objection, however, is not convincing. It assimilates the imagined cases to instances in which one finds oneself with two beliefs that cannot both be true. In such cases one usually takes oneself to be caught in a dilemma, being inclined to believe each of two things but knowing that they cannot both be true and being unable at the time to decide which inclination to trust. The imagined cases are different. These are cases in which one does not trust one's feelings and firmly believes that they are misleading. For example, having been raised to regard gay behavior as immoral, one finds oneself having negative feelings about such behavior even though one believes with complete conviction that nothing is wrong with it. It would be gratuitous to insist that in this case one has contradictory beliefs.

I do not wish to deny, however, that when one feels moral disapproval toward something, one's disapproval can function potentially as a reliable guide to forming true moral beliefs about the object of disapproval. The feeling itself can thus have a cognitive function without containing or implying a true or false moral belief. In this sense it can represent what is worthy of moral disapproval without having any propositional content. When the mechanisms underlying it are sufficiently reliable for the context in which the feeling arises and the feeling is a response to what is worthy of moral disapproval, the feeling can be a form of moral knowledge. The point on which I want to insist is that the feeling of moral disapproval can be a moral judgment without being a belief with propositional content. Here the hybrid theory parts company with standard cognitivist views, both internalist and externalist.

Nevertheless, the hybrid theory must be able to explain what it is about moral dispositions to act or feel that makes them moral rather than some other kind of disposition. I will not attempt to spell out the details in this regard, in part because the arguments to follow do not depend on them and also because I have nothing to add to the accounts already available that address this issue. David Copp, for example, gives a society-centered definition of what it is to subscribe to a standard of behavior or feeling as a moral standard.[7] The definition, too complex to set out here in full, entails being disposed to conform to the standard and to support conformity to it in one's society, being favorably disposed toward those who conform to it, including oneself, tending to have a negative response toward those who fail to conform to it, again including oneself, and regarding such failures "as creating a presumption of liability to a negative response."[8] Something like such an account seems plausible and nowhere presupposes that the person subscribing to a standard as a moral standard is making a true or false moral judgment.[9]

There are also cases in which one believes that something is true morally without having the disposition to behave and feel that would normally accompany one's belief. Externalists appeal to such cases to discredit the internalist.[10] Note that the hybrid theory has no problem with these cases of moral belief that are lacking the usual motivation. Indeed, this kind of example is implicit in the cases already covered, since in those one's disposition to behave and feel is contrary to what would normally accompany one's belief.

What needs to be explained, though, is what is normative about one's belief. Suppose that the hybrid theory can give a plausible story about the content of one's belief such that it is true or false and hence cognitive in the relevant sense. One wants to know what makes such factual beliefs normative in contrast to others. The hybrid theory, like externalism, needs a convincing answer to this question. The answer that it provides is like that of the externalism but only up to a certain point. In the case of externalism, the normativity of a moral belief is external to its content, and on this point the hybrid theory fully agrees. I have suggested, after Copp, that what is implied in the true or false content of a moral judgment is that what is judged meets or fails to meet a certain standard or norm and, further, that this standard together with the motivation (if any) that embodies this standard are justified. Even though on this account the justification of a norm is implied in the content of true or false moral judgment, according to externalism and the hybrid theory, there is nothing *necessarily* normative about such a judgment.

What, then, makes a moral judgment normative? The hybrid theory answers that it is the social context in which the judgment is made, in particular, that moral judgments normally function to motivate and guide people in their actions, feelings, and thoughts. It is, in short, their social function that makes them normative. Note that people need not agree in their moral judgments. The point is that people must normally be moved to respond appropriately to moral norms that they believe are justified. Apart from the fact that people normally respond in that way, the content of moral judgments has no normative status.[11]

Are externalism and the hybrid theory really that different? Where they diverge is around the centrality of the factual content of moral judgments. Externalism is a form of cognitivism in which moral judgments are *nothing more than* true or false beliefs or claims about moral reality. While the hybrid theory incorporates the usual cognitive dimension in its account of moral judgment, it places equal, if not more, emphasis on the cognitive but nonpropositional motivational element as an integral part of what a moral judgment normally is. What makes a moral judgment moral in its normative character is that it normally incorporates motivation with a certain structure (such as is contained in Copp's analysis of morally subscribing to a norm of conduct). In

cases in which this motivation is absent, the cognitive remainder has normative status and indeed moral content only in relation to its normal association
in society with specifically moral motivation. The hybrid theory is thus not a
form of cognitivism as ordinarily understood. By the same token, it is not a
form of noncognitivism either, since the latter denies that moral judgments
are ever strictly true or false. In effect, the hybrid theory rejects the standard
dichotomy.

Realism and Contractarianism

Is it really possible that the same mental state can function both as disposition
to behave and feel and as true or false belief? The stability of the standard
dichotomy rests on the apparent impossibility of a state with this dual function, yet the thesis of meaning-value holism, defended in the previous chapter,
implies that such a state is possible and cannot be ruled out on the ground that
states that represent how the world is may not simultaneously function to
guide behavior and feeling. Meaning-value holism thus sustains the possibility
of a moral realism in which motivation has a central place in the theory of
moral judgment.

Within this framework, contractarianism can be understood as a specific
theory about how norms, along with the motivations that embody them, can
be justified. At least this is the approach that I want to take. It may be objected
that contractarianism does not ground morals in a reality that is independent
of social conventions and hence cannot, properly speaking, be part of a realist
account of moral truth. The basis for a reply to this objection has been set out
in the previous chapter, where I reviewed five different conceptions of moral
realism and gave a principled basis for rejecting the four conceptions that
would rule out the possibility of a moral realism in which moral reality is
socially constructed. The upshot is that contractarian theory of moral justification will fit within the realist theory of moral judgment developed here
provided that it would explain how some moral judgments can turn out to be
true in just the same sense that we regard some scientific judgments as being
true. A theory that explains how moral standards are justified when members
of society would agree (under certain conditions) to impose them on themselves has the potential of meeting this requirement. It would allow the possibility that we can be mistaken individually and collectively about what is true
morally. That moral reality should be contained in our potential as social
beings is fully compatible with its existing independently of our representations of it.

The idea that moral reality might be contained in our potential as social
beings suggests how a contractarian theory of the kind defended here could
dispense with the notion of moral truth and still be realist. The theory identi-

fies moral justification with how members of society would respond under certain ideal conditions. As with scientific models, we can think of our representations of how we should be morally as models of how the world is in certain respects, and these models can be similar in structure to the world or not. When moral representations are understood in this way, the realist has no need to insist that they are propositional in content, no more than the realist has such a need in the case of models in science. This conception of moral representations comports well with the theory of moral judgment just set forth, since the theory entails that a person can represent moral reality accurately without forming true beliefs about it.

By the same token, a contractarian realism need not imply that moral reality is defined for every conceivable representation that we might make about morals. The theory of moral justification may imply that there is no fact of the matter with respect to some moral disputes, for the system of norms that is justified for a given society may not contain standards that are sufficiently discriminating to decide the issue at hand. It is possible, then, to be mistaken even about whether answers to certain moral questions exist. Contractarian realism need not be committed to the view that every moral question has a definite answer.

At what level does realist contractarianism bear on the truth of moral claims? The theory of justification is to be linked to the truth of specific moral claims but only indirectly. Consider an example given by David Copp. In claiming that slavery is morally wrong, one says that slavery fails to meet a certain standard (in particular, it violates a standard prohibiting slavery); one also implies that such a standard is justified.[12] If this is so, a theory that explains how a standard is justified should explain why slavery is morally wrong. Still, the connection between the justification of norms and the truth of individual moral claims is indirect. Merely knowing that a relevant norm is justified—say, one prohibiting rape—may not settle a moral dispute because people differ about whether a particular act constitutes rape. A realist theory of moral justification, then, should not be thought of as offering an algorithm for adjudicating moral differences. From a feminist standpoint this is both good news and bad. On the positive side it may help to disassociate realism with dogmatism, but it also runs the risk on not being able to do interesting moral work. I hope to give good reasons why it can.

In the following discussion I will think of the justification of moral norms as being relative to a society. This will have the effect of combining realism with relativism. To some this combination will seem odd, but there is no contradiction in the idea and good reason to favor it. It is possible that there are societal differences such that the norms that people in one society can autonomously impose on themselves will not match in every way the norms that people in another society can autonomously impose on themselves. In that case there will be norms that are justified for one society and not the other and hence moral truths about what is right or wrong that are relative to a given society. There are no grounds to rule out this possibility a priori and hence no basis to suppose that the form of realist contractarianism defended here must be incompatible with a relativism of this minimal sort.

Notice, however, that relativism of this kind does not rule out the possibility that there are norms that are justified in every known society. There is every reason, indeed, to think that a prohibition on, for example, slavery or rape would be justified in every society. For who would freely choose to make themselves vulnerable to these harms, knowing what they entail, if she or he had the option to prohibit them altogether? To concede the truth of relativism in the sense intended is not to imply that no universal norms exist; it is only to imply that some norms may not be universal. This distinction may render the combination of realism and relativism more appealing than it may appear to be at first.

What about the case, though, in which a norm is acceptable to one group but not another? Consider a norm that permits or requires the practice of clitoridectomy and infibulation on young girls. Though deeply troubling to members of our society, especially feminists, it appears to be accepted by members of some societies. Do we want to say that in this case the justification of the norm is simply relative? From the perspective of the present theory, the critical question is whether all the members of any society, and hence all its female members, could accept this norm and impose it freely on themselves knowing what it entails. For reasons that I will turn to soon, this is an enormously difficult question that calls for an adequate theory of autonomous choice. It is far from clear to me that the norm in this case can be justified for any society in the relevant sense. If, however, the norm can be justified to all members of society, in the sense that each would join with the others in autonomously choosing to live by it, then I cannot see how we can reasonably demand any deeper justification for it. I simply doubt that it can be.

Another difficult case arises when the norms of a society direct its members to treat outsiders oppressively. Could not such norms be "justified" to a society and not be genuinely justified? This problem arises because contractarians think of a society's norms as governing the relations among its members, not relations of its members to those of other societies. But societies have always had normative views about how to treat outsiders, and here the contractarian conception of society-relative justification gives very counterintuitive results. The natural remedy is to take seriously the basic insight that norms are to be justified *to those persons whose relations are affected by the norms*. Hence, outsiders must be included among those whose agreement is necessary in order for the norms affecting their relations to be justified. Norms are to be justified to the widest social group whose relations would be shaped by the general acceptance of the norms within some part of it. For some norms, then, such as one prohibiting the oppression of one group by another, the relevant "society" will be all humanity.

Reconciling Justice with Care

The remedy just offered presupposes that morals based on agreement will not be oppressive. But is this presupposition at all plausible? Is it reasonable to suppose, for example, that moral norms that are justified on a contractarian basis will not be biased against women? Feminists have found contractarianism wanting on at least two closely related grounds. First, it is objected that people's reasons for treating one another morally would be purely instrumental, since according to contractarianism the sole basis for morality is its usefulness as a means to satisfy their prior preferences.[13] A direct consequence is that gender equality has a moral basis only to the extent that it is useful. But this puts gender equality on a precarious basis. What will count as useful to society will always depend on current preferences and available information, and both, because of gender prejudice, can weigh against counting women as equal to men in the distribution of rights, powers, and privileges.[14] Second, it is objected that contractarianism is based on a one-sided moral perspective that excludes the ethic of care, in which people take responsibility for the well-being of each other, in favor of the ethic of justice, in which being moral is pursuing one's own well-being without damaging that of others.[15] Hampton puts the objection this way:

> In contrast [to the ethic of justice], a perspective on morality that emphasizes caring for and fostering the well-being of others appears to be not only a richer, sounder theory of what genuine moral behavior is all about but also a better guide to behavior that enables one to live a life full of friendship and love. Such a perspective is one that women (and especially mothers) are frequently thought to exhibit more than men.[16]

Contractarianism is thus deemed unacceptable because it derives from an excessively narrow, characteristically male conception of morality.

Hampton does not, however, accept these objections as decisive. She concedes that "the Hobbesian moral theory gives us no reason outside of contingent moral sentiment to respect those with whom we have no need of cooperating or those whom we are strong enough to dominate, such as the elderly, the physically handicapped, mentally disabled children whom we do not want to rear, or people from other societies with whom we have no interest in trading."[17] But she takes Kantian contractarianism to be an alternative that is not open to these objections. In all forms of social contract theory, she argues, the notion of a social contract does not itself do any real justificatory work but serves merely as a metaphor. This can be seen in the fact that even Hobbesians like Gauthier reject actual contracts if they violate principles that are justified from the standpoint of a particular hypothetical "original" position.[18] What does the justificatory work is always to be found in the way that position is constructed. In the Kantian version, contingent differences among people that are apt to give some an advantage over others are systematically set aside in determining the content of morality. Everyone chooses as if they were assuming that all, including themselves, have intrinsic worth.

Kantian contractarianism thus avoids the first difficulty, since the basis for treating people morally is not simply their instrumental worth. One may also argue that it meets the second, because from its perspective people's moral obligations to each other are seen to extend beyond merely not damaging others. Each person, recognizing the intrinsic worth of each other person, takes her- or himself to have positive duties of care toward each other person. But is this reply really convincing? Is it credible to suppose that a Kantian contractarianism contains within it the basis for what has become known as an ethic of care?

Since Carol Gilligan introduced the thesis that girls undergo a different kind of moral development than boys and learn to reason about morals differently, psychologists have disagreed about whether the two kinds of moral thinking that Gilligan distinguished—an ethic of care and an ethic of justice—correlate with differences in gender. Lawrence Walker has argued, for example, that when one controls for education and occupation, girls and boys tend to score similarly on the tests Gilligan used.[19] Whether such gender differences exist, however, is not as important for our purposes as the significance of her distinction between two moral voices for the possibility of a viable feminist contractarianism. Might it not be argued that an ethic of care must be central in any feminist moral theory but that it cannot be central in any contractarian account of morality? This argument, advanced by Virginia Held,[20] does not depend on Gilligan's original thesis of gender difference.

To assess this objection to contractarianism, we need to be clearer about what an ethic of care entails. Joan Tronto lists three characteristics that distinguish Gilligan's ethic of care from a morality of justice: (1) an ethic of care revolves around the moral concepts of responsibility and relationships of interdependency rather than those of rights and moral rules; (2) it is "tied to concrete circumstances rather than being formal and abstract;" and (3) it is "best expressed not as a set of principles but as an activity, the 'activity of care.' "[21] Let us accept this characterization as being roughly accurate and also concede Marilyn Friedman's observation,[22] which Held and Tronto have independently endorsed,[23] that an ethic of care does not stand on its own but would have to be supplemented by considerations of justice. Still, if an ethic of justice needs, in turn, to be supplemented by an ethic of care or if, indeed, its place in morality should not be central, is there not a serious problem for contractarianism as a general theory of morals, since the latter appears to be based purely on an ethic of justice?

My reply comes in three parts. First, we need to make a clear distinction between the normative system that members of a society would autonomously agree to impose on themselves and the contractarian reasoning that constitutes the justification for that system of norms. The difference is as fundamental as that between the conclusion of an argument and the reasoning that leads to it. Given this difference, it is entirely possible that the normative system that would be justified for a given society on contractarian grounds contains an ethic of care as a central part of it, as Tronto characterizes it. The normative system need not privilege rights over responsibilities in an interdependent relationship, nor need it be learned as formal or abstract rules. Moreover, the system may be lived in large part as the "practice of care" in the sense that Tronto intended by that phrase. Contractarian reasoning cannot by its nature preclude this possibility, as long as the reasoning that justifies a normative system is not confused with the system itself.

It may be objected that contractarian reasoning, because it is based on a hypothetical choice by mutually disinterested agents, must inevitably privilege considerations of justice over those of care. The second part of my general reply is to distinguish the form of contractarian reasoning defended here from reasoning that is often associated with social contract theory. The image of men and women gathered around a table negotiating a social contract, as Hampton has stressed, is merely a metaphor. Until the conditions of choice are spelled out, there is no real theory. In the present case the conditions of choice that I shall stipulate do not, in fact, imply that the parties to the contract are uncaring, isolated individuals. On the contrary, I shall argue in the next chapter that, unless the parties to the agreement care about how their interests are jointly served by the agreement, contractarian reasoning will not issue in a workable normative system. What makes the reasoning "contractarian" is that it aims at reaching an *agreement* about norms that is acceptable to all members of society. Nothing in this idea requires that their motivation be merely self-interested or even that the parties to the agreement be uncaring about each other or have no strong bonds with particular others.

Finally, it is important to note, as almost anyone advocating an ethic of care will acknowledge, that considerations of care can conflict with themselves and also conflict with considerations of rights. How are these conflicts to be adjudicated at the level of deciding on a balanced normative system? Contractarian reasoning offers a mechanism to sort through the potential areas of conflict and significant protection for those whose socialization in a society where the burdens of care are unequally distributed may incline them to accept more responsibility for others than justice should allow. The Kantian perspective, in emphasizing that the choice of norms must be autonomous, serves as a

corrective to the tendency among some to valorize the characteristically female virtue of caring.

The voices of Jake and Amy in Carol Gilligan's *In a Different Voice* illustrate this point well. These children are presented with a hypothetical situation
in which a man with little money must decide whether to steal a drug for his
seriously ill wife. Their responses to the dilemma are remarkably different.
Amy's view of the situation is often taken to exemplify an ethic of care and
Jake's an ethic of justice. But Hampton believes that it would be a mistake to
treat Amy's perspective as morally superior:

> I find it striking that these children's answers betray perspectives that seem to fit
> them perfectly for the kind of gendered roles that prevail in our society. In their
> archetypal forms, I hear the voice of a child who is preparing to be a member of
> a dominating group and the voice of another who is preparing to be a member of
> a group that is dominated.[24]

It is arguable that, from the standpoint of Kantian social contract theory, Jake
fails to be sufficiently sensitive to the intrinsic worth of others, but Amy fails
to be sufficiently sensitive to her own. Hampton sees the Kantian theory as
offering a balance between the two. How this balance is to be struck is obviously not a trivial matter. The point here, however, is that reasoning that leads
to autonomous agreement has the potential of reaching a balance that will not
yield a gendered distribution of the burdens of care.

The Need for an Archimedean Point

I say it has the potential of reaching such a balance. Not all forms of Kantian
contractarianism are equal from a feminist point of view. Rawls's theory of
justice as fairness is a good example. Though it is a form of Kantian social
contract theory, Okin shows that his original position is so structured that the
question of justice within families, particularly in regard to gender inequality,
cannot arise. In Rawls's theory the parties to the original contract are heads
of households. The fundamental problem is not that Rawls thought of families
hierarchically, with males, in most cases, representing families in the original
position. That problem might be easily remedied by having the representative
member from each family chosen by lot. Nor is it that Rawls failed to stipulate
that the "veil of ignorance" would prevent the contractors from knowing their
sex. Obviously that is easily remedied too. The problem is that Rawls conceived the contract as an agreement between families about principles of justice and one that would apply only in the *public* sphere. So construed, such
principles, no matter how impartial they are, would inevitably not address
injustice arising from gendered roles inside the family. They would not ad-

dress, for example, the fact that responsibility for primary child care and housework falls at present mainly on women rather than on men, or the fact that the life prospects of women are thereby diminished to a significant degree, or the fact the status quo in this regard is strongly reinforced by the social and economic structures in the public realm.[25]

Though Rawls's social contract theory is Kantian in that it is designed to make the parties to the original contract choose principles that treat everyone as ends in themselves, the position from which they choose is not structured to provide a perspective that is external and prior to conventional morality. Providing such a perspective is essential to a feminist social contract theory if it is to offer a corrective to the sexist features of conventional moral thinking. Seeing the promise of this kind of theory, Okin tries to reconstruct Rawls's theory so that it is not vulnerable to this difficulty. In her version the parties to the agreement represent individuals rather than family units. Most important, while they do not know their sex or any of the other characteristics that jointly distinguish them as individuals, they are to have knowledge of the causes and effects of conventional gender roles and of possible alternative social arrangements in this regard. Okin believes, not without good reason, that an agreement about principles formed on this basis would be external and prior to conventional moral thinking in a way that could provide a feminist foundation for morality.

This completes my sketch of two of the main motivations behind the Kantian form of feminist contractarianism exemplified in the work of Hampton and Okin. In the next three sections I present reasons why any contractarianism that perfectly reflects both motivations cannot be fully coherent.

Embodied Knowledge

For an agreement to be a foundation for morality—to explain and justify it—the parties to it must be free of coercion and not acting out of ignorance. This is the autonomy requirement. The fact that people have agreed or would agree to act in accordance with certain principles would not lend credibility to those principles if we doubted that the agreement would have been made freely with knowledge of its consequences. Moreover, principles agreed to by some only because of coercion or ignorance cannot be trusted to reflect the equal intrinsic worth of all parties to the agreement. In short, to accord with the Kantian conception of a social contract, the agreement must be free and informed.

Problems arise, however, when we ask how to interpret the idea of free and informed agreement. Consider first the requirement that the parties agree out of knowledge rather than ignorance. This requirement cannot mean that they must have merely true beliefs about the relevant facts, such as about the consequences of applying alternative sets of principles. That condition is simply too weak to characterize a reliable form of contractarian reasoning if such reasoning is to constitute the *justification* of norms. To play this role, the reasoning should be based on beliefs that are at least justified on the evidence. Feminists and others who want to base morality on reasoning from a position of equality expect this reasoning to do epistemic work. If it is to do this work, the beliefs on which the agreement rests had better be justified, if not known to be true.

Here, with the notion of "justified on the evidence," we enter hotly contested territory. In the heyday of positivism, a consensus prevailed in many quarters that the contexts of discovery and justification were utterly distinct and that values other than truth have no place in the latter context. While philosophy of science after Kuhn has conceded the place of values, such as simplicity and consistency with past practice, in evaluating evidence, considerable resistance remains to allowing moral and political values to play a role as well. Like other feminist theorists, such as Helen Longino, Lynn Hankinson Nelson, and Kathleen Okruhlik, I have argued that there is no way to separate evaluation of evidence from the influence of moral and political values.[26] Indeed, the position developed in the preceding parts of this book is that even in very conservative assumptions about the logic of confirmation, the context of discovery will have to play a role. For example, whether evidence e supports a hypothesis h depends on whether there is an alterative hypothesis h* that explains e just as well, but the capacity of a person or, indeed, a community of researchers to think of a suitable h* can depend on their moral and political commitments. In this way the context of discovery can enter directly into determining whether e supports h, for any evidence e and any hypothesis h. I have called this and other forms of interdependence between fact and value *fact-value holism.*

As I have already indicated, apt illustrations may be found in the voluminous and growing scientific literature discussing hypotheses comparing the moral and intellectual capacities of men and women. Beliefs in this regard would have a profound bearing on what principles one might choose to govern society if one were in an original position of choice of the kind postulated by social contract theorists. It would make considerable difference, for example, if one thought that women tended on average to be unsuited for science, business, and politics, as some sociobiologists have suggested.[27] In evaluating the evidence, feminist researchers often suggest explanations that are inconsistent with those put forward by others. I have cited the analyses that the biologist Anne Fausto-Sterling has made of evidence purporting to show the superiority of males in various respects.[28] I have argued that her ability to produce plausible alternative explanations of the evidence springs in part from a feminist conception of social justice.

The import of this result for feminists who want to appeal to informed (and free) agreement as being an independent standard for evaluating conventional morality should now be clear. There is a dilemma. If the conception of social

justice leading feminists to provide alternative explanations of the evidence
(and to devise and test alternative hypotheses) is merely conventional, then the
project of providing an external and prior standard for evaluating conventional
morality is undermined. It is undermined simply because the agreement itself
would be based on the conventional morality that the standard of justice is
meant to evaluate. On the other hand, if the conception is not conventional,
the project of founding morality on a hypothetical original agreement fails
anyway, since it is not the agreement as such but an independent idea of
justice that is foundational. In this case contract theory is not functioning as a
foundation for justice. Either way, the motivations for contractarianism with
which we began turn out not to be completely coherent when taken together.

Transformational Experiences

So far we have focused on the need for the agreement to be based on justified
beliefs about the relevant facts. But in social contract theory the need to have
the relevant facts—say, about the consequences of choosing one set of principles rather than another—stems from the need to know which principles will
best serve the *interests* of the parties to the agreement. In a recent critique of
the liberal model of interests, Susan Babbitt has shown that experiential or
nonpropositional knowledge is crucial to knowing what one's interests are,
and hence, for an agreement to serve as a foundation for morality, it must be
based on this kind of knowledge as well.[29] This result can be easily seen to
raise a problem similar to the one before for the project of founding morality
on agreement.

To explain the connection, I will first summarize the liberal model and
Babbitt's critique. According to this model, what is in one's interest is whatever will satisfy the preferences that one would have if one were to have all
the relevant facts and were deliberating rationally (in a purely instrumental
sense).[30] A virtue of this model is that it implies a distinction between satisfying immediate preferences and acting in one's interest, since the preferences
that one has now need not be the preferences that one would have if one knew
better the nature of one's choice. A difficulty is that in this model knowing
better what one is choosing is construed merely in terms of knowing the truth
of certain propositions and does not include as relevant the very different
knowledge that comes from knowing from experience what certain options
are like. Babbitt argues that it may at times be necessary to know what something is like through some form of direct experience of it to determine whether
it is what one really wants.

Plato and Mill have made parallel points about judging the relative worth
of different types of lives and pleasures. Where Babbitt's proposal differs
markedly is in applying this insight about the importance of experience to

determining whether certain alternative social arrangements would be in one's interest. She is thinking particularly of arrangements that are distant from one's present experience. Though Babbitt's concern is not with social contract theory, knowledge of whether such arrangements are in one's interest would be obviously essential to the parties to a foundational agreement. The difficulty is in understanding how the parties can have access to this knowledge given the role that experience must play in gaining it. Although we can easily imagine a person with lots of general propositional knowledge, it is quite another thing to imagine someone who has experienced living within vastly different social arrangements, especially when the most salient ones from a feminist standpoint have not been realized in any general way. Yet if the original position is to fulfill its epistemic role, our imaginations must be up to exactly this feat. It is difficult to see how we can succeed in this regard without having some prior insight into what just social arrangements are like, since the experience that one could have under such arrangement is apt to be highly relevant to knowing what one's interests are. But then, of course, we are faced with the very same dilemma that arose before. If the idea of justice is conventional, Okin's requirement is violated; if it is not, then the ultimate justification for claims about justice is, contrary to Hampton, not some form of Kantian social contract but rather some prior conception of justice.

The Baseline Problem

I turn finally to the problem created by the condition that the parties to the agreement are to act freely, without coercion of any kind. The analysis of coercion that I shall draw on is very basic but defensible nonetheless, at least in outline.[31] Simply put: I coerce you to do X when I so manipulate your circumstances that you have fewer options than before, and the best of them, X, which is what I want you to do, is one you would not have chosen in the prethreat situation. For example, when I say credibly, "Your money or your life." I coerce you to relinquish your money by reducing your prethreat options of keeping your money and your life, knowing that you will choose to keep living and that you would not have given me your money had you retained both options. A virtue of this analysis is that it allows a clear distinction between threats and bribes, since the latter can be seen to expand options, even though some bribes can be equally compelling psychologically. Another virtue, one particularly relevant to feminism, is that this analysis does not impugn the free will of the person coerced.[32] Though in an important sense the person coerced does not act freely, the person's power to choose among the options in the postthreat situation need not be diminished in any way.

Although I believe that this line of analysis is basically on the right track, an aspect that has not received adequate attention, to my knowledge, is the way in which it presupposes a baseline of "normality" that is required by justice, other things equal. Take a person serving a twenty year sentence. Her obedience while in prison is clearly coerced, and we might say that she is continually under threat: obey or else (such and such bad thing will happen to you). But, *contrary* to the analysis, her options do not get less and less with each threat. We can imagine that they remain more or less constant, day after day, year after year. Perhaps we can reply as follows: Imagine that each threat is just a restatement of the original threat when she was first imprisoned, so that thereafter her options are less compared with what they were before that time. But we would not regard her as less under coercion had she been imprisoned since birth! What is crucial, then, is that we take her options, however long she has been in prison, to be less that what justice *normally* requires—say, for someone not deserving of punishment. Coercion is fully intelligible, in other words, only against an assumption of what are the usually legitimate options, ones that are normally safeguarded by justice.

What should count as an appropriate baseline for comparison is a matter open to considerable debate. Feminist work on the subjects of "compulsory" heterosexuality, free speech, sexual harassment, the gendered division of labor, and informed consent for medical procedures, to name but a few relevant topics, typically calls into question conventional assumptions about what should count as a proper baseline for comparison in deciding whether a particular practice or institution is coercive.[33] I will not pursue the details. My objective here is to underscore how this issue bears on the contractarian ideal of a free, uncoerced original agreement. My claim is that, however hypothetical, this agreement cannot be usefully spelled out in light of the analysis of coercion just sketched without a *prior* understanding of the nature of social justice, and then we are again stuck with the dilemma set out earlier.

Morality without Foundations

I see no way out of the dilemma posed by the considerations of the last three sections if we adhere to the idea that a feminist contractarianism provides a foundation for morality or, to be more precise, a foundation for the justification of moral norms. There is, in essence, no way to explain uncoerced and relevantly informed choice apart from the very moral concepts that the idea of a social contract based on uncoerced, relevantly informed choice is supposed to explain and justify. What, then, might we give up if we want to hold onto feminist contractarianism for the reasons urged by Okin and Hampton?

We need to give up the idea that a feminist contractarianism can provide a foundation for morality. If Hampton and Okin are right about what a feminist contractarianism should be like, as I think they are, the further requirement that it not presuppose in any way the moral norms that it is designed to justify

Feminist Contractarianism 187

and thus be "foundational" in relation to them turns out, as we have seen, to be incompatible with the requirement that the agreement about morals be formed autonomously, free of coercion and relevantly informed. But, it might be asked, is it really possible to keep Okin's requirement but not the foundational idea? After all, is not her requirement really the demand that there be some way to assess conventional morals that is external and prior to them? And is this anything less than the traditional demand for a foundation for morals?

What is feminist and morally unconventional about Okin's moral perspective is that justice pertains in part to relations within families and to how family relations are structured by relations in the public realm. The original agreement in her theory is designed to include this perspective and thus a standpoint that is external to conventional morality from which even aspects of conventional justice can be evaluated and revised. In this respect hers is like a foundational theory. But in two important respects it is not, at least not foundational in a way that leads to paradox. First, nothing in Okin's conception of the agreement, or indeed in Hampton's, requires that *all* reference to conventional notions of justice be excluded from our understanding of how the agreement is reached. But second, and more important, even those elements that suggest a foundational theory are *defeasible* and thus open to revision.[34]

How is the latter possible? Clearly, the part of Okin's theory that makes it external and prior to conventional morality cannot be open to rejection because it fails to cohere with today's morals. If that were a legitimate ground for rejection or even revision, then Okin's condition on justification would be no requirement at all. How then? The answer lies in the three aspects of informed and uncoerced agreement outlined earlier. Though these concepts cannot be made sense of without some reference to justice, each involves an independent source of grounds for revision. In the case of justified belief, the source is the truth that can be uncovered through empirical investigation. For example, Okin's project will succeed only if her claims about the causal relationships between the public and domestic realms can be sustained. Though an inquiry of this kind, I have argued, is guided by assumptions about the nature of justice, the latter will not ensure that her causal hypotheses will be confirmed by experience. If they are not, then part of the foundation of her contractarianism will be defeated. Similarly, the experiential knowledge to which Babbitt refers might not support Okin's vision of what a just society would be like, and what baseline will seem reasonable in light of new information, both propositional and experiential, cannot be guaranteed beforehand. In short, Okin's perspective is in the end defeasible, independently of whether it agrees with conventional morality.

The upshot is an understanding of contractarian reasoning that is responsive to the feminist theoretical constraints imposed by Hampton and Okin, but at the same time it is not foundational in the strong sense that would lead to

paradox. What remains to be asked is whether this understanding of contractarian reasoning amounts to a justification of moral norms. Is it possible, that
is, to have a justification of moral norms without foundations? I turn to this
question in the next chapter.

Notes

1. Jean Hampton, "Feminist Contractarianism," in *A Mind of One's Own: Feminist Essays on Reason and Objectivity*, Louise M. Antony and Charlotte Witt, eds.
(Boulder, Colo.: Westview, 1993), 227–55.

2. Susan Moller Okin, *Justice, Gender, and the Family* (New York: Basic Books,
1989).

3. Robert Nozick, *Anarchy, State, and Utopia* (New York: Basic Books, 1974).
Nozick presents a contractarian justification of a minimal state rather than of morality;
Okin's critique focuses on the Lockean concept of property rights embedded in Nozick's moral presuppositions and argues that it leads to paradox when it is applied to
women's labor in reproduction.

4. John Rawls, *A Theory of Justice* (Cambridge, Mass.: Harvard University Press,
1971). Okin's critique, summarized later, extends also to Rawls's more recent work.
See her *"Political Liberalism*, Justice, and Gender," *Ethics* 105 (1994): 23–43.

5. Here I borrow from David Copp's account of the cognitive content of certain
standard forms of moral judgment; see David Copp, *Morality, Normativity, and Society*
(Oxford: Clarendon, 1995), 9–36. In his view, to claim behavior is wrong is to imply
that it violates a moral standard for behavior and that this standard is justified. Unlike
Copp, I propose a contractarian account of justification and take what is justified to be
not merely the standard or norm that is applied but also the attitude and motives appropriate to it.

6. Here I adapt for realist purposes a suggestion developed by Allan Gibbard in
his *Wise Choices, Apt Feelings* (Cambridge, Mass.: Harvard University Press, 1990),
chapter 4.

7. Copp, *Morality*, 82–94.

8. Copp, *Morality*, 84.

9. It should be noted, however, that Copp is a cognitivist regarding moral judgments. I am assimilating his account of subscribing to a moral standard to an account
of moral judgment that is hybrid rather than strictly cognitivist.

10. See David O. Brink, *Moral Realism and the Foundations of Ethics* (Cambridge:
Cambridge University Press, 1989), 45–50.

11. This is contrary to Copp, who believes that normativity is inherent in the content
of a normative judgment; see Copp, *Morality*, 32–36. A problem for Copp is that he
has no satisfying explanation of why justification, as he conceives it, is normative
per se. See my "Critical Notice of David Copp, *Morality, Normativity, and Society*,"
Canadian Journal of Philosophy 27 (1997): 423–44.

12. Copp, *Morality*, 24–25.

13. See, for example, Virginia Held, *Feminist Morality: Transforming Culture, Society, and Politics* (Chicago: University of Chicago Press, 1993), 70–73.

14. In formulating this objection, I am not presupposing a purely distributive conception of justice. Iris Marion Young has argued against such a conception in the first chapter of her *Justice and the Politics of Difference* (Princeton, N.J.: Princeton University Press, 1990). She has argued that rights, powers, and privileges cannot be distributed in the same way that material goods can be. But all I intend is that it is possible for men to have more of such goods than women and that this would be a source of injustice. At least that much seems to be implied by Young's own account of oppression in her second chapter.

15. The distinction between the ethics of care and justice is made in Carol Gilligan, *In a Different Voice: Psychological Theory and Women's Development* (Cambridge, Mass.: Harvard University Press, 1982).

16. Hampton, "Feminist Contractarianism," 229.

17. Hampton, "Feminist Contractarianism," 234.

18. For example, contracts based on fraud or coercion have no moral standing according to David Gauthier; see his *Morals by Agreement* (Oxford: Clarendon, 1986), 195–98.

19. See Lawrence J. Walker, "Sex Differences in the Development of Moral Reasoning: A Critical Review," *Child Development* 55 (1984): 677–91.

20. Held, *Feminist Morality*, chapter 4.

21. Joan C. Tronto, *Moral Boundaries: A Political Argument for an Ethic of Care* (New York: Routledge 1993), 79.

22. See Marilyn Friedman, "Beyond Caring: The De-Moralization of Gender" in *Science, Morality, and Feminist Theory* (*Canadian Journal of Philosophy*, suppl. vol. 13), Marsha Hanen and Kai Nielsen, eds. (Calgary: University of Calgary Press, 1987), 98–105.

23. See Held, *Feminist Morality*, 76, and Tronto, *Moral Boundaries*, 126.

24. Hampton, 231.

25. Okin's evidence that these are indeed facts is developed especially in the seventh chapter of *Justice*.

26. Helen Longino, *Science as Social Knowledge* (Princeton, N.J.: Princeton University Press, 1990); Lynn Hankinson Nelson, *Who Knows: From Quine to Feminist Empiricism* (Philadelphia: Temple University Press, 1990); Kathleen Okruhlik, "Birth of a New Physics or Death of Nature?" in *Women and Reason*, Elizabeth D. Harvey and Kathleen Okruhlik, eds. (Ann Arbor: University of Michigan Press, 1992), 63–76.

27. For example, Edward O. Wilson, "Human Decency Is Animal," *The New York Times Magazine*, 12 October 1975.

28. Anne Fausto-Sterling, *Myths of Gender* (New York: Basic Books, 1985).

29. Susan Babbitt, "Feminism and Objective Interests: The Role of Transformation Experiences in Rational Deliberation," in *Feminist Epistemologies*, Elizabeth Potter and Linda Alcoff, eds. (New York: Routledge, 1992), 245–64. The argument is developed in more detail in her *Impossible Dreams: Rationality, Integrity, and Moral Imagination* (Boulder, Colo.: Westview, 1996).

30. A version of this model may be found in Rawls, *A Theory of Justice*. It is also present in the work of many other liberal theorists.

31. For less basic versions of this view, see, Robert Nozick, "Coercion," in *Philosophy, Science, and Method: Essays in Honor of Ernest Nagel* (New York: St. Martin's,

1969), 440–71. See also Wright Neely, "Freedom and Desire," *Philosophical Review* 83 (1974): 32–54, and my *Self-Love and Self-Respect: A Philosophical Study of Egoism* (Ottawa: Canadian Library of Philosophy 1979), 166–70.

32. A common mistake made about sexual harassment is to suppose that thinking of harassment as coercive impugns the agency of the victim and hence itself demeans the victim. But to think of a person as coerced implies that her or his options have been unfairly diminished; it does not imply that the person is unable to choose rationally among the diminished set. The analysis offered here makes the difference clear.

33. To illustrate how the baseline problem arises regarding free speech, for example, see Rae Langdon's brilliant discussions: "Whose Right? Ronald Dworkin, Women, and Pornographers," *Philosophy and Public Affairs* 19 (1990): 311–59; "Speech Acts and Unspeakable Acts," *Philosophy and Public Affairs* 22 (1993): 293–330. See also Daniel Jacobson, "Freedom of Speech Acts? A Response to Langdon," *Philosophy and Public Affairs* 24 (1995): 64–79.

34. I say this aspect is not foundational because in traditional foundationalism the foundational parts of a justification are not defeasible, but sometimes the term is used more broadly. See Robert Audi, "Fallibilist Foundationalism and Holistic Coherentism," in *The Theory of Knowledge*, Louis P. Pojman, ed. (Belmont, Calif.: Wadsworth, 1993), 263–79.

Chapter 10

Feminist Contractarianism Naturalized

Analogy with Induction

How do we know what is right or wrong? We often feel the pressure of moral demands, but we are free to ask in any given case whether this or that moral pressure corresponds to something that would justify responding to it. How do we know that the felt demand is not misleading, that nothing in reality justifies responding to it? How do we know, in other words, that what *appears* morally right or wrong really is so?

Contractarianism has an answer. A moral demand is justified if it derives from a system of moral demands that we can agree together to impose on ourselves. There are feminist reasons, as we have seen, for qualifying this answer. In Hampton's Kantian interpretation, women and men must be able to agree to impose the system when they are motivated to treat each other as ends. This approach involves, at minimum, imposing it freely, with knowledge of the consequences of their choice, particularly regarding those that would result in oppression. In Okin's Rawlsian interpretation, they must be able to do this when their agreement does not derive from the demands of conventional morality. But we discovered that these interpretations conflict if the agreement is to be a foundation for morality. We can escape the conflict by supposing that there is no ultimate foundation for morals, but now we must wonder whether moral knowledge is truly possible after all. If no foundation for an agreement about morals exists that is truly independent of the moral norms in question—no foundation that would justify our allegiance to certain moral norms rather than others—why assume that the contractarian answer explains when and how what appears morally right really is right?

The burden of this chapter will be in part to resolve this puzzle, but I also have a deeper goal. I want to locate the present contractarian moral theory within feminist naturalized epistemology. I will argue that once this is done, it is possible to answer the last question by appeal to this larger picture of how knowledge is possible. As a first step, I return to Quine's Darwinian vindication of inductive reasoning and draw an analogy between inductive and moral reasoning.

In drawing this analogy, I shall continue to suppose that contractarianism can be viewed as a method of reasoning about which moral norms are justified. Contractarianism asks us to imagine what norms we would agree to impose collectively on ourselves. This thought experiment is supposed to function as a method of gaining insight into what is actually morally required of us. As just noted, we can wonder whether the method is any good in this regard, especially if the method is not supposed to function as a foundation for morality. But notice that we can ask a parallel question of inductive reasoning. Inductive reasoning can be understood as a method for gaining insight into the causal order of the world around and inside us. Does this method yield any genuine insight? Though the aim in each case is different, the form of question is the same: Is the method employed successful in achieving the understood aim? The analogy that I want to draw concerns how we might evaluate the worth of each method given their distinctive aims.

My discussion will proceed in two stages. First, I will draw an analogy between evaluating our intuitive sense of right and wrong and evaluating our innate capacity to reason inductively. Then, after addressing a worry about the Darwinian assumptions being made, I will extend the analogy to bring in contractarian reasoning specifically.

Recall Quine's explicit appeal to natural selection as a way of explaining how inductive reasoning in its primitive forms does better than chance at getting it right about what to expect in situations such as those in which those forms of reasoning evolved. Could anything like this appeal be made to vindicate primitive forms of moral thinking? Sometimes natural selection is used to explain how morals evolved by pointing out how moral dispositions tend on average to contribute to individual fitness.[1] In these explanations moral dispositions are often likened to dispositions to cooperate reciprocally in iterated Prisoner's Dilemma games.[2] Given a very rough correlation between increases in fitness and individual well-being, the story about how morals evolved might then be used to justify in purely prudential terms why we should be disposed to think morally as we do.[3]

Notice, however, that this justification for our tendency to think morally does not really purport to provide a justification of this tendency in a way that is parallel to Quine's vindication of our tendency to think inductively. This is because Quine wants to explain why our innate inductive methods work better than chance at accomplishing what we are trying to accomplish when we use induction, such as figuring out what will happen next. To be parallel, an appeal to Darwin in the case of morals would have to show that our innate sense of morals would be more likely than chance to get it right *about what is morally required of us*. Why? Because getting it right about what is morally required of us is our aim in moral reasoning, just as getting it right about what to expect is our aim in inductive reasoning. The two explanations would be parallel only if we assume that what is morally required of us is to maximize our individual fitness or well-being. Few would find this assumption plausible.

It may appear, then, that the familiar speculation about how morals might have evolved presents no parallel to Quine's appeal to natural selection to help vindicate induction. In fact, if one looks carefully at Quine's argument, a surprisingly close analogy exists, though different from the one already described. Natural selection favors our mode of inductive reasoning only if this way of thinking matters to survival and reproduction. We suppose that normally it would. For example, we suppose that if we fail to get it right about what will happen if we do not flee from a predator, we would not be able to survive and reproduce. What we are supposing in these cases? We suppose that we know what coming out right is in certain particular cases and see that coming out right in these cases makes one more biologically fit than one would be otherwise. Though it hardly needs saying that getting it right about whether a lion is going to charge or whether one mushroom is made of the same stuff as another increases chances of survival, Quine's argument depends on our knowing the contingent fact that getting it right in these cases will aid survival. The argument simply assumes, at the outset, that we know some facts about cause and effect of the very kind that inductive reasoning allows us to infer. These facts are in addition to the general contingent fact of natural selection itself, which is, of course, also based on inductive reasoning.

To construct a similar argument to vindicate our methods of moral reasoning, we would have to assume at the outset some basic facts about what is morally required of us. That is, before the argument can get off the ground, we would need to assume that we already know something of what it is like for our sense of right and wrong to come out right about the moral facts. Would not this assumption be question begging? We have addressed the question of whether assuming Darwin's theory is question begging in the case of Quine's attempt to vindicate induction; we will revisit this circularity issue shortly. The point I want to stress here is that if the structure of argument is to be the same for induction and morals, we need to assume in the case of morals that we already know certain moral facts. We need to assume, at least tentatively, that we know certain moral facts that we now think are perfectly obvious—for example, that it is wrong to murder, rape, and steal. A consequence is that our epistemology for moral knowledge will not be foundational. Within a naturalized epistemology, vindication of our ways of knowing must proceed from assumptions about some of the very facts, in this case moral facts, about which our methods of knowing are supposed to inform us, even though those methods are themselves in question.

In each case the success of the method is correlated with improved fitness. In successful induction chances of achieving one's immediate ends are improved because one has better beliefs than one would have otherwise about how to reach them. The tie with fitness exists because one's ends are apt to correspond roughly with what will improve on average one's reproductive success. For example, the desire for food, shelter, and sex tends to lead to doing things that aid survival and reproduction. The case in moral thinking is similar. Believing certain acts are wrong is tied to wanting to avoid them. (Recall the hybrid theory of moral judgment.) Mutual avoidance of these acts is at the same time correlated with improved fitness. Thus, moral thinking, at least in its most basic forms, is correlated roughly with selective advantage. While this standard speculation about the evolution of moral thinking explains why moral thinking exists in the first place, it also explains, in a way exactly parallel to the Darwinian explanation of inductive reasoning, how this thinking can be expected *to get it right* much of the time about what is morally required. The evolutionary account, to the extent that it is historically accurate, serves to vindicate this way of thinking. Vindicate it how? This way: It shows why our method of moral thinking, at least in its most primitive forms, is apt to be successful in its aim—namely, to discern right and wrong.

Biology in "Man's" Image?

The preceding story relies on natural selection having a role in the evolution of primitive forms of moral thinking. But do we not know that attempts by sociobiologists to explain human behavior by appeal to natural selection have been fraught with sexism and other oppressive distortions of reality?[4] If so, it would appear to be seriously question begging to use sociobiological thinking to vindicate patterns of moral thinking. How is this concern to be answered? I want to concede the premise but suggest that the conclusion does not follow. Sociobiology and indeed much of the biological sciences involve sexist thinking of various kinds, yet the speculation that primitive forms of moral thinking were in the past conducive to survival and reproduction does not seem to me to be inherently sexist, or oppressive in some other way. Let me offer three reasons why I do not condemn the use of Darwinian theory in the present context.

Three conditions are sufficient for biological evolution: variation in biological forms, differential reproduction, and heredity. Modern Darwinian theory postulates natural selection as one, but not the only, explanation for differential reproduction. When some biological forms "are selected" (interact with their environment, including the other organisms in that environment, in such a way that they leave more offspring than other forms do in the same environment) and the offspring tend to be more like their parent or parents than they are like other forms in that environment, distribution of forms in the population evolves. At this level of abstraction, politically suspect assumptions are not in evidence. They emerge, however, in how natural selection and heredity are often specifically understood.

Take the case of heredity. Much has been written on how masculinist assumptions enter into the ways that genes are characterized in models of heredity—for example, where the function and significance of genes are described in patriarchal metaphors of control and dominance.[5] In reality, bits of DNA do nothing by themselves apart from a specific cell environment and the various causal factors operating there. By themselves, genes do not control or produce anything.[6] Yet, because genes are considered to be the main units of heredity, people lapse into thinking that genes can alone "determine" heredity—a claim that is biological nonsense. The point I want to stress, however, is that a Darwinian explanation of evolution, though it presupposes *some* mechanism of heredity, is not committed to any such nonsense regarding biological determinism. One can discredit sexist models of heredity and allow that heredity itself is not an illusion and that there are mechanisms to explain it.

A second place where politically suspect assumptions enter into the Darwinian account is in characterizing the nature of selection, especially when it is conceived as being essentially individual and competitive. Though no doubt competition in the sense of struggling to gain control of resources can be and has been a factor in accounting for differential reproduction, it need not always be so. For example, the reciprocal altruism model for the evolution of cooperation is intrinsically cooperative in its interactions.[7] (In iterated Prisoner's Dilemmas, the "tit- for-tat" reciprocator never does better than the other "party" in any interaction and many times worse, yet that strategy evolves in ecological simulations.) An appeal to natural selection does not, therefore, necessarily imply that evolution occurs through competitive interactions.

The question of whether the principal "unit of selection" is individual is highly contested at the moment. Some hold that selection occurs at the level of genes (alleles); others believe that it occurs at some "higher" level (genotype, whole organism, group).[8] We need not enter into this debate, however. The very fact that the debate exists is evidence that modern Darwinian theory, at the level of generality as I have presented it, is not committed to selection being individual, except in the trivial sense that it is individual organisms that differentially reproduce and pass their genes onto the next generation. The causal factors influencing the direction of selection, which is a nontrivial matter with important political implications, can be and are perhaps best conceived in nonindividual terms.[9]

Finally, it is worth emphasizing that the appeal to Darwin's theory is made here at a fairly high level of abstraction, which means that the argument I am making lacks the detail needed for a more developed naturalized epistemology. Like many theories that advocate naturalized epistemology, my epistemology is less naturalized than the kind I recommend.[10] By the same token, though, I am not committed to the specific sociobiological stories about, for

example, "parental investment" and "sexual selection," which support gender
stereotypes and derive from questionable assumptions. What I am committed
to, of course, is that there is some plausible way to explain how morals
evolved within the Darwinian paradigm. In keeping with the general argument
of this book, I believe that this explanatory project is best approached from a
feminist perspective.

Extending the Analogy

An important complication is that mutual effort to do the right and avoid the
wrong is what improves individual fitness, not unilateral effort on the part of
the individual whose fitness is in question. In this respect the connection between morals and selective advantage seems less direct than that between induction and selective advantage. We have already touched on this point in the
first section. In effect, individuals confront situations in which they stand in
iterated Prisoner's Dilemmas with respect to meeting their desires and obtain-
ing the correlated improvement in fitness. To succeed in this situation, they
must coordinate their behavior in mutually beneficial ways. What gets selected
for is a form of moral thinking about how they should act. Though some
"cheaters" will always exist in a system of moral constraints, the selective
forces favoring compliance to these moral demands are powerful and yield a
stable pattern of behavior.

The complication has noteworthy implications. The need for cooperation
and mutual restraint in the pursuit of ends suggests that responsiveness to
moral demands is in its origins not an absolute and unqualified adherence to
specific rules of behavior. There is reason to cooperate *provided that others
do likewise*, but if nobody else is prepared to cooperate, adherence to a set of
cooperative rules would be unmotivated and irrational. This thought captures
a significant part of how a contractarian might reason about the ultimate basis
of morality. One can think of the social contract as a hypothetical construct
that is designed to capture the cooperative basis for morality already implicit
in the long evolution of moral thinking. Though hypothetical rather than historical, the contract is a simple and useful way to represent the product of a
evolutionary process that was not contractual.

There is reason to believe, however, that the idea of a social contract bears
a more direct relation to thinking about right and wrong, one that extends the
analogy with induction. The reason is the well-known fact that simple moral
directives, such as "Keep your word" or "Don't tell lies," often come into
conflict. Even if everyone is prepared to adhere to moral rules when everyone
else does, cooperation in this respect does nothing to guide action in cases in
which moral rules give directions that are mutually incompatible under the
circumstances. Theoretically, it is possible to devise specific rules to decide

specific conflicts, but occasions of conflict are different enough in nontrivial respects to make it impractical to have different rules for all the different occasions of moral conflict. What people do in such cases is try to "balance" the importance of the various competing moral demands and arrive at a judgment that best reflects their comparative weight. There is no generally agreed-on procedure to follow in arriving at this judgment, though, of course, many theories describe how it might best be accomplished. We may view contractarianism as one among many moral theories that purport to shed light on not only the ultimate basis of moral demands but also how conflict among moral demands ought to be resolved.

Taken in this light, contractarianism is analogous to an explicitly formulated, sophisticated methodology for inductive reasoning. Instead of a largely biologically based and intuitive, though socially cultivated, moral sense, analogous to the innate similarity space that Quine discusses in his effort to vindicate induction, we have instead abstract, sometimes highly technical, formulations of moral reasoning such as in the current literature on moral theory. These formulations, I want now to suggest, are continuous with moral common sense. Naturalized epistemology, as Quine conceived it, postulates a degree of continuity between the two levels in the case of induction. Why should we not expect the same for morals?

That Quine supposes such continuity to obtain in the case of induction is clear from the following passage.

> [O]ne's sense of similarity or one's system of kinds develops and changes and even turns multiple as one matures, making perhaps for increasingly dependable prediction. And at length standards of similarity set in which are geared to theoretical science. This development is a development away from the immediate, subjective, animal sense of similarity to the remoter objectivity of a similarity determined by scientific hypotheses and posits and constructs.[11]

As Kornblith has observed, we must be able to explain how this development is possible, "how we got here from there."[12] It is one thing to postulate a continuity, another to explain it. Kornblith attempts to do this (and here diverges from Quine) by postulating an innate propensity to look for natural kinds that he characterizes as a homeostatic clustering of often hidden properties that underlie and explain the more readily observable ones. If the continuity reaches to our ability to recognize moral similarities, a corresponding explanation should be forthcoming to explain the transition from the basic recognition of moral categories to sophisticated moral reflection.

The search for continuity is complicated by the fact that the levels of thinking—for example, instinctive patterns of inductive inference versus modern statistical methods—appear to be very different. Indeed, the more sophisticated methods are apt to conflict in many places with our primitive moral and

inductive inclinations. The literature is full of studies showing how our intuitive sense of how to reason inductively leads most people to draw mistaken
inferences in specially contrived circumstances.[13] Parallel points could surely
be made regarding moral feelings, such as the desire for vengeance. Still, it is
a task of naturalized epistemology to explain how these sophisticated methods
evolved from the more primitive and where possible to shed light on their
reliability.

In particular, we need to ask how the motivation to treat someone as an end
might have evolved if our best method of moral reasoning is captured by a
feminist Kantian contractarianism. I want to suggest that this motivation is
more closely connected to the actual evolution of morals than its Hobbesian
alternative. In an explanation of the evolution of moral dispositions, especially
those associated with justice, there is, up to a point, no need to postulate more
than some form of reciprocal altruism to account for the convergence toward
cooperation. But when moral dispositions come into conflict, coordination for
mutual advantage is far more difficult, and agreements based on such dispositions alone are apt to prove unstable. In these cases we should expect natural
selection to favor some degree, perhaps only a minimal degree, of treating
others as more than merely a means, even if they are strangers. Individuals
who are able to feel this motivation toward others, especially for those who
are similarly motivated, are apt to do better in cooperating with them in circumstances that call for balancing contrary moral inclinations than those who
lack this capacity.[14] We should then expect this motivation to evolve. Its basis
would not be pure practical reason, as Kant thought, but our nature as crea-
tures shaped by natural selection.

But what is it exactly to be motivated to treat another as an end in the
context of trying to figure what is morally right by seeing what moral demands
we can agree together to impose on each other? Part of what is meant, I have
suggested, is that each person wants the other to choose on the basis of all
relevant information and wants the other's choice to be uncoerced. The evolutionary reason for this construal is not hard to see. Only such agreements are
going to be stable and sustain future cooperation. For this reason those who
think about agreements in this way, finding them attractive in their own right,
will have an advantage over those who think otherwise. It appears, therefore,
that the Kantian maxim of treating humanity, in ourselves and others, never
as a means only—or equivalently, treating humanity as autonomous self-legis-
lators—has a basis in evolution.

We need now to understand how this basis permits us to escape the dilemma
with which we began. We have seen in the last chapter how the requirements
of being informed and uncoerced cannot be fully explained without presupposing considerations of justice as we now conceive it and thus contradicting
the feminist constraint that the present conception of morals has a basis inde-

pendent of justice as we now conceive it. Is there a way out of this impasse in light of the analogy drawn with induction?

Coping with Circularity

Recall the charge of circularity leveled against the attempt to vindicate inductive reasoning by appeal to Darwin. I replied that the circularity is not stultifying, since, as Quine notes, there is no guarantee that induction would be vindicated in the end. Whether it is depends on how science develops, on the extent to which science is capable of understanding itself. If Darwinian theory is overturned or if auxiliary hypotheses on which we rely to explain induction (that, e.g., our basic inductive tendencies are gene linked) are not borne out, then the appeal to Darwin simply fails. Science may find an alternative explanation that is better confirmed and does the job as well. But it may not. Science may ultimately fail to explain itself. The circularity of the appeal does not, therefore, guarantee the success of the argument simply by assuming its conclusion. The mode of vindication is open to test and revision, as in the case of any other theory.

But a deeper ground of reply exists that goes to the heart of the present dilemma regarding contractarianism. Appealing to Darwin to vindicate innate inductive tendencies only goes so far. It does not vindicate them absolutely. In fact, it contains within itself the means to predict when the tendencies will go wrong and to explain why. The tendencies were selected according to the theory for survival and reproduction within a certain range of environment and against a background of options with associated evolutionary costs. This means that the tendencies have definite limitations. We reason very conservatively and are prone to make various kinds of elementary sampling errors, as numerous studies have revealed. If, however, we were not able to reason at all appropriately regarding inductive problems, we would not, of course, be able to devise better inductive strategies. Moreover, were it not for Darwin's theory, we would not be able to understand how our evolutionary past has made us naturally blind in certain respects. Inductive reasoning has proved, in sum, that it has the power to revise itself. This is a second respect in which the apparent circularity in the appeal to Darwin is not vicious or stultifying. Indeed, given that no alternative means of evaluation is possible, no a priori truths or first philosophy, the kind of self-corrective circularity in the naturalizing approach to induction is as much a virtue as a fault.

Can a parallel claim be made for contractarian thinking? The problem of circularity this time is that informed and uncoerced agreement cannot be understood without having some conception of justice, whose merits contractarian thinking is supposed to test. To appeal to the very moral demands whose legitimacy is in doubt is structurally a problem of the same type that faces the appeal to Darwinian theory to vindicate inductive reasoning. However, a structurally similar reply is available. There is no guarantee that the appeal to informed, uncoerced agreement, even if that depends to some degree on conventional ideas of justice, will in the end vindicate those ideas. Moreover, the process of applying the contractarian standard can be seen to be self-corrective.

Consider again the three respects in which the ideal of informed and unco-erced agreement depends on ideas of conventional justice. First, we cannot figure out what informed agreement is in any particular application of the contractarian method without justified beliefs about the relevant circum-stances. The problem is that, for reasons given in the previous chapter, justi-fied beliefs relevant to the question cannot be fully ascertained without some understanding of considerations of justice. Notice, though, that the source of these beliefs contain independent grounds for revision. For example, as noted in chapter 9, Okin's project will succeed only if her claims about the causal relationships between the public and domestic realms can be sustained. Though such an investigation, I have argued, is guided by assumptions about the nature of justice, the latter will not ensure that her causal hypotheses will be confirmed by experience. If they are not, then her contractarianism would have to be revised.

Second, consider the experiential dimensions of informed agreement that were brought out by Babbitt's analysis of transformational experiences. The experiential knowledge to which Babbitt refers might not support Okin's vi-sion of what a just society would be like; here, too, is an independent source of revision. Finally, there is the problem that what will constitute uncoerced agreement is relative to a baseline of normality that is in keeping with what justice requires. Location of a baseline, however, can be influenced by new information. What baseline will seem reasonable will change in light of new information, both propositional and experiential; the outcome cannot be guar-anteed beforehand. In sum, Okin's model, as well as any other feminist model of morality that might issue from the contractarian process of thinking out-lined here, is in the end defeasible, and this is so whether or not the model agrees with conventional morality.

The transition from Rawls's contractarian vision to Okin's illustrates the process of revision on all three counts. The baseline of comparison in Rawls's theory is the point of view of heads of households for whom child care is not supposed to be a matter of pressing concern. Although no mention is made of sex in the original theory, the point of view is clearly that of males, particu-larly those for whom justice can be conceived as primarily a matter of fair distribution of primary goods within a public realm external to the relation-ships among members of families. This conception of justice is at odds with the experience of females, for whom justice within families is a concern that is not subordinate but in fact is inextricably linked to justice in the public realm. To see the two as linked and indeed to feel the unfairness in excluding the one may well depend in part on understanding justice as it is conventionally taught. But, importantly, these perceptions are not limited to the latter. They depend on experiences different from those typical for men, on information about the consequences of the present gendered division of labor, and on being able to think of a baseline of comparison in which women and men have equal choices about how the labor of child rearing will be divided.

In Okin's revised formulation of contractarian thinking, the agreement is conceived as applying as much to relations within families as to those between families, and the parties to the agreement cannot assume that they will be immune to arrangements that are detrimental to women. Moreover, they will have information that is specific regarding the consequences in this regard. Two points are worth emphasis. First and most obvious, the revision moves in the direction of ensuring that the agreement is based on relevant information, with respect to both experience and facts about the consequences of the options, and that the agreement is uncoerced. The coercion that is implicit in Rawls's version is a consequence of the fact that women (and men also) have no say about the arrangements that pertain to justice within families. If the relevant baseline is a position from which these are options, then to choose under circumstances where these options are closed is coercion. Okin's revision alters the presumed baseline and thus adds stability to the agreement. It challenges conventional thinking about justice while preserving its apparent intent, to treat all parties as potentially free and equal.

Second, though much less obvious, the revision involves the contractarian conception of morality being applied to its own construction in order to revise its import and application. Okin does not describe herself as following this methodology, but her revision, for the reasons just given, can be usefully understood to involve an attempt to think about the ways in which women in Rawls's original position would be neither relevantly informed about nor free to choose among relevant options. The notions of relevant information and freedom from coercion are, of course, open to interpretation in light of experience. This allows the contractarian conception of morality to be both dependent on previous understandings of justice and at the same time able to revise them. There is no a priori way to know what the revisions should be. Experience will shape the transition from one stage of thinking to the next, and there is no reason to believe that Okin's formulation is beyond further revision in light of other kinds of experience.

Foundationalism or Coherentism?

Feminist contractarianism, despite its inevitable partial reliance on conventional ideas of justice, has the capacity to revise itself in accord with new information and new insights regarding options previously not recognized. Because the theory is structured to allow for this revision—indeed, to encourage it by putting a premium on informed, uncoerced choice of self-imposed norms—the theory can both explain and vindicate the thinking that gives rise to the theory and its revisions. In this fact lies my argument that the circularity contained in the theory is not vicious or stultifying and that the paradox developed in the last chapter can be entirely avoided.

Nevertheless, an important concern remains. There are limits to which the theory can be revised and continue to be a form of contractarianism. If I am assuming that in broad terms the theory itself is invulnerable to criticism, that it must always be the case that moral norms are justified for a people by their being willing to apply the norms to themselves when they are informed and uncoerced, am I not giving foundational status to the theory? Is not feminist contractarianism, despite its capacity for self-revision, a form of moral foundationalism?

We might conceive of foundationalism in a number of ways.[15] Perhaps the most common conception is that certain beliefs serve a "foundational" role with respect to the justification of other beliefs. These *basic* beliefs, as they are called, have this role because (1) they are not justified by reference to any other beliefs, and (2) all other beliefs are justified ultimately by reference to them. In the moral case, certain moral beliefs would be basic because their justification does not depend on any other moral beliefs, and all other moral beliefs are justified ultimately by reference to them. There might, of course, be just one basic moral belief, such as a belief that a certain form of utilitarianism is true. In the present instance the claim would be that feminist contractarianism entails that there is one basic moral belief—namely, the belief in feminist contractarianism—that explains how moral norms in a society are to be justified and hence how any other moral beliefs are to be justified by reference to justified moral norms.

It should be fairly clear that feminist contractarianism, as it has been conceived in this chapter and the last, would not be foundational in this sense. There are two main reasons that it is not. First, contractarianism is conceived by analogy with induction as a method of moral reasoning that may fail to get it right about what is morally required of us. Its vindication as a method of moral thinking, in other words, depends in part on how well it does in matching our initial assumptions about what really is morally required. Thus, its justification as a method depends on other moral beliefs. Second, and equally important, the very factors that allow its formulation to be adjusted in detail are factors involving other moral beliefs that can result in its being overturned altogether as a sound method of moral reasoning. By definition, basic beliefs cannot be vulnerable in this way.

In the next two sections, I will consider two objections that threaten to overthrow feminism contractarianism in the last way. The communitarian objection (really a collection of related concerns) centers on the apparently individualistic character of contractarian thinking and argues that the method presupposes a false conception of human motivation and social relations and is in fact the product of androcentric thinking about moral life. The objection can be conceived as appealing to information more readily available to the less privileged members of society, information that is propositional and experiential, which feminist contractarianism indeed seeks but which ultimately undermines this way of thinking about moral issues. The second objection focuses on information about the consequences of thinking about hypothetical rather than actual consent as a test of moral permissibility and argues that contractarianism in depending on the former yields a gender-biased moral perspective. Both objections can be conceived as difficulties internal to the contractarian method that purport defeat it on its own terms. In sum, the justification of feminist contractarianism itself depends on the theory's being consistent, given everything else we know, with *other* moral beliefs (e.g., that gender bias in evaluating moral norms is a moral error), and therefore the theory by its own terms violates one of the conditions defining moral foundationalism.

The term *foundationalism* can be used metaepistemically to refer not to a theory of justification (or knowledge) but to a style of doing epistemology. In fact, as Susan Haack observes, there are two distinct uses of the latter kind.[16] One is to refer to the idea that epistemology is an a priori discipline designed to provide a sound basis for our presumed empirical knowledge. It should be obvious that feminist contractarian does not begin to fit this sense of the term, even if we substitute "moral" for "empirical," since naturalized epistemology rejects the category of the a priori altogether. The other use is to refer to the idea that epistemic standards (perhaps epistemic standards for justifying moral beliefs) have an objective basis. This use of the term may seem to fit the theory and cannot be dismissed out of hand.

The epistemology advocated in this book is realist in that it assumes that a reality exists independently of our representations of it and that it can be known. Moreover, I have argued in chapter 8 that there is no a priori way to exclude the possibility of moral realism, that there is value that exists independently of our representations of it. Our epistemic norms are to be judged by how well they can guide us in discovering what is real. Feminist contractarianism would be no exception. It appears, therefore, that the present theory is committed to foundationalism in one of the metaepistemological uses of the term. But there is danger of serious confusion. To say that the epistemic norm of feminist contractarianism has an "objective basis" may suggest that the norm is somehow "basic" in the sense spelled out earlier—that the epistemic norm itself needs no justification and serves instead as a foundation for norms that are subject to error and depend on it for their justification. I have already argued, however, that feminist contractarianism does not and cannot be basic or foundational in *this* sense.

To say that feminist contractarianism has an objective basis is not to imply that it is infallible or even that it is by its nature or necessarily likely not to be mistaken. If it is likely not to be mistaken, that is in virtue of its causal role in the context of its use and the justification that arises from that context. I prefer, therefore, not to use the term to describe feminist contractarianism. Suppose that I am a moral realist, believing that some actions are wrong independently of whether anyone thinks that they are wrong. It would seem to invite confusion to label myself as a foundationalist just by virtue of the fact that I am a moral realist, especially if I thought that moral beliefs are prone to error and that no moral beliefs are basic. Nevertheless, I do believe that feminist contractarianism has an objective basis, however fallible that method is.

Part of the problem is that one can be a coherentist in one's theory of justification and still hold consistently that epistemic norms have an objective basis, though *coherentism* is normally a term used to designate an epistemology different from foundationalism. It might be thought, in fact, that the present theory of justification is coherentist in structure. I want to argue that it is not. First, what is coherentism? I take it to be the view that a belief is justified just in case it belongs to a coherent set of beliefs. What constitutes a coherent set of beliefs is, of course, a very long story, and there are many different theories of what constitutes coherence in this context, each corresponding to different version of coherentism. However it is defined, though, coherence is a relation among beliefs, not a relation of beliefs to something else, such as an independent reality. A central problem for this approach, therefore, is to explain how coherence itself can provide any genuine support for the beliefs that comprise a coherent set. To provide genuine support, coherence would have to give us a reason to expect that coherent beliefs have a better chance of accurately representing reality than beliefs that are not coherent or less coherent. It would have to give us a reason, that is, why they are more likely to have an objective basis.

It is not necessary to settle that issue to see that feminist contractarianism does not face this problem and hence that it has to be distinct from coherentism. Here is why. For feminist contractarianism to be justified (to any degree) just *is* in the final analysis for it to be likely to get it right (to that degree) about what is morally required. Justification is not essentially a matter of coherence, though coherence with beliefs that one thinks antecedently are right is obviously relevant. In naturalized epistemology we begin with views about what reality is like and then within our evolving theory try to explain how we can come to be justified in believing what we think we are justified in believing. Coherence of itself has no epistemic status, however defined. Whether or not feminist contractarianism has an objective basis, then, it is not a coherentist theory of justification.

The Communitarian Objection

I now want to address directly the communitarian objection alluded to earlier. For many feminists what is objectionable about the contractarian point of view, more than anything else, is its apparent presupposition that persons are essentially independent of others or at least should be conceived in this fashion for the purpose of justifying a system of morals.[17] In fact, according to these critics, persons are anything but independent. They are instead social creations who are deeply dependent on others for significant periods of their lives if not throughout. The illusion of independence is a product of social privilege and serves to rationalize a conception of minimal moral obligation that protects privilege and maintains the oppression of those on whose labor the privileged depend for their sense of freedom and power. Once the illusion is broken, the idea of morality as being based on the choices of fully independent contractors loses its relevance, if not its intelligibility.

I have considerable sympathy with this objection and have addressed it indirectly in the discussion of an ethic of care in the last chapter. I want now to address it more directly. The literature in which the objection occurs is immense and embodies many different forms. To provide a thorough reply, it will be helpful to disentangle six complaints that exemplify various aspects of the main objection and deal with each in turn. I do not believe that any of them occur in a pure form, but if, as I shall argue, none of them has any force against the version of contractarianism that I defend, then they do not have force when they occur in combination, either.

Egoism

Though contractarianism is not itself a form of ethical egoism (it does not argue that each person ought to do the best possible for her- or himself), it is often conceived as founding morals on the agreement among persons who are motivated to benefit just themselves individually. In other words, morals are founded on a compromise among egoists or at least persons who are assumed hypothetically to have no direct interest in each other. Thus, in Rawls's version each contractor is motivated to maximize her or his share of primary goods. For Rawls, what protects the weak from exploitation by the powerful is that the contractors must choose their principles behind a Veil of Ignorance hiding their identity as individuals, so that egoistic motives get translated into nonegoistic principles. Even though in his case the egoism is muted to a large extent by the conditions imposed on the contract, it is argued with some justice that making the starting point be one of mutual unconcern means that any movement away from it as the result of extra conditions being imposed requires a special reason, with the burden of proof being to show that a further condition is justified. The fundamental norm that lies behind the idea of social contract is, therefore, that of mutual unconcern and lack of any shared responsibility for each other. Though modification to the norm is possible, as in the case of Rawls, it is apt to appear arbitrary, unmotivated, and in tension with the spirit of contractarian thinking.

It should be clear from the last chapter, however, that the idea of a social contract need not begin with the assumption of mutual unconcern. Feminist contractarianism, in fact, begins with the opposite assumption. It assumes that the parties to the agreement care about what others who are similarly motivated can agree to when they are relevantly informed and uncoerced. They are motivated, in other words, to respond to what others want or would want if they are choosing freely and not out of ignorance and are similarly motivated. The norm in this conception, one could say, is that of mutual concern and shared responsibility. Moreover, this is seen, from the standpoint of naturalized theory to be consistent with the natural evolution of moral capacity as a response to the need for a stable basis for cooperation. It is from this perspective not arbitrary or unmotivated.

Abstraction

A related but different concern is the evident abstractness of the contractarian ideal, notably in its Kantian formulation from which the present theory receives inspiration. The communitarian focus in this regard is on how the character, personality, and cultural location of particular individuals is left out of account in the choice situation. To take an extreme case, the contractors in Rawls's Original Position do not know their own identities behind the Veil of Ignorance. The problem, on the nonpolitical side, is partly one of relevance and partly one of intelligibility. Relevance comes in because it is far from obvious why the imagined choices of an abstract shell of a person should have any bearing on how actual persons should behave, and intelligibility does because it may seem to make no sense for an abstract person, devoid of real preferences, to choose at all. On the political side, which will be addressed later in "Privilege" and in the next section, there is the worry that the abstraction is camouflage for the choice of an individual of privilege who only pretends (self-deceived though she or he may be) to imagine the choice of a purely abstract person.

Postponing an answer to the political objection, I find it easy to answer the abstractness charge with respect to relevance and intelligibility. Feminist contractarianism is a methodology for actual persons to apply in thinking about *actual* persons. People are to consider what they, as actual, identifiable persons with a history, cultural location, preferences, and so on, would freely and knowingly agree to impose on themselves when they are motivated to treat each other as ends. Issues regarding relevance and intelligibility may arise here. How do I know what I would choose if I were to be autonomous?

But these issues do not arise in virtue of the abstractness of the parties to the agreement.

Impersonality

The problem of impersonality can arise in dealing with actual persons when they are treated impersonally. It must be distinguished, therefore, from the previous complaint. The difficulty has been articulated in many different ways, but I find Michael Stocker's discussion of the schizophrenia of modern ethical theories the most persuasive.[18] Stocker's critique is very general, applying to modern utilitarian and deontological theories as well as to some formulations of contractarian theory, such as Gauthier's.[19] These theories separate our most powerful motives, like love, friendship, and community, and thus our deepest sources of personal pleasure and fulfilment, from the reasons we would have to act if we were perfectly moral. Stocker believes that, to the extent that we try to embody such reasons in our motives, our lives will fail to realize these essential human values and we will find our chosen goods "hollow, bitter, and inhumane."[20] He gives the example of visiting a friend in the hospital for the reason that doing this is in the circumstances the best means to maximize utility, or the only way to fulfill one's duty given the present balance of prima facie obligations, or perhaps what an ideal social contract requires. Something is lacking in one's reason for acting—indeed, lacking in moral merit and value.[21] What is lacking is that one is not acting for the sake of one's friend. Moreover, one's reason and motive for acting in this case, though morally ideal according to these theories, reveal a serious deficiency in character if one acts on this reason because one is incapable of acting from the motive of friendship.

Again, the complaint, though powerful against its intended target, is not pertinent to the present form of contractarianism. This is because the moral attitude toward others from which the theory flows is continuous with, and where relevant incorporates, caring about particular persons for their own sakes. One is not expected, in applying this way of moral thinking, to ignore for the moment one's bonds of love, friendship, and community. On the contrary, these bonds as well as personal projects will bear on what one can agree to, when choosing freely and knowingly, and this bearing will be legitimate as long as one is motivated to make the agreement by respect for the parties as ends. Far from excluding these considerations, the agreement would be ultimately founded on precisely those projects and bonds that give meaning to our lives and distinguish us from each other.

Individualism

The picture that the social contract tends to evoke is one of strangers seated around a negotiating table and bargaining for having some say in what the social contract will be like. They may be conceived as being actual persons who are not selfishly motivated and who care about each other as ends. Still, something is wrong with this picture, some will say, because the contractors are torn out of their social contexts, and it is these alone that give their lives moral significance. Indeed, it may be contended that apart from these contexts, they are not persons at all, since persons are essentially relational in their being.[22] In sum, contractarianism presupposes a false metaphysics of persons, treating them for the purpose of the theory as merely mental atoms floating in a social void and thus distorting their nature as moral beings.

This is another version of the objection to abstraction, this time focusing on abstraction from social context rather than on abstraction from an individual's (other) distinguishing features. It deserves to be considered in its own right, since the previous rejoinder does not apply. This is because the two requirements that the person have all relevant information and be uncoerced will inevitably entail a consideration of what the person would be like *apart* from her or his present social context in which her or his information and freedom of choice are imperfect. The fact that we are talking about an actual individual complete with all distinguishing characteristics is beside the point. The issue here is whether thinking of persons apart from those social limitations, regarding access to relevant information and new options, is to cease to think of them as genuine persons.

It is clear that we do not think of people as ceasing to be persons when they gain by degrees new information or new options. Incrementally, there does not seem to be a problem. If there is a difficulty, it must arise when the change in information or options is drastic. Feminist contractarianism does contemplate this kind of case. For example, we reflect on how people might modify their present social arrangements regarding child care if people were genuinely free to choose alternatives and the consequences of doing so were plainly in view. Though it will be difficult to ascertain for such large changes what people would choose if they could do so freely and knowingly, I do not see that there is any reason to suppose that contemplation of these complex empirical questions necessarily calls into question the idea that it would be particular, historical persons whose choices are at issue.

What the objection to individualism brings to the fore is the need to think of contractarianism as a method for gaining moral knowledge that is to be applied incrementally and socially. To avoid moral conservatism, we should make the increments as large as possible. That is, we want the method to suggest social arrangements that are as good as we can conceive them under the method. Still, there will be limits to our ability to envision options and get relevant information, given the social contexts in which we understand ourselves. This is why the method must be incremental. It must not purport to define once and for all what is morally best. The best that we can conceive now may be less than the best that we can conceive tomorrow. Moreover, progress toward better understanding will be a social undertaking, since individuals by themselves will be far more limited in ability to conceive options and gain information. For the method to succeed in practice, those that apply it must exemplify the moral virtues of cooperation and trustworthiness. This kind of incremental and social approach to moral knowledge, however, accords well with feminist contractarianism.

Rationality

Most often contractarian theories emphasize the need for the contractual agreement to be founded on reason. This is especially clear in contemporary versions, for example, in Gauthier's Hobbesian and Rawls's Kantian theories. The problem with emphasizing reason or rationality is partly that it calls to mind the objections to egoism, abstraction, impersonality, and individualism already addressed. Both Gauthier and Rawls think of rationality as being the maximization of individual preference satisfaction, thus linking rationality to the objections against individualism and egoism. Since in each case rationality is formulated in abstraction from actual individuals and their bonds with particular other individuals, the objections to abstraction and impersonality are also brought into play. There is, however, another aspect to the emphasis on rationality that I have not discussed: the traditional contrast between reason and emotion. Because the dichotomy between reason and emotion is gendered in our culture, the emphasis on reason and rationality has tended to associate contractarian theories in the minds of many feminists with a male-biased viewpoint. The objection here is not, of course, that feminists think men tend to be rational and women tend not to be but that emotional dimensions of our moral lives, dimensions that are crucial to our sense of social responsibility, are virtually invisible in modern contractarian theory and that this result is in large part a consequence of a sexist disassociation of reason from emotion.

It should be clear that the contractarianism defended here does not buy into that dichotomy. Indeed, there is no reference to reason or rationality in the formulation of my theory. As was made plain in the last chapter, the parties must agree knowingly, but their information about the nature of their choice should be no less emotional and experiential than it is rational and well reasoned. A brief account of emotional knowledge was sketched in the fourth chapter. The importance of this kind of knowledge is clear in the hybrid theory of moral judgment set forth in the previous chapter. Its importance is also aptly illustrated in Okin's critique of Rawls's theory of justice. If justice does not extend to the family, and for Rawls it does not, then children may not be raised knowing experientially what it is like to do the tasks now assigned largely to their opposite sex and hence will not develop the "sense of justice" that Rawls rightly believes is essential to acting justly in situations in which one must be able to put oneself in another's place. The psychological underpinning of his theory—namely, the emotional information that can only be acquired experientially—Okin argues, is denied by the sexist restriction of his theory to the public realm. Unfortunately, Okin herself, while recognizing the great importance of this emotional knowledge, does not in her revision of Rawls indicate how this knowledge enters into her conception of his Original Position. In the present theory the concept of information has been broadened to exclude the artificial division between reason and emotion.

Privilege

Finally, we come to what may be the most serious aspect of the feminist communitarian complaint. This is that the very idea of a social contract between persons who are to a very significant extent independent of others for their material and emotional needs is based on an illusion enjoyed by the privileged members of society who do not realize that their sense of power and agency depends more or less directly on the oppression of those to whom such independence is all too plainly not an option. For reasons developed in response to the other objections, the parties to the contract conceived in the present theory are not assumed to be independent in the ways imagined. Quite to the contrary, they are supposed, when considering alternative social arrangements, to learn about the costs that are incurred by many in sustaining the illusion of independence that some enjoy. But this reply is not to the point. The problem is that the illusion is remarkably impervious to contrary information when persons are entertaining merely hypothetical scenarios that they are able to construct from their own perspective. A privileged male, putting himself hypothetically into the place of a female in present society, may say to himself, "If I were in her shoes, I would be lucky." He may say this even if he has been informed that the woman does not count herself lucky. Because hypothetical consent is so easily misconceived, the hypothetical nature of the imagined contract makes it of limited practical relevance in the present circumstances of male domination and privilege. The problem is important enough to devote a separate section to it.

Taking Consent Seriously

In an important essay[23] Alison Jaggar raises a number of potentially damaging criticisms directed against the hypothetical character of contractarianism and then argues that, if one wishes to take consent seriously, one should seek actual rather than hypothetical consent. Some of the criticisms have been dealt with already, at least implicitly, such as her point that rationality is philosophically contested, so that social contract theory puts weight on this notion at its own peril. Her criticism that the theory is impractical, however, bears directly on our present concern. It is worth addressing, not only for its own sake but for the light it sheds on the problem of how privilege distorts projections into a hypothetical choice situation.

After pointing out that contractarians typically aim at elaborating what Rawls calls "perfect justice" (principles that characterize well-ordered societies in favorable circumstances), Jaggar raises the following objection:

> The very notion of developing a distinctively feminist perspective in practical ethics, however, presupposes our habitation of a pre-feminist world that by definition is far from ideal. This world is characterized by male domination and its inevitable concomitants of brutality, exploitation, and ideological distortion. Feminists daily confront the realities of rape, prostitution, pornography, and incest, as well as environmental destruction, war, and grotesquely unequal access to world resources. Reflection on the notion of hypothetical consent may be able to demonstrate (if demonstration is needed) that these atrocities would not characterize the perfectly just society, that they are morally wrong, unjust, and/or irrational; but it seems capable of giving little moral guidance in dealing with them when they occur.[24]

The practical problem for Jaggar is how the ideal world of the hypothetical contract can guide us, "very concrete people who are only partially free, rational, and informed—often, indeed, quite ignorant, damaged, and corrupted."[25] Jaggar believes that our best strategy is to seek actual rather than hypothetical dialogue, recognizing that "consent given hypothetically is never the moral equivalent of actual consent" having "no independent moral force, any more than hypothetical experiments have independent evidential force."[26]

An important truth is contained here that helps resolve the problem of privilege with which we began. At the same time serious confusion appears about how actual and hypothetical consent are related. Jaggar counsels us to work together to obtain actual rather than hypothetical consent to figure out what to do. We are, in other words, to seek actual moral consensus: "feminists (and others) who work in practical ethics and who are inspired by the egalitarian and anti-authoritarian ideals that motivate the contract tradition should refrain from speculations about hypothetical consent and devote their energy instead to reflecting on and indeed actively pursuing real-life moral consensus."[27] But not any actual moral consensus will do. As Jaggar notes in the same paragraph, what is needed is "consensus reached legitimately, in the sense recognized by the contract tradition."[28] The difficulty is that to figure out whether a consensus has been reached legitimately, it will be necessary to reach that consensus in a "dialogue under fair conditions, a requirement necessary to ensure that all points of view are given equal consideration."[29] These are, in fact, the contractarian conditions of informed, uncoerced consent, the very conditions that Jaggar worries cannot even be approximated in actuality. What practical point can there be in seeking this consensus if we know that it is practically impossible to obtain?

The way out of this confusion is to recognize that when we seek to get actual consensus or agreement under "fair" conditions of inquiry, we are doing exactly what we should be doing if we want to know what we *would* consent to (hypothetically) under such conditions. Actual consent under these conditions is precisely what would confirm the hypothetical. Ironically, it is because we value this knowledge (knowing whether we would agree under ideal conditions) that we attempt to approximate ideal conditions of inquiry in seeking actual agreement. Contrary to Jaggar, the two pursuits, actual and hypothetical, are tightly tied together. To learn about the actual under ideal conditions is at the same time to learn about the hypothetical under ideal conditions.

The truth is, however, that we are unable to achieve the ideal conditions in practice. As Jaggar makes clear, most of the time we are far from being able to carry out dialogue under ideal conditions of inquiry. What we can do instead is attempt to approximate these conditions as best we can and then try to extrapolate from what we know under imperfect conditions to a conclusion about what we would agree to under better conditions, being prepared to revise our judgment as we get new information. This practice is, of course, entirely consistent with what the feminist contractarianism defended here implies. If we want to know what is morally required, not merely in the obvious cases but also in the more difficult, morally complex choices, we should, following the contractarian method, seek actual moral consensus under conditions that come as close as we can make them be to those of informed, uncoerced consent. Actual consensus under conditions as fair as we can make them is, in the model before us, the best evidence we can possibly have about what is morally required of us.

This result sheds light on the problem of privilege and its attendant illusions regarding independence. It is all too easy to speculate about a hypothetical moral consensus without seeking any actual moral consensus—that is, without having any good evidence for one's speculations. Those in positions of privilege who want moral insight will have a strong motive for doing so if the process of seeking actual consensus is apt to reveal oppression as a basis for privilege. A hypothetical contract among persons with positions of privilege may therefore tend to acquire normative status, even though *this* hypothetical situation is not relevant to finding what the relevant persons would freely and knowingly agree to accept as norms governing everyone. Contractarian theory often looks as if it is based on such irrelevant purely hypothetical situations. For example, in Rawls and Gauthier the actual method of calculating the agreement or collective choice is so structured as to make actual agreement irrelevant. Against this way of thinking, Jaggar's approach makes excellent moral and theoretical sense. Any conception of hypothetical agreement that makes actual agreement of all kinds morally irrelevant is going to be contrary to the emancipatory and antiauthoritarian spirit of the contractarian ideal. The hypothetical of privilege, as we might call it, has no moral standing. But hypotheticals about what actual persons would consent to if their options were greater and their information more complete does have moral standing. Jaggar's point, reinterpreted in light of the present theory, is that the most honest method for learning what that consent would look like is to endeavor to seek it in actuality under conditions that come as close as possible to the ideal.

Notes

1. A summary of how the reasoning goes may be found in my "Can Biology Make Ethics Objective?" *Biology and Philosophy* 11 (1996): 21–31. For a critical review of biological accounts of ethics, see Alexander Rosenberg, "The Biological Justification of Ethics: A Best-Case Scenario," *Social Philosophy and Policy* 8 (1990): 86–101.

2. See Robert Axelrod, *The Evolution of Cooperation* (New York: Basic Books, 1984), for a clear exposition of the relevance of iterated Prisoner's Dilemma games for the evolution of a disposition to cooperate. For a recent illuminating study of how game theory can help explain the evolution of morals naturalistically, see Brian Skyrms, *Evolution of the Social Contract* (Cambridge: Cambridge University Press, 1996).

3. Something like this strategy is adopted in my "Can Biology Make Ethics Objective?" and "Sociobiology and the Possibility of Ethical Naturalism," in *Morality, Reason, and Truth*, David Copp and David Zimmerman, eds. (Totowa, N.J.: Rowman & Allanheld, 1985), 270–96. See also Michael Ruse, "Evolution and Ethics: The Sociobiological Approach," in *Ethical Theory: Classical and Contemporary Writings*, 2d ed., Louis P. Pojman, ed. (Belmont, Calif.: Wadsworth, 1995), 91–107.

4. See, for example, Ruth Hubbard, *The Politics of Women's Biology* (New Brunswick, N.J.: Rutgers University Press, 1992), 109–13. For a good guide to the feminist literature on this topic, see the extensive bibliographic essay by Faye Chadwell in Sue V. Rosser, *Biology and Feminism: A Dynamic Interaction* (New York: Twayne, 1992), 175–85. A rigorous general critique of sociobiology, especially in its application to human behavior, is Philip Kitcher, *Vaulting Ambition* (Cambridge, Mass.: MIT Press, 1985).

5. For a thorough, up-to-date discussion, see Bonnie B. Spanier, *Im/partial Science: Gender Ideology in Molecular Biology* (Bloomington: Indiana University Press, 1995).

6. I take it that this point is too well established to need argument. For the details, see Spanier, *Im/partial Science*.

7. Axelrod, *The Evolution of Cooperation*.

8. A good discussion of the units of selection debate may be found in Elliott Sober, *The Nature of Selection: Evolutionary Theory in Philosophical Focus* (Cambridge, Mass.: MIT Press, 1984).

9. A sophisticated argument in this direction is in David Sloan Wilson and Elliott

Sober, "Reintroducing Group Selection to the Human Behavior Sciences," *Behavior and Brain Sciences* 17 (1994): 585–608.

10. The general point is made in Phyllis Rooney, "Putting Naturalized Epistemology to Work" in *Epistemology: The Big Questions,* Linda Alcoff, ed. (Oxford: Blackwell, in press).

11. "Natural Kinds," in W. V. Quine, *Ontological Relativity and Other Essays* (New York: Columbia University Press, 1969), 133.

12. Hilary Kornblith, *Inductive Inference and Its Natural Ground: An Essay in Naturalistic Epistemology* (Cambridge, Mass.: MIT Press, 1993), 63.

13. See "Native Inferential Tendencies" section of chapter 5.

14. There is the problem in contract theory of the unreasonable holdout, someone who does not care about reaching an agreement and can veto any reasonable efforts to reach agreement. The suggestion is that we are motivated to reach a "reasonable" agreement—that is, one that would be reached if at all possible by those who are motivated to reach agreement, at least with those who are similarly motivated. This general idea and indeed my general approach to contractarian thinking has much in common with Richard W. Miller's concept of justice as social freedom; see his *Moral Differences: Truth, Justice, and Conscience in a World of Conflict* (Princeton, N.J.: Princeton University Press, 1992), 185. Miller attributes the basic idea to Thomas M. Scanlon, "Contractualism and Utilitarianism," in *Utilitarianism and Beyond,* Amartya Sen and Bernard Williams, eds. (Cambridge: Cambridge University Press, 1982).

15. Here I follow the distinctions made in Susan Haack, *Evidence and Inquiry: Towards Reconstruction in Epistemology* (Cambridge, Mass.: Blackwell, 1993).

16. Haack, *Evidence and Inquiry,* 186.

17. This and related concerns are expressed by feminist critics, many of whom would not classify themselves as "communitarian." I use the term for convenience to stand for the various kinds of complaints about contractarian thinking that are described in this section. Some of the places where they are voiced are, Seyla Benhabib, "The Generalized and the Concrete Other: The Kohlberg-Gilligan Controversy and Feminist Theory," in *Women and Moral Theory,* Eva Feder Kittay and Diana T. Meyers, eds. (Totowa, N.J.: Rowman & Littlefield, 1987); Annette Baier, "What Do Women Want in a Moral Theory?" *Nous* 19 (1985): 53–64; Annette Baier, "The Need for More Than Justice," in *Science, Morality, and Feminist Theory,* Marsha Hanen and Kai Nielsen, eds. (Calgary: University of Calgary Press, 1987), 41–56; Carole Pateman, *The Sexual Contract* (Palo Alto, Calif.: Stanford University Press, 1988); Virgina Held, *Feminist Morality: Transforming Culture, Society, and Politics* (Chicago: University of Chicago Press, 1993); Joan C. Tronto, *Moral Boundaries: A Political Argument for an Ethic of Care* (New York: Routledge, 1993); and Iris Marion Young, *Justice and the Politics of Difference* (Princeton, N.J.: Princeton University Press, 1990). The worries are also expressed by many nonfeminist theorists.

18. Michael Stocker, "The Schizophrenia of Modern Ethical Theories," *Journal of Philosophy* 73 (1976): 453–66.

19. David Gauthier, *Morals by Agreement* (Oxford: Clarendon, 1986).

20. Stocker, "Schizophrenia," 466.

21. See his reference to moral merit; Stocker, "Schizophrenia," 462.

22. See Annette Baier, "Cartesian Persons," *Philosophia* 10 (1981): 169–88, and

Lorraine Code, "Second Persons," in *Science, Morality, and Feminist Theory*, Hanen and Nielsen, eds., 357–82.

23. Alison Jaggar, "Taking Consent Seriously: Feminist Ethics and Actual Moral Dialogue," in *The Applied Ethics Reader*, Earl Winkler and Jerrold Coombs, eds. (Oxford: Blackwell, 1993).

24. Jaggar, "Taking Consent Seriously," 79.

25. Jaggar, "Taking Consent Seriously," 80.

26. Jaggar, "Taking Consent Seriously," 81–82.

27. Jaggar, "Taking Consent Seriously," 82.

28. Jaggar, "Taking Consent Seriously," 82.

29. Jaggar, "Taking Consent Seriously," 82.

Chapter 11

Conclusion

The Paradoxes Are Illusions

I introduced in chapter 1 seven apparent contradictions or paradoxes that seem to be inherent in the concept of a naturalized feminist epistemology. In the intervening chapters I have offered resolutions of these paradoxes at various levels. I summarize here how I believe that they are to be resolved based on the foregoing distinctions and arguments.

The Problem of Normativity for Naturalized Epistemology

Naturalized epistemology, at least as Quine would have it, is epistemology pursued as part of science, but this appears to imply that an inherently normative inquiry about how we ought to form our beliefs should be reduced to a purely descriptive inquiry that can at best explain how we do form our beliefs. Though it is impossible that what is normative should be purely descriptive, the appearance of contradiction depends on the implausible assumption (shared by Quine among many others) that science, when it is doing its job, is merely engaged in describing how the world is. Countless studies of science make clear that contextual values of various kinds operate in science. But these studies, it may be argued, do not necessarily show us how science ought to proceed. Fact-value holism, however, has the implication that contextual values have a positive role to play in science and hence that, even when working ideally, science is in significant measure a normative enterprise.

Can science be normative, though, in the ultimate sense that epistemology is? Can it deal with the metanormative questions that are typically raised in epistemology, such as about the norms of inference and evaluation that we ought to heed? In fact, there is no way to argue, given meaning-value holism, that the concept of science precludes consideration of such questions, once we suppose that questions of value generally are relevant to the direction that science should take. The science question in feminism is in part how to mod-

217

ify the practice of science to make science more accurate and comprehensive in its depiction of social reality and more conducive to social justice. Changes of this order raise ultimate questions about which norms for scientific inquiry are best and how to answer such questions. These are matters internal to science in the view that meaning and value are interdependent.

The Problem of Normativity for Feminist Epistemology

The next problem is somewhat the reverse of the previous. While naturalizing epistemology seems to rob it of its normative power, making it feminist seems to make it normative in the wrong way. Epistemology, it is thought, should set aside political values and other aims that are not about pursuing truth for its own sake; it is, by its very nature, concerned with impartial inquiry after the truth. Politically motivated epistemology thus appears to be a contradiction in terms.

Some would avoid the apparent paradox by questioning the idea of epistemology as concerned with objective knowledge. This move has its own costs, however, both epistemic and political. A better solution is to question the supposed opposition between political commitment and the pursuit of objective knowledge. This is done by appeal to the same interdependence between fact and value used to resolve the first paradox. We suppose that there are structures in the world that obtain objectively—that is, whether or not anyone believes they obtain or has evidence that they do. We learn about these structures through empirical investigation. This includes the testing of hypotheses against the evidence. Because of the nature of the testing process, contextual values inevitably come into play. These can have a negative influence (e.g., making invisible alternative explanations of the evidence), but their influence can also be positive (e.g., making possible the recognition of alternative hypotheses that otherwise would have been missed). There is therefore no necessary incompatibility between inquiry guided by principles of evidence that lead to objective knowledge and inquiry guided also by values that are feminist. The apparent contradiction is an illusion based on a superficial understanding of objective inquiry.

The Problem of Circularity for Naturalized Epistemology

The fact that naturalized epistemology attempts to explain the possibility of knowledge by first assuming some knowledge creates the appearance of an untenable circularity. For example, to demonstrate how this epistemology can explain how our knowledge of the natural world is possible, Quine attempts to explain the reliability of induction by invoking Darwin's theory of natural selection. How can he begin to explain the possibility of such knowledge, including knowledge of how evolution occurred through natural selection, by assuming that we already have this knowledge, indeed, already have it by the use of inductive reasoning? He appears to assume understanding of the very thing he proposes to explain.

Though this problem may appear to be very different from the others, its solution also lies in recognizing the interdependence of facts and values. We seek to justify our factual claims about the natural world by appeal to norms of reasoning, but the latter are to be justified in turn by their guiding us more often than not to the facts. The thinking here is admittedly circular; the question is whether the circularity is objectionable. I have argued that it is not, provided that the assumptions made cannot guarantee their own justification and can genuinely explain why the norms at issue are as successful as they are. Quine's Darwinian explanation of why primitive forms of inductive reasoning often work provides a useful example. It does not guarantee that induction is justified; the skeptic, rather than these forms of induction, may be vindicated if the explanation is not inductively confirmed. Moreover, the explanation proposed, if confirmed, will be a genuine explanation, not a restatement in different words of what is to be explained.

The justification of norms for moral reasoning is similar with an important difference. The standard of success here is getting it right about how matters stand morally. To measure success, we must therefore make some assumptions about how matters do stand morally. We must begin by assuming that we have some moral knowledge when it is the possibility of moral knowledge that we want to explain. It does not follow, however, that the question is begged against the moral skeptic, for the explanation need not succeed in explaining how moral knowledge is possible, and in that case the assumptions with which we began would not be vindicated. Also, the explanation proposed, if confirmed, must genuinely explain the success of the moral reasoning rather than merely assert its success; the latter would be viciously circular. The last chapter develops this form of justification for a contractarian theory of social justice in which norms of moral reasoning are vindicated through an account of their origins along with preliminary assumptions about what is just.

From a feminist standpoint the deeply self-reflexive character of this mode of justification is particularly attractive, since it explains why it is appropriate to examine the origins of norms to see whether they are justified. Knowing their origins can enhance their credibility, but it can undermine them as well. Too often, norms thought by those in authority to be self-evident are normative because of the powerful interests that they serve rather than for reasons that would justify adherence to them. The origins of norms fall within the context of discovery and for that reason may be thought irrelevant. But it would be wrong to exclude this matter from the context of justification. The first three paradoxes rest precisely on that mistake. In assuming the independence of the two contexts, they deny fact-value holism.

The Problem of Circularity for Feminist Epistemology

Feminist epistemology begins with the knowledge that feminist goals are worth pursuing. The problem is how to explain knowledge of this kind without removing the justification for regarding the epistemology as feminist. If the value of pursuing feminist goals is explained without reference to feminism, theory that explains it appears not to be really feminist; but if the worth of feminist goals must be assumed, then the theory appears not to be a genuine epistemology, since it does not proceed from first principles. The resolution is implicit in those preceding. The worth of pursuing feminist goals can be explained by their role in gaining empirical knowledge of nature; this is possible because such value, given fact-value holism, may be inseparable from the discovery of other facts and thus may have an essential role in both epistemology and science. At the same time, assuming its value need not undercut its ability to help in explaining its own objective status, provided that it can do so without begging the question against the skeptic and the explanation offered is actually explanatory.

There is, however, a possible source of puzzlement regarding the proposed resolution. Though I have emphasized at various points in the book that the assumption that feminist goals are worth pursuing should not be interpreted as being beyond question—and cannot be, given the interdependence of fact and value—puzzlement may persist about how the assumption can play an essential role and still not be held dogmatically. How is the question not begged against someone who is skeptical about the value of pursuing feminist goals?

Feminists have a multiplicity of goals and frequently disagree about what they should be, how to achieve them, what their relative value is, and so on. The assumption that feminist goals are worth pursuing has to be understood as meaning that the most basic are worth achieving, such as eliminating the systemic subordination of women to men. Let us, then, focus on whether such a basic goal has to be maintained dogmatically within feminist epistemology, as it is conceived here. The explanation of why this assumption would not be maintained dogmatically is to be found in how the assumption is supported. It is supported through myriad considerations, such as what norms governing the social, political, and economic relations between men and women women would freely choose to be guided by when relevant experiences and facts are brought to bear. To say that the assumption is not maintained dogmatically is just to allow that the assumption could be given up if the relevant justifying factors were fundamentally different than they are. This is not to suggest, I should add, that there is any remotely plausible reason to think that they are different. Soundly based conviction is not to be confused with dogmatism.

Even within this massive source of support, though, feminist values play a role, for access to relevant experiences and facts will depend on political motivation and even on one's conception of social justice, as I argued in chapter 9. It may appear, therefore, that there is still room for dogmatism, and the problem of circularity for feminist epistemology now reemerges. If knowledge of the worth of basic feminist values has an essential role to play in explaining such knowledge, can such a circular explanation really explain how this knowledge is possible?

The answer is fairly simple. Dogmatism has no place here, and the circularity is not question begging because the relevant facts and experiences that would give the support may not be forthcoming. Although feminist motives and values may be necessary in order for a person to locate the relevant data or to be in a position to have the relevant experiences, it does not follow that such commitment is *sufficient* to produce these facts and experiences. Whether a person has them will depend on what the facts are and how the world is structured to make possible the relevant experiences. Political motivation thus was needed to discover facts about the development of coronary heart disease in women, but these facts in themselves are not artifacts of that motivation. One begins with certain basic assumptions to get access to grounds of support that have explanatory power in their own right. The assumptions by themselves do not guarantee that those grounds of support will exist. Only if they did would the procedure be viciously circular and the grounds of support illusory.

The Problem of Naturalizing Value

The problems of normativity and circularity are problems of methodology and are resolved by appeal to the interdependence of fact and value. There is, however, the ontological question of what value is, and the problem for a naturalized epistemology is to say what value is within a naturalistic worldview. Philosophers who embrace a naturalized epistemology are divided on how to account for value. In one view no facts are intrinsically normative; the appearance that there are such facts—for example, that it is a moral fact that the subordination of women is wrong—is caused by a need to treat our normative commitments as if they were a response to moral facts. In the realist view, moral facts exist; in a naturalistic worldview this means that moral facts are natural facts, no different in kind from those revealed in science. I have argued that moral realism gives the most straightforward construal of feminist moral claims, but this view will appear paradoxical to many. Besides the standard arguments against naturalized moral realism, there is the worry that this position and the debate surrounding it abstracts from the political context of moral thinking. The idea that moral wrongness can exist apart from anyone's perspective, as moral realism implies, may indeed appear inconsistent with the interdependence of fact and value on which the previous resolutions depend.

The resolution of this problem in the later chapters proceeds on three different levels. In chapter 7 I counter the most serious arguments against moral realism, arguing that the arguments from internalism and explanatory impotence both depend on denying fact-value holism. Though in itself this defense offers no positive support for there being some natural facts that are intrinsically normative, when it is linked in chapter 8 to Quine's holism about meaning, the resulting meaning-value holism has the consequence that there is no way to preclude the possibility on the grounds of meaning that a factual claim might function to express normative commitment. This result opens the way to a normative realism in which the web of belief stretches farther than Quine concedes.

In chapters 9 and 10 I develop a contractarian form of feminist moral realism in which factual claims about hypothetical choice can serve to express moral commitment. This theory is based on a hybrid account of moral judgment that postulates two coordinated systems of social control. In the evolutionarily older one moral judgments function to motivate behavior; this system explains the intuitions that drive noncognitivism. In the other system moral judgments are true or false and function to evaluate whether such motivation and the norms embedded in them are socially justified. Contractarianism is interpreted in this context as a theory about what constitutes an adequate justification of this kind.

The theory does not fit the standard dichotomy of cognitive versus noncognitive, since it allows that a person can feel and hence judge that something is morally wrong without believing it to be wrong and that a person can believe something is morally wrong without feeling that it is and hence without being moved to act as if it is. Normally a person judges in both ways. This means that normally moral judgments have propositional content and can represent moral facts. The theory is, therefore, realist. This part does not, however, diminish the motivational dimension of moral judgment. In fact, moral beliefs have normative force only because it is normal that the moral judgments in which they figure function to move us to feel and act in morally relevant ways. Moreover, the theory implies that the so-called noncognitive elements that move us to feel and act have a cognitive function. They can provide reliable nonpropositional representations of our moral situation, making the theory realist even in the motivational dimension of moral judgment.

Feminist values are fundamental to the justification of moral norms on which the possibility of moral knowledge rests. Moral norms are justified only when they would be chosen under the right conditions of motivation, and determining whether they are met can depend on the operation of feminist values. The interdependence of fact and value is thus built into the realism even at the level of the conditions defining when a social choice would justify a moral norm. At the same time the theory is self-reflexive. It is possible for it to justify norms and thereby support moral claims that would undermine the feminist or other values that operate in determining whether the conditions of social choice are met. In keeping with its naturalism, the theory, though realist, cannot be construed as offering a foundation for morality.

But what about the method of contractarian reasoning itself? To meet the moral skeptic, I draw an analogy between justifying the methods of inductive reasoning and justifying the methods of moral reasoning. These methods themselves justify conclusions about the world. We are talking about justifications of justifications when we move to justifying these methods. The analogy provides insight into how one might proceed naturalistically to justify primitive modes of moral thinking by appeal to natural selection. As in the case of induction, preliminary assumptions are made about morals of the very kind that the moral thinking in question is supposed to justify, but the circularity is not vicious. Contractarian thinking builds on the previous conclusions about moral method. Included in this thinking is the motivation to treat others as ends. This idea is interpreted naturalistically as necessary to the evolution of stable social commitments. Finally, I defend this thinking, on its naturalistic interpretation, against communitarian objections and the worry that contractarianism does not take seriously the need for genuine consent.

The Bias Paradox

The contractarianism defended here contains the Kantian ideal of impartiality: that no person should be treated as a means only. The importance of this ideal is reflected in the complaint that an institution is gender biased, being "partial" to a standpoint that privileges men. Despite the value of impartiality for feminists, the ideal has received a bad name. This is because impartiality is often associated with value neutrality, especially in regard to political concerns. The effort to be value neutral can then mask the ways that pervasive norms reflecting dominant interests shape our thinking and make the views of those on the margins of society appear biased. The ideal of impartiality thus appears itself to be biased, implying paradoxically that impartiality is unacceptable as an ideal because it fails to be impartial.

Louise Antony, who recently called attention to this paradox, has argued that we need to distinguish between good biases and bad, suggesting that the good ones are the ones that lead to true conclusions and knowledge. The implication is that value neutrality as an ideal is indeed defective but that this need not impugn the ideal of impartiality provided that it is understood differently. I have argued that this resolution works but only if we understand knowledge from a realist perspective. Various reasons for accepting a realist understanding of knowledge are developed in chapter 3, including that it enables us to explain how "good science" can be systematically gender biased even when it follows all the rules of evidence. That realism provides a coherent resolution of the bias paradox is among these reasons.

Realism figures prominently in the exposition of a empiricism in which feminist values are internal to its methodology. Those values are seen to be conducive to achieving knowledge understood realistically. It would be a mistake to suppose, however, that this consideration is the only reason for wanting feminist values to be internal to empiricist methodology. That methodology, as argued in chapter 2, also affects the kinds of projects and aims that would be pursued in feminist science. One of those aims would be social justice. This makes sense once realism is extended to include moral values. End norms are, I have argued, as much a part of the fabric of scientific investigation as methodological norms. Among them is the end of understanding the natural world, including the value of social justice. Since to recognize the value of social justice is normally to be moved to pursue it, the end norm of social justice can become part of science and explain why feminist values should be part of it. These justified moral values, understood realistically, can thus help to resolve the bias paradox. They are themselves good biases.

The Paradox of Male Feminism

In the spirit of reflexivity, the standpoint of the book ought to be turned on its author. If the context of discovery, including one's sex, race, social position, and personal history, are key factors in determining one's chances at reaching an objective view of the world and if multiple privilege in these respects are apt to work against one, how is the feminist epistemology I advocate anything short of self-refuting, since I am privileged in these respects and many more? In particular, how is my male feminism possible, on even my own terms?

The book does not argue that privilege makes feminist insight impossible. That conclusion would indeed render this book a fraud, but it would also imply, ironically, that those who are privileged have an ironclad excuse for any lack of understanding they might have about their role in oppression. The book does argue, however, that the genesis of one's ideas is relevant to whether they are justified. This is certainly true in my own case. The book is an attempt to reconcile two approaches to epistemology that have been important to my own philosophical development. One, initiated by Quine, had its groundwork prepared for me when he was my teacher in the early sixties; the other became important to me through the feminist philosophers whose writings and conversations challenged the conception of philosophy in which I had been trained. A central concern has been whether the values that I have learned to respect in each of these approaches are distorting my understanding of the other or of the traditional approaches with which both conflicted. This concern has not been put to rest but rather heightened by the naturalized feminist epistemology that has come to make sense to me.

A worry that I anticipate on the feminist side is that the book is largely devoted to discussion of issues germane to those who are immersed in academic epistemology and thus addressed to an audience of experts with little relevance for anyone who is not interested in these matters or who wants to engage a wider audience in opposing the subordination of women. This book is self-consciously aimed at those who care about "strictly" academic philosophy. I so care, so the book reflects my preoccupations in this regard. I also care about more practical matters beyond the scope of this project and am grateful that so many feminist theorists and activists are pursuing them. Still, the focus that I have chosen is more narrow, addressed to those who are privileged. Does the book, then, not reflect my male socialization?

No doubt it does, yet my narrowness may be an advantage where "strictly" academic philosophy is a site of gender bias. The way to combat the dismissal of feminist concerns there, I have argued, is to transform such philosophy from the inside. I think of this book as an effort to collaborate with many other feminist philosophers who are committed to this project. What I add that might advance the discussion in one respect or another will probably indicate respects in which my history, training, and interlocutors are different from those of others. The theory of the book does not imply that a male feminist could not make a positive contribution in this way. What the theory does imply is that a male feminist would be unlikely to contribute anything useful if he were to attempt the project alone (or just in the company of good men) or if he were not expecting to be changed by feminists whom he studied and who questioned his thinking.

Is It Really Feminism? Or Philosophy?

When I first attempted, some ten years ago, to incorporate feminist concerns explicitly into my research and published work, skeptical colleagues tended to respond in one of two very different ways. First, they questioned whether what I was doing was really philosophy. I was taking as a given the legitimacy of a feminist political commitment and allowing it to guide my reasoning. A true philosopher, they thought, would base "her" conclusions on more general principles whose legitimacy should be evident to everyone. This response was familiar, since I heard it often enough when others had presented feminist philosophical views to the same audience. When my thought developed further and I was able to argue that my views were actually consistent with some of the very principles and insights shared by my critics, I was told that, though my position now made good sense and was indeed philosophical, there was nothing new or particularly feminist about it. This response, too, I had heard before when others defended their feminist views by appeal to assumptions that the audience shared. Together these responses present a dilemma: Basic feminist premises are either supported by an argument that a nonfeminist could accept or not. If they are not, the right to call a view based on them *philosophical* is denied; but if they are so supported, the right to call a view based on them *feminist* is denied. It would appear to follow that there can be no feminist philosophy.

The dilemma is a generalized version of the problem of circularity for feminist epistemology. Already I have indicated why I believe that this paradox is an illusion. May I not respond here in the same way? I believe that I can, but in my experience the illusion of paradox in this case is not easy to dispel. Let me, then, in conclusion, pursue it with some attention to the ways that it might apply to various parts of the book.

Because I have been perhaps too sensitive to the charge of not defending feminist assumptions, it may be argued that, in showing how feminist values are consistent with naturalized epistemology, I have produced philosophy that is not intrinsically feminist. I have heard this complaint, in fact, from a feminist standpoint theorist in criticism of my defense of feminist empiricism.[1] The feminism there (Part I) appears to her to be merely an accidental by-product of my empiricism and not intrinsic to my epistemology. A similar complaint might be raised about the incorporation of feminism in the naturalized epistemology of Parts II and III. There the main epistemological work is done, it might be argued, by Quinean holism, not by feminism per se. Finally, in Part IV, moral knowledge is to be explained by a form of Kantian social contract theory. Again, feminism may appear to be at best an accidental by-product of views that have no essential feminist content.

How is the dilemma an illusion? Consider the contention that in feminist empiricism the feminism there is merely a by-product of the empiricism and thus nothing is essentially feminist about this epistemology. The objection presupposes that the empiricist principles set forth in chapter 2, such as those that set standards for empirical testing, can be applied neutrally and thus involve no contextual values or commitments. If that were possible, we might suppose that the feminist values contained in feminist empiricism could be vindicated by appeal to a methodology that is not itself intrinsically feminist (or value laden in any other way) and could serve as foundation for feminist values. But it is an illusion that such neutrality exists. The empiricist principles cannot be applied independently of drawing on the context of discovery (to see, e.g., whether plausible alternatives explanations of the evidence are possible). This context, all sides agree, is shaped by contextual values. Moreover, without the supposition that this empiricism can be free of contextual values, the idea that the feminism contained in feminist empiricism can be vindicated by an empiricist half that is nonfeminist has no plausibility. For the only way there could be a nonfeminist empiricism is for the principles of empiricism to be applied in conjunction with *other* values, and such empiricism, the record shows, does not tend to support feminist values.

That the feminism in feminist empiricism is nonredundant answers one objection, but it does not dissolve the dilemma. There is the other horn. If the feminism is internal to the empiricism, how then can feminist empiricism offer any objective and hence noncircular justification for the feminist values that are internal to it? The question, taken rhetorically, presupposes that the presence of feminist values within empiricist methodology makes it viciously circular and unobjective. In Part I, I argued (I hope cogently) that this supposition is false: it is possible for empirical inquiry to be both objective in a realist sense and guided by feminist (as well as other) political values. When empirical inquiry is guided in this way, feminist values allow us to represent reality more accurately and are thus justified through an empiricism in which they play a nonredundant role. There is not a guarantee that they will be vindicated in this way. But the basic presupposition of the dilemma—that feminist values *cannot* be so justified—has no real basis. It is an illusion, and without it the dilemma that argues for the impossibility of feminist empiricism as a viable position in philosophy dissolves.

It might be objected, however, that the argument just given depends on the interdependence of fact and value and that this thesis—fact-value holism—does not depend in any essential way on feminism. Since this holism together with meaning-value holism form the backbone of the naturalized feminist epistemology defended here and neither is based on feminism, the appearance is that feminism does not function as a fundamental premise of the epistemology. Even if feminism plays an essential role in feminist empiricism, this form of empiricism depends on a more basic epistemological position that is not itself feminist. Thus, the objection that the proposed epistemology is not really feminist returns in a new form.

The objection may appear compelling because the holisms can be stated without reference to feminism. Does this mean, though, that feminism is not involved in their discovery and justification? Note that the holisms themselves purport to be facts about the nature of evidence and meaning. If they are facts, as I have argued they are, then they apply to themselves; their discovery and justification, as well as their meaning, is value dependent and, in particular, may depend significantly on feminism. If, in fact, feminism did not help in tracking reality, fact-value holism (and by implication meaning-value holism which includes it) would have less credibility than it has. The holisms do not stand as independent theses whose truth and meaning are to be ascertained independently of feminism. Not if they are, indeed, facts. They are themselves discovered from within a context of values.

Meaning-value holism adds a significant dimension, since it supports the possibility of a naturalized moral realism. Given a feminist form of such realism, it is possible to consider how much feminism helps track moral reality. Though, as before, there is no a priori guarantee that feminism will succeed, to the extent that feminism helps to reveal moral facts, its doing so reinforces fact-value holism and by implication meaning-value holism also. Again, these holisms do not function as independent premises whose credibility is separable from the credibility of the values that are contained in this political movement. At the same time, the fact that the moral values contained there can find support in how matters figure morally—can adequately represent moral reality—entails that the moral values of feminism do not function as first principles that are themselves unsupported.

The argument just given raises, however, another concern. Is the specific form of moral realism proposed really feminist in any deep way? After all, it is a Kantian social contract theory. Such a theory is surely not intrinsically feminist. The answer to this worry is spelled out in the last two chapters. I argued in chapter 9 that there are three reasons that justified moral norms cannot be reduced to norms that would be chosen autonomously by members of society. Each involves the fact that autonomous choice (choice that is based on relevant knowledge in the absence of coercion) cannot be fully understood except by reference to social justice and hence to the very norms whose justification is to be shown. The upshot is that feminist values regarding social justice would inevitably play an essential role in any application of the theory. Of course, this reply immediately raises the other horn of the dilemma with which we began: Can those values be justified in a way that is objective and not viciously circular? I have tried to answer this concern in the last chapter. There I draw on the conceptual resources of naturalized epistemology and the holisms embedded in it to explain how moral norms assumed at the outset, like inductive norms, can be supported in a way that is not unacceptably circular. If correct, this approach explains how feminist moral values can have a role in moral epistemology that allows them to be both essential and at the same time not infallible or foundational assumptions.

I have now canvassed three versions of the basic dilemma that argues that feminist philosophy is impossible, and I have explained how the argument rests on various mistakes. Perhaps the most serious is the illusion that there are no facts to be revealed by objective inquiry whose knowledge depends on contextual values. This is an epistemic form of the fact-value dichotomy. Accepting it makes one vulnerable to both horns of the dilemma. Feminism, viewed as involving only nonepistemic values, can play no essential role in gaining knowledge of facts (the philosophy is not feminist), or else the knowledge gained cannot be of facts revealed by objective inquiry (the feminism is not philosophy). Some feminist theorists reject the separation of fact and value that the dichotomy implies but do not in fact reject the dichotomy as formulated. Though they hold that facts cannot be identified apart from political and other values, they deny objective status to both. They thus retain the version of the fact-value dichotomy just formulated (understanding objective factual inquiry not to depend on value commitments) and are, as a consequence, still subject to the dilemma.

Feminist philosophy is neither question begging nor redundant in addressing fundamental philosophical problems. How knowledge is possible and the place of value in nature are problems that are to be addressed within feminist philosophy—indeed, within science transformed by feminist thought. Feminist epistemology, in particular, is inquiry to be carried out within a naturalistic worldview but not limited by present conceptions of naturalized epistemology or science or by the paradoxes that are inherent in those conceptions.

Note

1. See Catherine Hundleby, "Where Standpoint Stands Now," *Women & Politics* 18 (in press). She is responding to my "Virtues of Feminist Empiricism," *Hypatia* 9 (1994): 90–115.

Bibliography

Alcoff, Linda Martin. *Real Knowing: New Versions of the Coherence Theory*. Ithaca, N.Y.: Cornell University Press, 1996.

Alcoff, Linda Martin, and Elizabeth Potter, eds. *Feminist Epistemologies*. New York: Routledge, 1992.

Antony, Louise. "Quine as Feminist: The Radical Import of Naturalized Epistemology." In *A Mind of One's Own: Feminist Essays on Reason and Objectivity*, eds. Louise Antony and Charlotte Witt. Boulder, Colo.: Westview, 1993.

Antony, Louise, and Charlotte Witt, eds. *A Mind of One's Own: Feminist Essays on Reason and Objectivity*. Boulder, Colo.: Westview, 1993.

Audi, Robert. "Fallibilist Foundationalism and Holistic Coherentism." In *The Theory of Knowledge*, ed. Louis Pojman. Belmont, Calif.: Wadsworth, 1993.

Axelrod, Robert. *The Evolution of Cooperation*. New York: Basic Books, 1984.

Babbitt, Susan. "Feminism and Objective Interests: The Role of Transformation Experiences in Rational Deliberation." In *Feminist Epistemologies*, ed. Linda Martin Alcoff and Elizabeth Potter. New York: Routledge, 1993.

———. *Impossible Dreams: Rationality, Integrity, and Moral Imagination*. Boulder, Colo.: Westview, 1996.

Baier, Annette. "Cartesian Persons." *Philosophia* 10 (1981): 169–88. (Reprint in Baier, *Postures of the Mind*.)

———. *Postures of the Mind: Essays on Mind and Morals*. Minneapolis: University of Minnesota Press, 1985.

———. "What Do Women Want in a Moral Theory?" *Nous* 19 (1985): 53–64.

———. "Trust and Anti-Trust." *Ethics* 96 (1986): 231–60.

———. "The Need for More Than Justice." In *Science, Morality, and Feminist Theory*, ed. Marsha Hanen and Kai Nielsen. Calgary: University of Calgary Press, 1987.

Barad, Karen. "Meeting the Universe Halfway: Realism and Social Constructivism without Contradiction." In *Feminism, Science, and the Philosophy of Science*, ed. Lynn Hankinson Nelson and Jack Nelson. Dordrecht: Kluwer, 1996.

Bartky, Sandra Lee. *Femininity and Domination: Studies in the Phenomenology of Oppression*. New York: Routledge, 1990.

Benhabib, Seyla. "The Generalized and the Concrete Other: The Kohlberg-Gilligan Controversy." In *Women and Moral Theory*, ed. Eva Feder Kittay and Diana T. Meyers. Totowa, N.J.: Roman & Littlefield, 1987.

Boyd, Richard. "How To Be a Moral Realist." In *Essays on Moral Realism*, ed. Geoffrey Sayre-McCord. Ithaca, N.Y.: Cornell University Press, 1988.

Boyd, Robert, and Peter J. Richerson. *Culture and the Evolutionary Process.* Chicago: University of Chicago Press, 1985.

Brandt, Richard. *A Theory of the Good and the Right.* Oxford: Clarendon, 1979.

Brink, David O. *Moral Realism and the Foundations of Ethics.* Cambridge: Cambridge University Press, 1989.

Calhoun, Cheshire. "Cognitive Emotions?" In *What Is an Emotion? Classic Readings in Philosophical Psychology*, ed. Cheshire Calhoun and Robert C. Solomon. New York: Oxford University Press, 1984.

Campbell, Richmond. *Self-Love and Self-Respect: A Philosophical Study of Egoism.* Ottawa: Canadian Library of Philosophy, 1979.

———. "Sociobiology and the Possibility of Ethical Naturalism." In *Morality, Reason, and Truth*, ed. David Copp and David Zimmerman. Totowa, N.J.: Rowman & Allanheld, 1985.

———. "Gauthier's Theory of Morals by Agreement." *Philosophical Quarterly* 38 (1988): 343–64.

———. "Moral Justification and Freedom." *Journal of Philosophy* 85 (1988): 192–213.

———. "Critical Notice of Allan Gibbard, *Wise Choices, Apt Feelings*." *Canadian Journal of Philosophy* 23 (1993): 299–323.

———. "The Virtues of Feminist Empiricism." *Hypatia* 9 (1994): 90–115.

———. "Can Biology Make Ethics Objective?" *Biology and Philosophy* 11 (1996): 21–31.

———. "Critical Notice of David Copp, *Morality, Normativity, and Society*." *Canadian Journal of Philosophy* 27 (1997): 423–44.

Churchland, Patricia S. *Neurophilosophy: Toward a Unified Understanding of the Mind-Brain.* Cambridge, Mass.: MIT Press, 1986.

Churchland, Paul M. "The Ontological Status of Observables: In Praise of Superempirical Virtues." In *Images of Science*, ed. Paul M. Churchland and Clifford A. Hooker. Chicago: University of Chicago Press, 1985.

———. *The Engine of Reason, the Seat of the Soul: A Philosophical Journey into the Brain.* Cambridge, Mass.: MIT Press, 1995.

Code, Lorraine. "Second Persons." In *Science, Morality, and Feminist Theory*, ed. Marsha Hanen and Kai Nielsen. Calgary: University of Calgary Press, 1987.

———. *What Can She Know? Feminist Theory and the Construction of Knowledge.* Ithaca, N.Y.: Cornell University Press, 1991.

———. "What Is Natural about Epistemology Naturalized?" *American Philosophical Quarterly* 33 (1996): 1–22.

Collier, John, and Michael Stingl. "Evolutionary Naturalism and the Objectivity of Morality." *Biology and Philosophy* 8 (1993): 47–60.

Committee on the Ethical and Legal Issues Relating to the Inclusion of Women in Clinical Studies. In *Women and Health Research Vol. 1: Ethical and Legal Issues of Including Women in Clinical Studies*, ed. Anna C. Mastroianni, Ruth Faden, and Daniel Federman. Washington, D.C.: National Academy Press, 1994.

Copp, David. *Morality, Normativity, and Society.* Oxford: Clarendon, 1995.

Crasnow, Sharon L. "Can Science be Objective? Longino's *Science as Social Knowledge*." *Hypatia* 8, no. 3 (1993): 194–201.

Darwall, Stephen. "Two Kinds of Self-Respect." *Ethics* 88 (1977): 34–49.

Darwall, Stephen, Allan Gibbard, and Peter Railton. "Toward *Fin de siècle* Ethics: Some Trends." *Philosophical Review* 101 (1992): 115–189.

Davidson, Donald. *Inquiries into Truth and Interpretation*. Cambridge, Mass.: Harvard University Press, 1984.

Dawkins, Richard. *The Blind Watchmaker*. New York: Norton, 1986.

Deigh, John. "Cognitivism in the Theory of Emotions." *Ethics* 104 (1994): 824–54.

Dillon, Robin. "Toward a Feminist Conception of Self-Respect." *Hypatia* 7 (1992): 52–69.

———. ed. *Dignity, Character, and Self-Respect*. New York: Routledge, 1995.

———. "Self-Respect: Moral, Emotional and Political." *Ethics* 107 (1997): 226–49.

Duhem, Pierre. *La theorie physique: son objet et sa structure*. Paris: Chevalier et Rivière, 1906.

Duran, Jane. *Toward a Feminist Epistemology*. Savage, Md.: Rowman & Littlefield, 1991.

———. *Knowledge in Context: Naturalized Epistemology and Sociolinguistics*. Lanham, Md.: Rowman & Littlefield, 1994.

Fausto-Sterling, Anne. *Myths of Gender: Biological Theories about Women and Men*. New York: Basic Books, 1985.

Fee, Elizabeth. "Woman's Nature and Scientific Objectivity." In *Woman's Nature: Rationalizations of Inequality*, ed. M. Lowe and R. Hubbard. New York: Pergamon, 1981.

Flax, Jane. "Postmodernism and Gender Relations in Feminist Theory." *Signs* 12 (1987): 621–43.

Fodor, Jerry. "The Dogma That Didn't Bark (A Fragment of a Naturalized Epistemology)." *Mind* 100 (1991): 201–20. (Reprint in *Naturalizing Epistemology*, ed. Hilary Kornblith, to which citations refer.)

Friedman, Marilyn. "Beyond Caring: The De-Moralization of Gender." In *Science, Morality, and Feminist Theory* (*Canadian Journal of Philosophy*, suppl. vol. 13), ed. Marsha Hanen and Kai Nielsen. Calgary: University of Calgary Press, 1987.

Gauthier, David. *Morals by Agreement*. Oxford: Clarendon, 1986.

Gibbard, Allan. *Wise Choices, Apt Feelings*. Cambridge, Mass.: Harvard University Press, 1990.

Giere, Ronald. "Causal Systems and Statistical Hypotheses." In *Applications of Inductive Logic*, ed. L. J. Cohen and M. B. Hesse. Oxford: Oxford University Press, 1980.

———. "Testing Theoretical Hypotheses." In *Testing Scientific Theories*, ed. J. Earman. Minnesota Studies in the Philosophy of Science, vol. 10. Minneapolis: University of Minnesota Press, 1983.

———. "Constructive Realism." In *Images of Science*, ed. Paul M. Churchland and Clifford A. Hooker. Chicago: University of Chicago Press, 1985.

———. *Explaining Science*. Chicago: University of Chicago Press, 1988.

———. *Understanding Scientific Reasoning*. New York: Holt, Rinehart, & Winston, 1997, 1991, 1984, 1979.

———. "Underdetermination, Relativism, and Perspective Realism." Paper presented as an Austin and Hempel Lecture, Dalhousie University, Halifax, Nova Scotia, 5 August 1993.

Gilligan, Carol. *In a Different Voice: Psychological Theory and Women's Development.* Cambridge, Mass.: Harvard University Press, 1982.

Goldman, Alvin I. *Liaisons: Philosophy Meets the Cognitive and Social Sciences.* Cambridge, Mass.: MIT Press, 1992.

Goldsworthy, Jeffrey. "Externalism, Internalism, and Moral Skepticism." *Australasian Journal of Philosophy* 70 (1992): 40–60.

Gorham, Geoffrey. "The Concept of Truth in Feminist Sciences." *Hypatia* 10 (1995): 99–116.

Gould, Stephen Jay. "Sociobiology and the Theory of Natural Selection." In *Beyond Nature/Nurture?* ed. G. W. Barlow and J. Silverberg. Boulder, Colo.: Westview, 1980.

Gould, Stephen Jay, and Richard C. Lewontin. "The Spandrels of San Marco and the Panglossian Paradigm: A Critique of the Adaptationist Programme." *Proceedings of the Royal Society of London* 205 (1978): 581–98.

Grice, H. P., and P. F. Strawson. "In Defense of a Dogma," *Philosophical Review* 65 (1956): 141–58.

Haack, Susan. *Evidence and Inquiry: Towards Reconstruction in Epistemology.* Cambridge, Mass: Blackwell, 1993.

———. "Science as Social?—Yes and No." In *Feminism, Science, and the Philosophy of Science*, ed. Lynn Hankinson Nelson and Jack Nelson. Dordrecht: Kluwer, 1996.

Hampton, Jean. "Feminist Contractarianism." In *A Mind of One's Own: Feminist Essays on Reason and Objectivity*, ed. Louise Antony and Charlotte Witt. Boulder, Colo.: Westview, 1993.

Harding, Sandra. *The Science Question in Feminism.* Ithaca, N.Y.: Cornell University Press, 1986.

———. "Feminist Justificatory Strategies." In *Women, Knowledge, and Reality*, ed. Ann Garry and Marilyn Pearsal. Boston: Unwin Hyman, 1989.

———. *Whose Science? Whose Knowledge?* Ithaca, N.Y.: Cornell University Press, 1991.

———. "Rethinking Standpoint Epistemology: What Is 'Strong Objectivity'?" In *Feminist Epistemologies*, ed. Linda Alcoff and Elizabeth Potter. New York: Routledge, 1993.

———. " 'Strong Objectivity': A Response to the New Objectivity Question." *Synthese* 104 (1995): 331–49.

Hardwig, John. "Epistemic Dependence." *Journal of Philosophy* 82 (1985): 335–49.

———. "The Role of Trust in Knowledge." *Journal of Philosophy* 88 (1991): 693–708.

Harman, Gilbert. "Inference to the Best Explanation." *Philosophical Review* 74 (1965): 88–95.

———. "Quine on Meaning and Existence, I." *Review of Metaphysics* 21 (1967): 124–51.

———. *The Nature of Morality: An Introduction to Ethics.* New York: Oxford University Press, 1977.

———. *Change in View: Principles of Reasoning.* Cambridge, Mass.: MIT Press, 1986.

Hartsock, Nancy. "The Feminist Standpoint: Developing the Ground for a Specifically Feminist Historical Materialism." In *Discovering Reality*, ed. Sandra Harding and Merrill Hintikka. Dordrecht: Reidel, 1983.

Harvey, Elizabeth, and Kathleen Okruhlik, eds. *Women and Reason*. Ann Arbor: University of Michigan Press, 1992.

Healy, B. "The Yentl Syndrome." *New England Journal of Medicine* 325 (1991): 274–76.

Held, Virgina. "Noncontractual Society: A Feminist View." In *Science, Morality, and Feminist Theory*, ed. Marsha Hanen and Kai Nielsen. Calgary: University of Calgary Press, 1987.

———. *Feminist Morality: Transforming Culture, Society, and Politics*. Chicago: University of Chicago Press, 1993.

Helke, Lisa. "Recipes for Theory Making." *Hypatia* 3 (1988): 15–29.

Hesse, Mary. *Revolutions and Reconstructions in the Philosophy of Science*. Bloomington: Indiana University Press, 1980.

Holland, John, Keith J. Holyoak, Richard E. Nisbett, and Paul Thagard. *Induction: Processes of Inference, Learning, and Discovery*. Cambridge, Mass.: MIT Press, 1986.

Hubbard, Ruth. *The Politics of Women's Biology*. New Brunswick, N.J.: Rutgers University Press, 1992.

Hume, David. *A Treatise of Human Nature*, ed. L. A. Selby-Bigge. Oxford: Clarendon, 1978.

Hundleby, Catherine. "Where Standpoint Stands Now." *Women & Politics* 18 (in press).

Jacobson, Daniel. "Freedom of Speech Acts? A Response to Langdon." *Philosophy and Public Affairs* 24 (1995): 64–79.

Jaggar, Alison. *Feminist Politics and Human Nature*. Totowa, N.J.: Rowman & Allanheld, 1983.

———. "Love and Knowledge: Emotion in Feminist Epistemology." In *Gender/Body/Knowledge*, ed. Susan Bordo and Alison Jaggar. New Brunswick, N.J.: Rutgers University Press, 1989.

———. "Taking Consent Seriously: Feminist Ethics and Actual Moral Dialogue." In *The Applied Ethics Reader*, ed. Earl Winkler and Jerrold Coombs. Oxford: Blackwell, 1993.

Kahneman, Daniel, Paul Slovic, and Amos Tversky, eds. *Judgment under Uncertainty: Heuristics and Biases*. Cambridge: Cambridge University Press, 1982.

Kant, Immanuel. *Immanuel Kant's Critique of Pure Reason*, tr. Norman Kemp Smith. New York: St. Martin's, 1961.

Keller, Evelyn Fox. *Reflections on Gender and Science*. New Haven, Conn.: Yale University Press, 1985.

———. "Feminism and Science." In *Sex and Scientific Inquiry*, ed. Sandra Harding and John O'Barr. Chicago: University of Chicago Press, 1987.

Kim, Jaegwon. "What Is 'Naturalized Epistemology'?" In *Philosophical Perspectives, 2, Epistemology*, ed. James E. Tomberlin. Atascadero, Calif.: Ridgeview, 1988. (Reprint in *Naturalizing Epistemology*, ed. Hilary Kornblith.)

Kitcher Philip. "A Priori Knowledge." *Philosophical Review* 86 (1980): 3–23. (Reprint in *Naturalizing Epistemology*, ed. Hilary Kornblith.)

———. *Vaulting Ambition*. Cambridge, Mass.: MIT Press, 1985.

———. *The Advancement of Science*. Oxford: Oxford University Press, 1993.

Klein, Ellen R. *Feminism under Fire*. Amherst, N.Y.: Prometheus, 1996.

Kornblith, Hilary. "Beyond Foundationalism and the Coherence Theory." *Journal of Philosophy* 72 (1980): 597–612. (Reprint in *Naturalizing Epistemology*, ed. Hilary Kornblith.)

———. *Inductive Inference and Its Natural Ground: An Essay in Naturalistic Epistemology*. Cambridge, Mass.: MIT Press, 1993.

———, ed. *Naturalizing Epistemology*, 2d ed. Cambridge, Mass.: MIT Press, 1994.

Kuhn, Thomas. *The Structure of Scientific Revolutions*, 2d ed. Chicago: University of Chicago Press, 1970.

———. *The Essential Tension*. Chicago: University of Chicago Press, 1977.

Langdon, Rae. "Whose Right? Ronald Dworkin, Women, and Pornographers." *Philosophy and Public Affairs* 19 (1990): 311–59.

———. "Speech Acts and Unspeakable Acts." *Philosophy and Public Affairs* 22 (1993): 293–330.

Lloyd, Elizabeth A. "Objectivity and the Double Standard for Feminist Epistemologies." *Synthese* 104 (1995): 351–81.

———. "Science and Anti-Science: Objectivity and Its Real Enemies." In *Feminism, Science, and the Philosophy of Science*, ed. Lynn Hankinson Nelson and Jack Nelson. Dordrecht: Kluwer, 1996.

Longino, Helen. *Science as Social Knowledge*. Princeton, N.J.: Princeton University Press, 1990.

———. "Subjects, Power and Knowledge: Description and Prescription in Feminist Philosophies of Science." In *Feminist Epistemologies*, ed. Linda Alcoff and Elizabeth Potter. New York: Routledge, 1993.

———. "Gender, Politics, and the Theoretical Virtues." *Synthese* 104 (1995): 383–97.

———. "Cognitive and Non-cognitive Values in Science: Rethinking the Dichotomy." In *Feminism, Science, and the Philosophy of Science*, ed. Lynn Hankinson Nelson and Jack Nelson. Dordrecht: Kluwer, 1996.

Longino, Helen, and Evelyn Hammonds. "Conflicts and Tensions in the Feminist Study of Gender and Science." In *Conflicts in Feminism*, ed. Marianne Hirsch and Evelyn Fox Keller. New York: Routledge, 1990.

Maccoby, Eleanor, and Carol Jacklin. *The Psychology of Sex Differences*. Stanford, Calif.: Stanford University Press, 1974.

Mackie, John L. *Ethics: Inventing Right and Wrong*. New York: Penguin, 1977.

MacKinnon, Catharine A. *Feminism Unmodified: Discourses on Life and Law*. Cambridge, Mass.: Harvard University Press, 1987.

———. "Sexuality, Pornography, and Method: 'Pleasure under Patriarchy.'" *Ethics* 99 (1989): 314–46.

Markman, Ellen. *Categorization and Naming in Children*. Cambridge, Mass.: MIT Press, 1989.

Mastroianni, Anna C., Ruth Faden, and Daniel Bederman, eds. *Women and Health Research. Vol. I: Ethical and Legal Issues of Including Women in Clinical Studies*. Washington, D.C.: National Academy Press, 1994.

McNaughton, David. *Moral Vision*. New York: Blackwell, 1988.

Miller, Richard W. *Moral Differences: Truth, Justice, and Conscience in a World of Conflict*. Princeton, N.J.: Princeton University Press, 1992.

Milo, Ronald. "Contractarian Constructivism." *Journal of Philosophy* 92 (1995): 181–204.

Moore, George Edward. *Principia Ethica*. Cambridge: Cambridge University Press, 1903.

Multiple Risk-Factor Intervention Group. "Statistical Design Considerations in the NHLI Multiple Risk-Factor Trial (MRFIT)." *Journal of Chronic Diseases* 30 (1977): 261–75.

Murphy, Jeffrie. 1982. *Evolution, Morality, and the Meaning of Life*. Totowa, N.J.: Roman & Littlefield, 1982.

Neely, Wright. "Freedom and Desire." *Philosophical Review* 83 (1974): 32–54.

Nelson, Jack. "The Last Dogma of Empiricism?" In *Feminism, Science, and the Philosophy of Science*, ed. Lynn Hankinson Nelson and Jack Nelson. Dordrecht: Kluwer, 1996.

Nelson, Lynn Hankinson. *Who Knows: From Quine to a Feminist Empiricism*. Philadelphia: Temple University Press, 1990.

———. "Epistemological Communities." In *Feminist Epistemologies*, ed. Linda Alcoff and Elizabeth Potter. New York: Routledge, 1993.

———. ed. *Feminism and Science, Synthese* Vol. 104 (Dordrecht: Kluwer, 1995).

———. "A Feminist Naturalized Philosophy of Science." *Synthese* 104 (1995): 399–421.

———. "Empiricism without Dogmas." In *Feminism, Science, and the Philosophy of Science*, ed. Lynn Hankinson Nelson and Jack Nelson. Dordrecht: Kluwer, 1996.

Nelson, Lynn Hankinson, and Jack Nelson, eds. *Feminism, Science, and the Philosophy of Science*. Dordrecht: Kluwer, 1996.

Nozick, Robert. "Coercion." In *Philosophy, Science, and Method: Essays in Honor of Ernest Nagel*. New York: St. Martins, 1969.

———. *Anarchy, State, and Utopia*. New York: Basic Books, 1974.

Okin, Susan Moller. *Justice, Gender, and the Family*. New York: Basic Books, 1989.

———. "*Political Liberalism*, Justice, and Gender." *Ethics* 105 (1994): 23–43.

Okruhlik, Kathleen. "Birth of a New Physics or Death of Nature?" In *Women and Reason*, ed. Elizabeth Harvey and Kathleen Okruhlik. Ann Arbor: University of Michigan Press, 1992.

Okruhlik, Kathleen, Sandra Morton, and Leslie Thielen-Wilson. "Philosophical Feminism: A Bibliographic Guide to Critiques of Science." *New Feminist Research* 19 (1990): 2–36.

Oldenquist, Andrew. "The Origins of Morality: An Essay in Philosophical Anthropology." *Social Philosophy and Policy* 8 (1990): 121–40.

Pateman, Carole. *The Sexual Contract*. Palo Alto, Calif.: Stanford University Press, 1988.

Popper, Karl. *The Logic of Scientific Discovery*. London: Hutchinson, 1959.

Potter, Elizabeth. "Good Science and Good Philosophy of Science." *Synthese* 104 (1995): 423–39.

———. "Undetermination Undeterred." In *Feminism, Science, and the Philosophy of Science*, ed. Lynn Hankinson Nelson and Jack Nelson. Dordrecht: Kluwer, 1996.

Putnam, Hilary. *Reason, Truth, and History*. Cambridge: Cambridge University Press, 1981.

Quine, W. V. *From a Logical Point of View*. Cambridge: Harvard University Press, 1953.

———. "On What There Is." In *From a Logical Point of View*. Cambridge, Mass.: Harvard University Press, 1953.

———. "Two Dogmas of Empiricism." In *From a Logical Point of View*. Cambridge, Mass.: Harvard University Press, 1953.

———. *Word and Object*. Cambridge, Mass.: MIT Press, 1960.

———. "Epistemology Naturalized." In *Ontological Relativity and Other Essays*. New York: Columbia University Press, 1969.

———. "Natural Kinds." In *Ontological Relativity and Other Essays*. New York: Columbia University Press, 1969.

———. "Ontological Relativity." In *Ontological Relativity and Other Essays*. New York: Columbia University Press, 1969.

———. *Ontological Relativity and Other Essays*. New York: Columbia University Press, 1969.

———. *The Roots of Reference*. La Salle, Ill.: Open Court, 1974.

———. "Posits and Reality." In *The Ways of Paradox and Other Essays*. Cambridge, Mass.: Harvard University Press, 1976.

———. "Five Milestones of Empiricism." In *Theories and Things*. Cambridge, Mass.: Harvard University Press, 1981.

———. "On the Nature of Moral Values." In *Theories and Things*. Cambridge, Mass.: Harvard University Press, 1981.

———. "On the Very Idea of a Third Dogma." In *Theories and Things*. Cambridge, Mass.: Harvard University Press, 1981.

———. *Theories and Things*. Cambridge, Mass.: Harvard University Press, 1981.

———. "Things and Their Place in Theories." In *Theories and Things*. Cambridge, Mass.: Harvard University Press, 1981.

———. *The Pursuit of Truth*. Cambridge, Mass.: Harvard University Press, 1992.

Quine, Willard V. O., and J. S. Ullian. *The Web of Belief*. New York: Random House, 1970.

Railton, Peter. "Moral Realism." *Philosophical Review* 95 (1986): 163–207.

Rawls, John. *A Theory of Justice*. Cambridge, Mass.: Harvard University Press, 1971.

Richards, Robert. *Darwin and the Emergence of Evolutionary Theories of Mind and Behavior*. Chicago: University of Chicago Press, 1987.

Rooney, Phyllis. "Putting Naturalized Epistemology to Work." In *Epistemology: The Big Questions*, ed. Linda Alcoff. Oxford: Blackwell (in press).

Rose, Hilary. "Hand, Brain, and Heart: A Feminist Epistemology for the Natural Sciences." *Signs* 9, no.1 (1983): 73–90.

Rosenberg, Alexander. "The Biological Justification of Ethics: A Best-Case Scenario." *Social Philosophy and Policy* 8 (1990): 86–101.

Rosser, Sue V. *Biology and Feminism: A Dynamic Interaction*. New York: Twayne, 1992.

Ruse, Michael. *Taking Darwin Seriously*. Oxford: Blackwell, 1986.

———. "Evolution and Ethics: The Sociobiological Approach." In *Ethical Theory: Classical and Contemporary Writings*, 2d. ed., ed. Louis P. Pojman. Belmont, Calif.: Wadsworth, 1995.

Russell, Diana E. H. *Rape in Marriage*. New York: Macmillan, 1982.

Sayre-McCord, Geoffrey, ed. *Essays on Moral Realism*. Ithaca, N.Y.: Cornell University Press, 1988.

———. "The Many Moral Realisms." In *Essays on Moral Realism*, ed. Geoffrey Sayre-McCord. Ithaca, N.Y.: Cornell University Press, 1988.

———. "Moral Theory and Explanatory Impotence." *Midwest Studies* 12 (1988): 433–57.

Scanlon, Thomas M. "Contractualism and Utilitarianism." In *Utilitarianism and Beyond*, ed. Amartya Sen and Bernard Williams. Cambridge: Cambridge University Press, 1982.

Scheman, Naomi. "Feeling Our Way toward Objectivity." In *Mind and Morals: Essays on Cognitive Science and Ethics*, ed. Larry May, Marilyn Friedman, and Andy Clark. Cambridge, Mass.: MIT Press, 1996.

Searle, John R. *The Social Construction of Reality*. New York: Free Press, 1995.

Seller, Anne. "Realism Versus Relativism: Towards a Politically Adequate Epistemology." In *Feminist Perspectives in Philosophy*, ed. Morwenna Griffiths and Margaret Whitford. Bloomington: Indiana University Press, 1988.

Sherwin, Susan. *No Longer Patient: Feminist Ethics and Health Care*. Philadelphia: Temple University Press, 1992.

———. "Theory Vs. Practice in Ethics: The Case Study of a Feminist Perspective on Health Care." In *Philosophical Perspectives on Bioethics*, ed. Wayne Sumner. Toronto: University of Toronto Press, 1996.

———. "A Relational Approach to Autonomy in Health Care." In The Feminist Health Care Ethics Research Network, Susan Sherwin, Coordinator, *The Politics of Women's Health: Exploring Agency and Autonomy*. Philadelphia: Temple University Press, 1998.

Skyrms, Brian. *Evolution of the Social Contract*. Cambridge: Cambridge University Press, 1996.

Smith, Dorothy. *The Everyday World as Problematic: A Feminist Sociology*. Boston: Northeastern University Press, 1987.

Sober, Elliott. *The Nature of Selection: Evolutionary Theory in Philosophical Focus*. Cambridge, Mass.: MIT Press, 1984.

Spanier, Bonnie B. *Im/partial Science: Gender Ideology in Molecular Biology*. Bloomington: Indiana University Press, 1995.

Spelman, Elizabeth. "Anger and Insubordination." In *Women, Knowledge, and Reality*, ed. Ann Garry and Marilyn Pearsall. Boston: Unwin Hyman, 1989.

Steering Committee of the Physicians' Health Study Research Group. "Final Report on the Aspirin Component of the Ongoing Physicians' Health Study." *New England Journal of Medicine* 321, no. 3 (1989): 129–35.

Stich, Stephen P. "Could Man Be an Irrational Animal? Some Notes on the Epistemology of Rationality." In *Naturalizing Epistemology*, 2d. ed., ed. Hilary Kornblith. Cambridge, Mass.: MIT Press, 1994.

Stocker, Michael. "The Schizophrenia of Modern Ethical Theories." *Journal of Philosophy* 73 (1976): 453–66.

Sturgeon, Nicholas L. "Moral Explanations." In *Morality, Reason, and Truth*, ed. David Copp and David Zimmerman. Totowa, N.J.: Rowman & Allanheld, 1985.

Suppe, Frederick. "What's Wrong with the Received View on the Structure of Scientific Theories?" *Philosophy of Science* 39 (1972): 1–19.

Tanner, Nancy Makepeace. *On Becoming Human*. New York: Cambridge University Press, 1981.

Thomas, Laurence. *Living Morally*. Philadelphia: Temple University Press, 1989.

Thompson, Paul. *The Structure of Biological Theories*. Albany: State University of New York Press, 1989.

Tronto, Joan C. *Moral Boundaries: A Political Argument for an Ethic of Care*. New York: Routledge, 1993.

Tuana, Nancy, ed. 1989. *Feminism and Science*. Bloomington: Indiana University Press, 1989.

———. "The Radical Future of Feminist Empiricism." *Hypatia* 7, no. 1 (1992): 100–13.

———. *The Less Noble Sex: Scientific, Religious, and Philosophical Conceptions of Woman's Nature*. Bloomington: Indiana University Press, 1993.

———. "The Values of Science: Empiricism from a Feminist Perspective." *Synthese* 104 (1995): 441–61.

Tversky, Amos and Daniel Kahneman. "Belief in the Law of Small Numbers." In *Judgment under Uncertainty: Heuristics and Biases*, ed. Daniel Kahneman, Paul Slovic, and Amos Tversky. Cambridge: Cambridge University Press, 1982.

Walker, Lawrence J. "Sex Differences in the Development of Moral Reasoning: A Critical Review." *Child Development* 55 (1984): 677–91.

White, Morton. "Normative Ethics, Normative Epistemology, and Quine's Holism." In *The Philosophy of W. V. Quine*, ed. Lewis Edwin Hahn and Paul Arthur Lewis. La Salle, Ill.: Open Court, 1986.

Wilson, David Sloan, and Elliott Sober. "Re-introducing Group Selection to the Human Behavioral Sciences." *Behavioral and Brain Sciences* 17 (1994): 585–608.

Wilson, Edward O. "Human Decency Is Animal." *New York Times Magazine*, 12 October 1975.

Wright, Larry. "Functions." *Philosophical Review* 82 (1973): 139–68.

Wylie, Alison. "The Constitution of Archaeological Evidence: Gender Politics and Science." In *Disunity and Contextualism: New Direction in the Philosophy of Science Studies*, ed. Peter Galison and David Stump. Stanford, Calif.: Stanford University Press, 1996.

Wylie, Alison, Kathleen Okruhlik, Sandra Morton, and Leslie Thielen-Wilson. "Philosophical Feminism: A Bibliographical Guide to Critiques of Science," *New Feminist Research* 9 (1980): 2–36.

Young, Iris Marion. *Justice and the Politics of Difference*. Princeton, N.J.: Princeton University Press, 1990.

Index

241

About the Author

Richmond Campbell is Professor and Chair of the Philosophy Department at Dalhousie University, Halifax, Nova Scotia, and an editor of *Canadian Journal of Philosophy*. He is the author of *Self-Love and Self-Respect: A Philosophical Study of Egoism* and coeditor of *Paradoxes of Rationality and Cooperation: Prisoner's Dilemma and Newcomb's Problem*. His publications include articles in logic, philosophy of science, philosophy of mind, moral epistemology, and feminist theory.